Cultural Policies for Sustainable Development

The concept of sustainable development is commonly divided into environmental, economic, social and cultural dimensions. While a variety of international actors have declared the importance of culture in sustainable development, jointly articulating this clearly has been difficult. For example, the Sustainable Development Goals (SDGs) that were adopted by the UN General Assembly in September 2015 contained only the most fleeting mention of culture. None of the SDGs referred directly to the case for integrating culture into sustainable development planning and decision-making. The role of cultural policy has remained unclear.

This book contributes to a better understanding of the role of culture in achieving sustainability, focusing on the particular roles for cultural policy in this context. Cultural sustainability is conceptualised as the sustainability of cultural and artistic practices and patterns, and to the role of cultural traits and actions to inform and compose part of the pathways towards more sustainable societies. The links between culture and sustainable development are analysed in ways that articulate and contemplate different roles for cultural policy. The contributors take up the concerns and perspectives of international, national, and local authorities and actors, illuminating ways in which these multi-scale efforts both intersect and diverge.

This book was originally published as a special issue of the *International Journal of Cultural Policy*.

Anita Kangas is Professor Emerita of Cultural Policy at the Department of Social Sciences and Philosophy, University of Jyväskylä, Finland.

Nancy Duxbury is Senior Researcher at the Centre for Social Studies, University of Coimbra, Portugal, and co-coordinator of its Cities, Cultures and Architecture Research Group.

Christiaan De Beukelaer is Lecturer in Cultural Policy at the School of Culture and Communication, University of Melbourne, Australia.

Cultural Policies for Sustainable Development

Edited by
Anita Kangas, Nancy Duxbury and
Christiaan De Beukelaer

LONDON AND NEW YORK

First published 2018 by Routledge

2 Park Square, Milton Park, Abingdon, Oxfordshire OX14 4RN
52 Vanderbilt Avenue, New York, NY 10017

Routledge is an imprint of the Taylor & Francis Group, an informa business

First issued in paperback 2020

Introduction, Chapters 1-4, 6-7 © 2018 Taylor & Francis
Chapter 5 © 2016 Kirsten Loach, Jennifer Rowley and Jillian Griffiths. Originally
published as Open Access.

British Library Cataloguing in Publication Data
A catalogue record for this book is available from the British Library

ISBN 13: 978-1-138-49481-7 (hbk)
ISBN 13: 978-0-367-53557-5 (pbk)

Typeset in Myriad Pro
by RefineCatch Limited, Bungay, Suffolk

Publisher's Note
The publisher accepts responsibility for any inconsistencies that may have
arisen during the conversion of this book from journal articles to book chapters,
namely the possible inclusion of journal terminology.

Disclaimer
Every effort has been made to contact copyright holders for their permission to
reprint material in this book. The publishers would be grateful to hear from any
copyright holder who is not here acknowledged and will undertake to rectify
any errors or omissions in future editions of this book.

Contents

Citation Information

The chapters in this book were originally published in the *International Journal of Cultural Policy*, volume 23, issue 2 (March 2017). When citing this material, please use the original page numbering for each article, as follows:

For any permission-related enquiries please visit:
http://www.tandfonline.com/page/help/permissions

Notes on Contributors

Christiaan De Beukelaer is Lecturer in Cultural Policy at the School of Culture and Communication, University of Melbourne, Australia.

Nancy Duxbury is Senior Researcher at the Centre for Social Studies, University of Coimbra, Portugal, and co-coordinator of its Cities, Cultures and Architecture Research Group.

Jillian Griffiths is Principal Lecturer in Information and Communications at Manchester Metropolitan University, UK.

Yudhishthir Raj Isar is Professor of Cultural Policy Studies at The American University of Paris, France.

M. Sharon Jeannotte is Senior Fellow at the Centre on Governance of the University of Ottawa, Canada.

Anita Kangas is Professor Emerita of Cultural Policy at the Department of Social Sciences and Philosophy, University of Jyväskylä, Finland.

Kirsten Loach is a PhD student at Manchester Metropolitan University, UK. Her work focuses on the sustainability of independent libraries.

Richard Maxwell is Professor and Chair of Media Studies at Queens College, City University of New York, USA.

Toby Miller is Emeritus Distinguished Professor at the University of California, Riverside, USA, and Professor of Cultural Policy Studies at Murdoch University, Perth, Australia.

Jordi Baltà Portolés is Researcher in cultural policy and international affairs, with an interest in the role of culture in sustainable development, cultural diversity and international cultural cooperation.

Jennifer Rowley is Professor of Information and Communications at Manchester Metropolitan University, UK.

Milena Dragićevic Šešić is Head of the UNESCO Chair in Cultural Policy and Management, and Professor of Cultural Policy and Cultural Management at the University of Arts, Belgrade, Serbia.

David Throsby is Distinguished Professor of Economics at Macquarie University, Sydney, Australia.

Introduction: cultural policies for sustainable development

Anita Kangas ⓘ, Nancy Duxbury ⓘ and Christiaan De Beukelaer ⓘ

ABSTRACT
Sustainable development has long conceptual roots, and international organisations have played a significant role in articulating the meaning of the term and the content of the dominant discourses. Within these frames, the concept of cultural sustainability tends to be diversely defined and operationalized. This article and special issue examine culture and sustainable development in ways that articulate and contemplate different roles for cultural policy.

In public policy-making at the national, regional, and local levels of government, the relation between cultural policy and sustainable development is highly topical, albeit under-researched. The recognition of this link is essential and could revitalize a new role for cultural actors (including arts, heritage, and socio-cultural activities) at all levels and potentially transform the politics of cultural policy. This special issue aims to advance the formation of principles for a new approach to culture and sustainability in the strategies of cultural policies.

The articles assembled in this special issue aim to address the question of how cultural policy/ies can contribute to sustainable development trajectories. The special issue brings international perspectives to this issue, presenting complementary frameworks of interpretation and considering different organizational levels and therefore different types of actors. The contributions to this special issue build on the multiple paths through which discussions about culture and sustainable development have emerged and travelled, and aim to identify attributes for clarifying and linking the debates more tightly to cultural policy.

Sustainable development has long conceptual roots, and international organisations have played a significant role in contesting the meaning of the term and the content of the dominant discourses. The term first came into prominence in 1980, when the International Union for the Conservation of Nature and Natural Resources presented the 'World Conservation Strategy' with 'the overall aim of achieving sustainable development through the conservation of living resources.'

The Brundtland Commission Report (WCED 1987) then significantly launched it forward by emphasizing the importance of sustainable development with a much wider scope of meaning, and in effect forcing it to the top of the agenda of the United Nations and the multilateral development banks. In its approach, there was no single focus (or object) of sustainable development but, instead, it asserted that all the economic, social, and environmental systems must be simultaneously sustainable. The Commission argued that perceived needs are socially and culturally determined, and sustainable development requires the promotion of values that encourage consumption standards that are within the bounds of the ecological possible and to which all can reasonably aspire. Paralleling the process that had led from the Brundtland Report to the Rio Summit (1992) and beyond, the World Commission on Culture and Development (WCCD) and UNESCO expanded from this discursive platform, promoting a new discussion about culture and development, and culturally sustainable development. The WCCD report (1995) linked cultural policy and sustainable development and connected culture to a range of economic, political, and societal issues. In this report, culture was defined broadly as 'ways of living together' and valued in 'giving meaning to our existence' (14). It was seen as having two roles: first, an instrumental role to promote economic progress, to integrate as an important dimension across all policy domains, and to add a cultural lens to all policy decisions; and second, a constituent role as a desirable end in itself, the characteristic of civilization that gives meaning to existence.

International organisations lay the foundations of their activities on four basic sources of legitimacy: rational-legal authority (their charters), delegated legitimacy (derived from states), moral legitimacy (their missions), and expert legitimacy (Barnett and Finnemore 2004). They are not consistent over time in their policy preferences because they are sensitive to a wide variety of influences and experts committed to competing ideas and paradigms. Ideas are accepted to provide guidance on institutional creation and reform to country-level policy actors. The international organisations' mode of governance is indirect and is often called an orchestration (Abbott et al. 2015). In practice, an orchestrator (for example, UNESCO) works through intermediaries, such as the third sector, business organisations, transgovernmental networks, and other international organisations. Intermediaries collaborate voluntarily with an orchestrator because they share basic goals and value its material and ideational support. In many ways they all profit from each other when orchestration serves to create and enforce common rules for the conduct of states.

Scientists tend to divide the concept of sustainable development into multiple dimensions: environmental, economic, social, cultural, and sometimes others. This conceptual practice of compartmentalization has been widely criticized, with the main difficulty building on the paradox that all these elements are equally part of sustainability, yet political discourse typically does not allow for the layered complexity that is needed to inclusively tackle these issues. As such, the tendency to define different dimensions of sustainable development reinforces administrative and policy separation in practice.

The concepts and frameworks that have evolved to situate culture in sustainability contexts have demonstrated multidisciplinarity, substantial flexibility, and a widening plurality of approaches over time. Cultural sustainability tends to be defined in two ways. On one hand, it refers to the sustainability of cultural and artistic practices and patterns, including, for example, identity formation and expression, cultural heritage conservation, and a sense of cultural continuity. On the other hand, cultural sustainability also refers to the role of cultural traits and actions to inform and compose part of the pathways towards more sustainable societies. Culture lies at the core of practices and beliefs that can support or inspire the necessary societal transition to more sustainable living. These narratives, values, and actions contribute to the emergence of a more culturally sensitive understanding of sustainable development and to clarifying the roles of art, culture, and cultural policy in this endeavour.

A central issue with the concept of cultural sustainability is that so many researchers share it as a common goal, that it has become a political catchword showing up in many discussions without anyone deeply considering what it really means, and tends to be diversely defined and operationalized. There is a very real danger of the term becoming a meaningless cliché, unless a concerted effort is made to add precision and content to the discussion. In addition, even if culture is gaining some currency in the sustainable development debate, the role of cultural policy remains unclear. Much more research in considering and clarifying the role of cultural policy in this context needs to be conducted. It is this gap in the academic literature and cultural policy on which the issue focuses.

Prior to introducing the articles that comprise this special issue, there are two final remarks we want to make. First, our primary focus is on culture as creative or artistic expression, as is common in cultural policy, but we connect this to a more anthropological notion of culture as a way of life because the unresolved tension between these two notions impedes a systematic engagement with culture for sustainable development. Second, while we use different notions of culture, in terms of policy, we focus on cultural policy alone. We do not explore other policy domains in which culture may have a role to play. This too is a necessary exploration, but one that remains beyond the scope of this special issue.

With these contexts as a backdrop, this special issue brings together a series of critical examinations of culture and sustainable development in ways that articulate and contemplate different roles for cultural policy. The articles take up the concerns and perspectives of international, national, and local authorities and actors, illuminating ways in which these multi-scale efforts both intersect and diverge.

The first three articles by David Throsby, Y. Raj Isar, and Jordi Baltà Portolés and Milena Dragićević Šešić provide insightful critical analyses and aim for greater conceptual clarity in defining the concepts of 'cultural sustainability', 'culture and sustainable development', and 'culturally sustainable development'. They also consider the conditions under which international organisations (such as UN and UNESCO) orchestrate intermediaries (such as UCLG, the United Cities and Local Governments, and other networks) to influence and monitor state behavior. The question is whether the concepts have become so-called floating signifiers. A growing number of issue-areas in globalized world concerning environmental, economic, social, and cultural changes have been a complicating factor in arts and cultural institutions. New arguments are needed for integrating culture into sustainable development processes. When the General Assembly of the UN approved seventeen Sustainable Development Goals in 2015, none of the goals referred to the cases for integrating culture into sustainable development planning and decision-making. One question is, how effective an instrument can UNESCO's Convention on the Protection and Promotion of the Diversity of Cultural Expressions (2005) be in these issues?

The next three articles by Richard Maxwell and Toby Miller; Kirsten Loach, Jennifer Rowley, and Jillian Griffiths; and M. Sharon Jeannotte challenge cultural institutions and local cultural administrations to operate as vital environmental participants with a stake in the future of the planet and all its inhabitants. One presumption is that the work of these institutions in sustaining culture should be valued according to its instrumental role in social, economic, and environmental sustainability, rather than according to its intrinsic cultural value. Emphasizing green cultural policy, one question comes up: Should, and how might, ecological criteria replace market criteria when determining the value of cultural production? Can environmentally truthful bookkeeping, for example, advanced through pressures from cultural funders, be widely implemented in the cultural sector by factoring in eco-system and atmospheric liabilities associated with all operations, from architecture to corporate sponsorship to digitization of cultural practices, performances, and exhibitions?

Another set of cultural policy issues also emerges. The integration of cultural rights in cultural policies and in sustainable development strategies has traditionally been hampered by a limited understanding of the concepts of cultural rights and the vagueness of their policy implications. In this regard, Jordi Baltà Portolés and Milena Dragićević Šešić argue that the goal divergence is relatively high in cultural rights and therefore states may be more reluctant to delegate resources and increase autonomy to develop those rights. Extending from this, M. Sharon Jeannotte discusses whether aboriginal perspectives on culture and nature can provide an alternative narrative that will advance our understanding of culture's role in community sustainability and counteract the monocultural perspective that is the legacy of colonialism throughout the world.

In the closing article, Nancy Duxbury, Anita Kangas, and Christiaan De Beukelaer argue that culture's absence from sustainable development debates is rooted in the *longue durée* of interplay among theoretical and policy debates on culture in sustainable development and on cultural policy since the mid-twentieth century. Based on their analysis and an assessment of the other articles in the special issue, they propose four roles cultural policy can play towards sustainable development: first, to safeguard and sustain cultural practices and rights; second, to 'green' the cultural sector's operations and impacts; third, to raise awareness and catalyse actions about sustainability and climate change; and fourth, to foster 'ecological citizenship'. In this regard, the challenge for cultural policy is to embody very different co-existing and overlapping roles in relation to sustainable development.

Disclosure statement

No potential conflict of interest was reported by the authors.

ORCID

Anita Kangas 🆔 http://orcid.org/0000-0002-7962-8225
Nancy Duxbury 🆔 http://orcid.org/0000-0002-5611-466X
Christiaan De Beukelaer 🆔 http://orcid.org/0000-0002-9045-9979

References

Abbott, K. W., P. Genschel, D. Snidal, and B. Zangl. 2015. *International Organizations as Orchestrators*. Cambridge: Cambridge University Press.
Barnett, M., and M. Finnemore. 2004. *Rules for the World: International Organizations in Global Politics*. Ithaca, NY: Cornell University Press.
International Union for the Conservation of Nature and Natural Resources. 1980. *World Conservation Strategy: Living Resource Conservation for Sustainable Development*. Gland: IUCNNR.
UNESCO. 2005. *Convention on the Protection and Promotion of the Diversity of Cultural Expressions*. Paris: UNESCO.
WCCD (World Commission on Culture and Development). 1995. *Our Creative Diversity*. Paris: UNESCO Publishing.
WCED (World Commission on Environment and Development). 1987. *Our Common Future*. New York: United Nations.

Culturally sustainable development: theoretical concept or practical policy instrument?

David Throsby

ABSTRACT

This paper outlines the concepts of sustainability and sustainable development, and considers the evolution of efforts to integrate culture into sustainable development policy and practice over recent years. The specific concept of culturally sustainable development (CSD), first promulgated more than 20 years ago, is re-assessed in the light of contemporary circumstances as a theoretically plausible proposition and as a basis for application to cultural policy formation. The paper proposes a set of principles by which consistency of a cultural policy or cultural development strategy with CSD can be judged. The application of each of the principles is discussed, drawing illustrations from particular policy areas in both developed and developing countries. The paper argues that CSD is a concept that has both theoretical substance and potential for practical policy application.

1. Introduction

Over the 30 years since the concepts of sustainability and sustainable development were articulated by the UN's World Commission on Environment and Development, usage of these terms in the political discourse has become so ubiquitous and applied in so many different circumstances that they are in danger of losing any semblance of meaning.[1] It is true that sustainability as an overarching paradigm within which to interpret biological and social interdependencies, and sustainable development as a specific application of this paradigm to processes of development, are well-established concepts. Moreover, their extension to embrace the role of culture in human affairs would appear to be well understood. Indeed so much has been written in recent times about culture in the context of sustainable development – or sustainable development in the context of culture – that it might be thought that all aspects of the field have been thoroughly ploughed and there is nothing left to say. Yet arguments in favour of a role for culture in sustainable development signally failed to impress the architects of the post-2015 Sustainable Development Goals which were adopted by the UN General Assembly in September 2015, as we shall discuss further below. Furthermore there remains some disconnect between the theory of sustainable development and of culture's role in it on the one hand, and practical policy strategies to secure development that is culturally sustainable on the other. Thus there are a number of issues in this vast territory that warrant further investigation, as this paper seeks to demonstrate.

In particular, it is unclear how proposals for the introduction of culture into the sustainable development discourse can be rationalised against more general sustainability models whose concerns are primarily environmental, economic and/or social. One possibility for resolving this disjunction is the articulation of a concept for the integration of culture in development that is specifically founded on the same basic principles that underlie other formal approaches to sustainability. Such a concept, which can be referred to as culturally sustainable development (CSD), was first promulgated more than 20 years ago, but has not been explored in detail, either theoretically or in regard to its possible relevance to the formation of cultural policy. There is a pre-history to this concept in the debate about what came to be known as ecologically sustainable development, an idea sufficiently precise for it to have become an element of public policy formation in a number of countries in the 1990s and beyond. So the following question arises: Are there any lessons in this experience that might enable us to decide whether or not CSD could eventually become similarly operational?

The purpose of this paper is threefold. First we provide a brief outline of ESD and how it migrated from the laboratory to the policy-making table. Second we aim to clarify and consolidate the theoretical basis of CSD. Finally we ask whether the concept of CSD could be interpreted as providing a guideline for integrating culture into sustainable development in the years ahead. The paper is structured as follows. In Section 2 the background to the emergence of sustainability as a framework for interpreting development processes is briefly outlined, and in Section 3 we discuss the ways in which culture became incorporated into this discourse. A formal statement of the principles of CSD is given in Section 4, followed by a consideration of how CSD can be interpreted in the context of cultural policy formation. We do so by demonstrating the application of each of the principles to cultural policy issues that arise in both developed and developing countries. Section 6 looks at three areas of current concern: culture in the UN's post-2015 development agenda, alternatives to maximising economic growth as an objective in sustainable development policy, and a possible role for the private sector in implementing the principles of CSD. The paper concludes with some speculations about the future.

2. Emerging paradigms

The origins of the concept of sustainable development are well known.[2] During the 1960s and 1970s widespread concerns were expressed at the negative environmental consequences of unrestrained economic growth. Books such as Carson (1962) and Mishan (1967), followed by the report of the Club of Rome on *The Limits to Growth* (Meadows et al. 1972), focussed these concerns, leading eventually to the establishment of the World Commission on Environment and Development (the Brundtland Commission). The Commission argued that poverty and lack of development in the global South was directly linked to exploitative resource use in the industrialised world, and that sustainability could be seen as an overarching paradigm enabling integration of the biosphere and the economy in a system-wide interpretation of development processes. In this context, the concept of *sustainable development* was seen as encapsulating the desirable features of a development path which would 'meet the needs of the present without compromising the ability of future generations to meet their own needs' (WCED 1987, 43). It was a concept that combined the ideas of sustainable *economic* development, meaning development that will not slow down or wither away but that will be in some sense self-perpetuating, with that of sustainable *environmental* development, meaning the preservation and enhancement of a range of environmental values upon which life on this planet depends. The sustainable development framework articulated by the Commission

> provided a basis on which the international community and national governments around the world could strive to reconcile the relentless drive for economic growth with the burgeoning problems of managing the air, land, biological and water resources for which they were responsible. (Harris and Throsby 1997, 1–2)

Not surprisingly, given the genesis and remit of the WCED, the focus of national and international policy interest arising from the Commission's recommendations was on dealing with pressing environmental issues. The outcomes of the so-called Earth Summit held in Rio in 1992, five years after the publication of *Our Common Future*, demonstrated this environmental orientation very clearly. This meeting of world leaders, which was convened to assess progress in implementing sustainable development precepts at the international level, generated several significant achievements, including a Framework Convention on Climate Change, a Convention on Biological Diversity, and a programme of action entitled Agenda 21 (United Nations 1997). Despite the concentration on environmental issues in the WCED, the interpretation of what it saw as a desirable development path was placed within a whole-systems framework linking biological, social and economic components in a single holistic model, the sort of interdependent-systems model characteristic of the science of ecology. Hence the term *ecologically* sustainable development (ESD) became accepted as the appropriate terminology to describe the way forward, widening the range of concern to include social and economic phenomena as well as purely environmental aspects.[3]

The report of the WCED threw down a significant challenge to the world to take action, and a number of countries responded by adopting ESD as a framework for implementing the Commission's recommendations.[4] But this was not a straightforward process. As an objective for public policy, ESD was a diverse and multi-faceted concept whose achievement could not be interpreted with reference to a single measurable goal, in contrast to other policy goals such as maximising economic growth or minimising unemployment, where single metrics provide an immediate and easily interpretable indicator. Sustainable development, like some other phenomena in the public policy arena such as security, justice, equity and freedom of expression, tends to be more readily noticeable when absent. So although the Brundtland definition of sustainable development quoted above provided an apparently clear directive, neither it nor any other of many similar definitions could be regarded as providing a workable basis for comprehensive policy determination.

A number of approaches to operationalizing sustainable development could be suggested. An obvious one is to disaggregate the concept into its component elements, enabling a general overarching framework to be distiled into a set of more specific propositions. In the case of ESD, this approach was adopted in Australia in a policy process initiated by the Australian Government in 1990–1991, three years after the publication of the Brundtland Report.[5] The process identified six principles of ESD that emerged from the WCED's deliberations (Hamilton and Throsby 1997, 7). In brief these principles were:

- improving material and non-material wellbeing
- improving intergenerational equity
- improving intragenerational equity
- maintaining biodiversity
- dealing cautiously with risk, uncertainty and irreversibility
- accounting for interconnectedness between systems.

In the Australian process these principles were applied to a series of nine industries to determine in each case whether the industry could be described as ecologically sustainable, and if not, what policy measures might be applied to remedy particular deficiencies.[6] It can be seen that these principles are sufficiently broad-ranging as to encompass the so-called 'three pillars' of sustainability: economic, social and environmental, a model that corresponds to the 'triple-bottom-line' of corporate accounting. A number of other countries have developed sustainable development strategies that incorporate all or most of the above principles in one form or another.[7]

3. Enter culture

The success of the Brundtland Commission in mobilising world opinion about significant environmental and developmental problems at a global level and in stimulating national governments to take action prompted a proposal that a similar investigative process could be set up to do the same for culture. Accordingly, the World Commission on Culture and Development was established, and had its first meeting in March 1993 under the chairmanship of Javier Pérez de Cuéllar. The Report on its proceedings was published in 1995 under the title *Our Creative Diversity*, a title that echoed that of its predecessor (WCCD 1995). But the hope that it might generate a similar groundswell of opinion recognising culture's place in discussion of serious developmental issues across the globe remained largely unrealised. The cultural 'summit' held in Stockholm in 1998, three years after the appearance of the Pérez de Cuéllar Report, failed to attract the level of presidential and ministerial attendance that was evident in the earlier Rio meeting (UNESCO 1998). Nevertheless the WCCD Report did at least succeed in laying the foundation for a gradually evolving debate on the role of culture in development, and on the importance of cultural diversity, matters that were taken up in the UNESCO *World Culture Reports* of 1998 and 2000, and later in the deliberations leading to the 2001 *Universal Declaration on Cultural Diversity* and the *2005 UNESCO Convention on the Promotion and Protection of the Diversity of Cultural Expressions* (hereafter the 'Cultural Diversity Convention').

Sustainability was certainly mentioned in *Our Creative Diversity*, but only in relation to an essentially environmental interpretation of sustainable development. Chapter 8 of the Report discusses the role of traditional cultures in maintaining ecosystem resilience and points to cultural issues in urbanisation processes.[8] But wider connections between sustainability and culture were not pursued. A paper prepared as a contribution to the WCCD process proposed for the first time the concept of CSD, recognising the links between cultural and natural capital and suggesting a set of principles by which CSD could be judged (Throsby 1994). However, despite support from some members of the Commission, the opportunity to incorporate CSD into its deliberations was not taken up, and it was left to subsequent articles in the academic literature to develop these ideas further.[9]

The relationship between CSD and its antecedent in the environmental arena raises the question: if ESD has worked as a basis for policy implementation in a variety of contexts, why could not CSD be operationalized in a similar fashion, transforming it from being simply a theoretical concept into a practical framework for making cultural policy? We consider this question below, but before doing so we set out a formal statement of CSD as a basis for our discussion.

4. Culturally sustainable development: a formal statement

The theoretical basis for CSD derives from the theory of cultural capital as it is understood in economics.[10] Tangible and intangible assets which embody or give rise to cultural value in addition to whatever economic value they possess can be interpreted as items of cultural capital. Such cultural assets may be long-lived, inherited from the past, and valued for their cultural significance. Alternatively, cultural goods and services being created in the present by artistic or cultural endeavours may endure as eventual contributions to the tangible or intangible cultural capital stock. However it arises, the stock of cultural capital available to a community or a nation comprises a valued resource that has somehow to be managed, and it is this management function that can be interpreted within a sustainability framework.

The phenomenon of cultural capital as it is understood in economic terms bears a close parallel with natural capital (Costanza 1992; Jansson et al. 1994; Tisdell 2003). The latter includes renewable and non-renewable natural resources, biodiversity, and natural ecosystems. Correspondingly, the elements of cultural capital comprise tangible and intangible cultural resources, cultural diversity, and cultural networks and support systems.[11] These similarities suggest that many of the propositions that have been explored in the theory of natural capital will find, *mutatis mutandis*, some correspondence in the theory of cultural capital. For example, the distinction between 'weak' and 'strong' sustainability that revolves around the substitutability between different forms of natural capital (Neumayer 2013) has a direct counterpart in a cultural context (Rizzo and Throsby 2006, 988–994). The parallel continues in the applied area: if ESD policies are described as the sustainable management of natural capital, we can represent CSD similarly as the sustainable management of cultural capital.

In addressing the question of how to translate these theoretical propositions into practical terms, we come upon the same obstacle as was encountered in operationalizing ESD, namely there is no single definition against which achievement of sustainable development of any sort can be judged. Hence we follow the same path with CSD as was followed with its counterpart in the ecological sphere, i.e. we disaggregate the concept into a set of principles expressing the main dimensions of what sustainable development in the cultural sphere is thought to entail. There are several ways in which these principles might be expressed. A succinct summary following Throsby (2010, 195; 2012b, 356) is as follows:

- *intergenerational equity*: development must take a long-term view and not be such as to compromise the capacities of future generations to access cultural resources and meet their cultural needs; this requires particular concern for protecting and enhancing a nation's tangible and intangible cultural capital.
- *intragenerational equity*: development must provide equity in access to cultural production, participation and enjoyment to all members of the community on a fair and non-discriminatory basis; in particular, attention must be paid to the poorest members of society to ensure that development is consistent with the objectives of poverty alleviation.
- *importance of diversity*: just as environmentally sustainable development requires the protection of biodiversity, so also should account be taken of the value of cultural diversity to the processes of economic, social and cultural development.
- *precautionary principle*: when facing decisions with irreversible consequences such as the destruction of cultural heritage or the extinction of valued cultural practices, a risk-averse position must be adopted.
- *interconnectedness*: economic, social, cultural and environmental systems should not be seen in isolation; rather, a holistic approach is required, i.e. one that recognises interconnectedness, particularly between economic and cultural development.

This set of principles comprises not so much a definition of CSD as a checklist against which any particular development strategy can be judged in order to assess the extent to which it can be regarded as culturally sustainable. Interpreting the principles as a checklist in this way offers a means for translating theory into policy application.

5. From principles to policy

In practical terms, the integration of culture into sustainable development policy may take a number of different forms (UNESCO 2015, 151–169). In some countries efforts are made to include the cultural sector in processes of national macroeconomic planning; such 5-year or 10-year plans may or may not make reference to sustainability goals. In other cases the cultural sector may be a specific target for the implementation of sustainable development measures. The checklist could be applied to any of these policy strategies either across the board or in instances where a particular criterion is the focus of concern. Alternatively the checklist might be used to assess policies which have some other intent but which could have some cultural impact: do they meet the CSD criteria? It is apparent that in any application a degree of latitude will be required, with no simple yes/no answer to whether consistency with CSD has been or is likely to be achieved. Policies may deliver completely, only to some extent, or not at all; in some cases only one or two of the criteria may be relevant. In other words, transforming CSD into policy terms will require judgement tailored to specific circumstances.

In this section we take each of the above five principles in turn and discuss some of the issues in its application in particular policy areas, with illustrations drawn from cultural policy experience in both developed and developing countries.

5.1. Intergenerational equity

If one principle could be taken as the central proposition in the concept of sustainability, it would be that dealing with continuity and concern for the long term – indeed it is in these senses that word 'sustainable' is used in everyday parlance. But the idea that the present generation might or should be willing to make sacrifices in order to bestow a benefit upon future inhabitants of the earth is one that presents some difficulty to economists. How should intergenerational equity be taken on board in the corpus of economic theory and analysis? Is it possible to construe it as an efficiency question, one of determining optimal strategies for intertemporal resource allocation (Hartwig 1977; Solow 1986)? Or is it simply a moral or ethical issue, dependent on people's subjective value judgements and thus beyond the reach of a strictly-defined economic calculus (Attfield 1998; O'Connor 2009)? Either way, it is a matter beset with problems relating to such aspects as uncertainty about the tastes of generations to come, and the impossibility of predicting how technological changes might affect future patterns of consumption.

In the cultural arena these problems are no less confronting. The injunction in the intergenerational equity principle of CSD concerning future generations' capacities 'to access cultural resources and meet their cultural needs' asks us to define what those resources are and how those needs might be assessed. For want of a better alternative in such circumstances, we frequently assume that future generations will have much the same motivations and preferences as ourselves; if so, the equity principle would suggest that we should leave them a cultural capital stock at least as great as that to which we ourselves have access. But there may still remain a question as to whether the cultural value of that stock has changed – it may have been improved, but equally it may have been degraded in some way, before it is passed on.

Consider the conservation of tangible cultural heritage. From the viewpoint of economics, an efficiency-based interpretation of whether it is justifiable to devote current resources towards the preservation of heritage items to service the cultural needs of the future might see the present generation as gaining some public-good benefit from the knowledge that the cultural opportunities for our children and our children's children are being looked after (Rangel 2003; Sandler 2009). If so, there could be a market-failure case for collective intervention to allocate resources specifically to realise this current benefit. Such intervention could be voluntary, as is evident in community support for national trusts and similar organisations set up to safeguard cultural heritage,[12] or it could be mandatory through publicly-funded programmes for heritage conservation, always assuming in either case that the costs of intervention are outweighed by the benefits secured.

But in the end a rationalisation of heritage policy on efficiency grounds may be unnecessary, if one accepts that a concern for the future is an ethical position that is widely enough held by citizens for it to be invoked as justifying private or public action. We are all the beneficiaries of the historic buildings, the artworks and the cultural traditions that have been passed to us intact by our predecessors, so the argument runs, and we have a moral obligation to behave in similar fashion in handing the capital stock on to the future. A difficulty remains, of course, in determining how much action is warranted on these grounds, and some sort of decision rule is needed. In the global South, decisions on heritage rehabilitation, whilst recognising the intergenerational benefits to be realised in the future, may be driven as much by immediate concerns for economic and social development in the present. For example, the rehabilitation of historic monuments and buildings in the Aga Khan Trust's Azhar Park project in Cairo included, alongside the heritage conservation goals, important objectives to address social and economic needs of local residents in regard to housing, health, education and so on (Aga Khan Trust for Culture 2005).

It is apparent that judging the consistency of any cultural policy with the intergenerational equity criterion of CSD will always be somewhat problematical, since an assessment must be based on future impacts that can only be speculated upon. Nevertheless the principle remains of crucial importance, and indeed crops up again and again in considering the application of the other principles, as we shall see below.

5.2. Intragenerational equity

The pursuit of fairness and non-discrimination in the provision of access to cultural participation for the present generation may be an explicit objective of cultural policies, or may be an incidental impact – positive or negative – of policies directed towards other goals. We consider three situations where these considerations arise.

First, there has been considerable interest in seeing the cultural industries as a target for integrating culture into sustainable development strategies in the developing world (UNCTAD 2008, 2010). Amongst many specific policies in this area, support for creative SMEs, whilst primarily provided to boost incomes, employment etc. in the cultural sector, can also have possibly significant effects on intragenerational equity. Small-scale cultural production at a local level frequently has a potential for raising the incomes of the poorest strata in the community and providing economic opportunity for women. Programmes to support the establishment and operation of SMEs may be able to mobilise traditional skills and link the economic development of the community to the preservation and enhancement of the local culture. All of these outcomes are consistent with the intragenerational equity principle of CSD.

The second illustration of the application of this principle in cultural policy is drawn from the developed world. It is often argued that public subsidies to the creative arts are regressive in their incidence, since the so-called 'high arts' are patronised mainly by wealthy consumers, whereas the taxes that provide the financial support are paid by everyone. This argument is weakened somewhat if the arts as a whole can be shown to generate widespread public-good benefits for which the community is prepared to pay.[13] Moreover it is also argued that an intergenerational issue arises if arts subsidies have the effect of preserving valued artforms such as grand opera which might otherwise die out. An additional consequence of arts subsidies that may be seen to counter their regressive incidence is the impact they may have on the incomes of creative artists. These workers are traditionally among the lowest-paid members of the labour force (Alper and Wassall 2006; Menger 2014), so a policy that improves their economic circumstances could be regarded as consistent with the intragenerational equity principle.

Nevertheless it seems that none of the above arguments, alone or in combination, will be sufficient to dispel continuing concerns about the possible regressivity of public support for the arts. Thus there opens up an opportunity for remedial action. For example, private finance could be directed specifically for the purpose of correcting the imbalance. It is also true that cultural institutions such as theatres, opera companies, galleries and museums in many countries, prompted by the persistence of an immediately observable and apparently inequitable outcome in the impact of the subsidies they receive, adopt free or reduced-price admission policies in an effort to offset any financial barrier to cultural access (Martin 2003; Rentschler, Hede, and White 2007).

Finally, an issue where the intragenerational equity principle of CSD comes into stark relief is that of cultural rights (Stamatopoulou 2007). Economic and social policies with a focus elsewhere may inadvertently infringe the cultural rights of particular groups in society. For example indigenous people living on their customary lands may find their cultural rights compromised when mining projects are located in areas containing sites of traditional spiritual significance (Hilson 2002). A further example arises when cultural rights are invoked as a justification for setting aside certain provisions of the legal framework governing civil behaviour. Such a proposition has been advanced, for instance, in order to sanction such practices as female genital mutilation. Application of the equity principle in such a case requires a determination of how rights are to be defined; in these circumstances the charter of human rights is frequently referred to as a basis for asserting that in conditions where cultural and human rights are in conflict, the latter should prevail.

5.3. Cultural diversity

Inclusion of the preservation of cultural diversity as a CSD principle mirrors the treatment of biodiversity as an important consideration in ESD. The reasons are somewhat similar. Biological diversity is valued because the multiplicity of species in the natural world provides a richly satisfying environment in which people live. Likewise the 'human mosaic' that is the essence of cultural diversity is valued uniquely for its own sake. Moreover there is a potential economic value in the preservation of species, as the future exploitation of genetic material extracted from possibly endangered species might yield a subsequent payoff. Such a proposition may have relevance to cultural diversity if it can be argued that uncertainty surrounds the possible ways in which particular cultural traditions or practices may one day prove useful for reasons not yet apparent. At the very least the stimulus to creativity that cultural diversity can be shown to generate constitutes a source of value that should not be overlooked; maintenance of diversity could indeed be rationalised on these grounds.

Policies designed to stimulate the production and celebration of the benefits of cultural diversity include, for example, strategies to promote intercultural dialogue either within or between countries, through artistic and cultural exchanges, cultural diplomacy and so on (Council of Europe 2008). A particular avenue for promoting the positive aspects of cultural diversity is via the media. Governments can play an important role here if publicly operated or financed media organisations are given a specific policy objective of commissioning, producing and disseminating diverse cultural content (Merkel 2015). Such efforts are likely to be consistent with the pursuit of CSD and may indeed be relevant to more than one of its principles – for example they may contribute to longer-run objectives of peace and reconciliation.

Application of the diversity principle as an item in a checklist for CSD could expose threats to the diversity of cultural expressions arising from policies implemented elsewhere in pursuit of economic efficiency. An obvious example can be found in the international arena, where measures aimed at trade liberalisation may result in a diminution in the diversity of cultural production; local cultural industries may be forced to reduce operations or to close as result of competition from dominant firms in the global marketplace (Hahn 2006; Iapadre 2013). Domestic production of film and television programmes in some countries is a clear case in point.[14] Action to counter these effects can be supported by a broad appeal to the principles of CSD, again with reference to more than one of them.

5.4. Precautionary principle

Dealing cautiously with risk, in particular when facing decisions that may have irreversible consequences, is an issue that arises especially in relation to tangible and intangible cultural heritage. The classic illustration in the case of tangible heritage is when a valued historic building or buildings stand in the way of a development proposal such as for a freeway, an airport, or an urban renewal project. Consistency with CSD would require cultural impacts of any decision to be weighed up in terms that allow them to be brought explicitly into the overall assessment. Assuming there is no possibility of relocating the historic structure(s), an appropriate approach is to incorporate the cultural value preserved or lost alongside the economic value gained or forgone, so that the relative benefits and costs can be evaluated on a comprehensive basis.[15] In these circumstances the precautionary principle applies – a bias towards a strictly risk-averse position if the irreversibility involved is absolute. Such an argument may be entertained on the grounds that whilst economic loss from destruction of a heritage asset could possibly be made good elsewhere, this particular cultural loss could not.

In the case of intangible cultural expressions, the precautionary principle applies in similar fashion. Cultural traditions may be in danger of dying out altogether unless maintained; even in circumstances where such traditions are not regarded as especially important by the present generation, there may be an argument that they could become more valuable in the future. Indigenous languages that have lost their utilitarian purpose are an example – they may be preserved for their intrinsic cultural value, or they may be recognised as the vehicle whereby indigenous cultural knowledge is transmitted between generations. Application of the precautionary principle of CSD in the latter situation reflects a wider sense of a holistic cultural system whose sustainability is important and in which language is just one component. Mention of holism in this context leads naturally to the next and final principle of CSD, interconnectedness.

5.5. Interconnectedness

This principle encapsulates the system-wide characteristic of any sustainability model. In the case of the CSD framework it provides for a holistic interpretation of development where no one component of the system should be seen in isolation. It requires that the various interconnections between parts of the system be recognised, such that the overall attainment of CSD in a given situation will involve accounting for all of them. The interconnectedness invoked in this principle thus relates across the board to economic, social, cultural and environmental interdependencies, the distinctive feature of CSD being that it includes culture as an integral part of the system – in other words its precepts are specifically formulated to incorporate cultural needs and aspirations alongside other requirements for a sustainable development process. In this respect the range of concerns embraced by CSD mirrors that incorporated in concepts of sustainability as understood by indigenous societies, where culture is integral to life, and the characteristic of holism is reflected in the fundamental association between humanity and the natural world (Throsby and Petetskaya 2016).

In policy terms, the principle of interconnectedness relates particularly to the desirability of seeing economic and cultural development as proceeding hand in hand. The interconnections observable in urban environments provide an apt illustration. Cities can be seen as complex systems where economic, social, cultural and environmental variables interact. The desired outcome may be described as a 'sustainable city' or a 'liveable city' where all these variables work in harmony to allow citizens to enjoy satisfying and rewarding lives.[16] Cultural considerations have a particular significance in this context. For example, local cultural industries may provide creative employment opportunities; artistic organisations may create a stimulating cultural atmosphere in the city; the activities of artists may contribute to encouraging cultural participation and creativity; and community cultural centres, perhaps built in and around heritage assets, may enhance social cohesion and reduce intercultural tensions (Bailey, Miles, and Stark 2004; Vickery 2007; Throsby 2010, 131–145). In short, cultural interconnectedness – reflected in the sorts of cultural networks and ecosystems referred to earlier – links all stakeholders in the city. Its effects may be realised in a more creative, dynamic, innovative and fulfilling urban environment.[17]

6. Current issues and future prospects

We turn now to a brief consideration of three current issues that are related to the discussion of CSD in this paper. The first concerns the effort mentioned earlier that was made by UNESCO, several international organisations and some national governments to argue for the integration of culture into the UN's post-2015 development agenda. In 2012 an international meeting was held in Rio de Janeiro on the twentieth anniversary of the original Earth Summit, with the objective of formulating a draft set of international development goals to replace the Millennium Development Goals which were due to expire in 2015. It was decided to incorporate the concept of sustainability into the new goals, which duly became designated as Sustainable Development Goals (SDGs). The focus of Rio+20, as the meeting was named, was on coming to terms with pressing environmental issues such as climate change. Hence it was clearly an environmental interpretation of sustainable development that underpinned the agenda of the meeting and informed the proceedings of the Task Team charged with drafting the goals. Nevertheless the Task Team directed its approach towards the broad concerns of the ESD model, with social and economic outcomes from development processes as the principal targets.[18]

Despite this wide-ranging remit, it was plain from the outset that the concept of sustainability recognised by the Task Team referred to the so-called 'three-pillars' model (economic, social, environmental) that was mentioned earlier, ignoring the arguments long promulgated in cultural circles that a fourth pillar, culture, should be added to provide a complete coverage of what sustainability stands for (Hawkes 2001). The international cultural community, aware of the direction the SDGs were taking, responded by mounting a vigorous campaign to articulate the contribution that culture could make to sustainable development and to persuade the UN to incorporate culture into the formulation of the goals.

The essential argument put forward was that culture can be seen as both a facilitator and a driver of development. The facilitator role derives from the fact that all development takes place in a cultural context, such that the successful implementation of development policies across the board depends importantly on the cultural circumstances in which the policies are being applied. The culture-as-driver argument was based primarily on the potential of the cultural industries to generate growth, incomes and employment in developing economies in a manner consistent with the preservation and enhancement of local cultures. The case for integrating culture into the SDG process was promulgated through a series of international forums and meetings, including those held in Hang Zhou in May 2013, Bali in November of that year, and Florence in October 2014. Each of these published a declaration articulating the case and urging the UN to take action.[19]

Despite the fact that the General Assembly of the UN had on more than one occasion passed resolutions clearly acknowledging the importance of accounting for culture in development strategies,[20] the set of seventeen SDGs finally approved by the Assembly in September 2015[21] contained only the most fleeting mention of culture. References to culture in sustainable development and to the role of cultural heritage were consigned to three minor paragraphs dealing with education and tourism. None of the goals referred either directly or by implication to the case for integrating culture into sustainable development planning and decision-making.

Why did such an energetic campaign, backed by evidence-based argument and spearheaded by the UN's own cultural organisation, have so little impact on the international decision-making processes? Three possible reasons might be suggested. Firstly, the concept of sustainability that informed the discussion leading to the new goals was very much the traditional interpretation traceable back to the Brundtland Commission. Indeed the path towards the formulation of the goals could be viewed as a reversion to Brundtland, where the major problems of poverty, malnutrition and lack of development in the Third World were seen to come from unsustainable resource use in industrialised countries; it is apparent that these problems were identified in the goal-setting process as economic and social issues, and correcting them would be expected to have a payoff in economic and social terms. In this scenario, culture does not figure, indeed is regarded as not necessary.

Secondly, a belief that culture was peripheral to the main thrust of the SDGs could also reflect a view that art and culture are simply an adornment to human life, involving aesthetic and spiritual aspirations that are unrelated to the stern realities of survival. Such a view, if indeed it was in any way influential, has been strongly challenged by a number of economists including Amartya Sen,[22] but the challenge has gone unheeded in mainstream sustainable development thinking, despite the commitment of sustainability theory to holistic systems and the principle of interconnectedness.

Finally, it may be that the SDG outcomes in 2015 may have had more to do with political considerations inside the UN than with matters of principle, a result that some would regard as inevitable in the complex internal workings of the world body. No doubt this and other explanations of the way in which the SDG process turned out will continue to be speculated upon in the days and years ahead.

Ultimately, however, the advancement of a role for culture in sustainable development might never have been achievable if this objective had been left simply as a component of goals such as the SDGs. Rather, it can be suggested that an international framework specifically oriented towards culture and development is likely to be more effective. Such a set of guidelines is provided by the 2005 Cultural Diversity Convention, to which more than 140 Member States of UNESCO are signatories. It has the considerable advantage of being an international treaty, not a set of aspirations. Despite some criticisms of the Convention and of its sustainability provisions,[23] the evidence provided by a wide range of countries reporting back to UNESCO on their experience in implementing the various articles of the Convention provides many examples where efforts to link cultural and economic development in accordance with sustainability guidelines have brought results; in general these results can be judged to be consistent with CSD principles.[24]

The second issue raised by this paper's discussion of CSD concerns the continuing appropriateness of economic growth, measured as increases in real per capita Gross Domestic Product (GDP), as a major objective of public policy around the world. The many deficiencies of GDP as an indicator of human welfare are well understood, including its arbitrariness, its dependence on dubious assumptions, and its failure to account for much of what contributes to human happiness (Coyle 2015). Its relentless focus on the quantity of material production as the determinant of welfare ignores the quality of people's lives as a basic contributor of their wellbeing. Yet governments around the world continue to use it as a measure of economic success and regard increasing per capita GDP as an essential policy objective, despite the fact that economists from Adam Smith to Keynes have not seen continued growth as inevitable or even desirable.

Many alternatives to GDP have been put forward, most of which recognise the multi-faceted nature of economic, social and cultural life, and propose a range of indicators rather than a single statistic. Such a 'dashboard' approach has been used, for example, by the OECD in its 'Better Life Index'[25] which includes variables evaluating citizens' access to food, shelter and clothing, their opportunities for civic participation, and the availability of adequate healthcare, education, and so on. These sorts of metrics could easily be extended to include cultural considerations in their assessment; in their wide-ranging interpretation of what contributes to human welfare, they could provide a basis for assessing sustainable development strategies in general and the application of CSD principles in particular. Indeed the use of multidimensional evaluation measures could help in due course to shift the attention of policy-makers away from an obsession with GDP growth and to encourage them towards a development path more in line with sustainability principles, including appropriate recognition of the role of culture.

The re-interpretation of growth within the context of sustainability could lead to a rebalancing of development objectives towards a more comprehensive and integrated view of human wellbeing. Philipsen (2015, 250), for example, sees prospects for a 'much broader and creative concept of sustainability, one that shows how our well-being depends not only on a healthy ecosystem, but also on justice, vibrant communities, stable cultures, political openness, and safety'. Such a vision is entirely consistent with the principles of CSD.

The third and final issue to be considered here is the role of the private sector in engaging with sustainable development. So far in this paper we have been concerned primarily with public-sector policy-making, but business firms are constantly making decisions and taking action that may have an impact one way or another on sustainability. At a general level, corporations have an incentive to behave in ways that are legal, ethical and socially responsible towards consumers, employees and members of the community. Such behaviour, brought together under the rubric of corporate social responsibility (CSR), is regarded as consistent with corporate objectives of increasing long-term profits, reducing risk, enhancing shareholder value and building the trust of stakeholders.[26] But it can also be regarded as fulfilling the precepts of sustainable development interpreted at the firm level –equitable treatment of staff and customers, concern for the long run, environmentally responsible resource use, and so on (Payne 2006; Moon 2007; Costantino, Marchello, and Mezzano 2010).

We can extend this observation to suggest that the principles of CSD enunciated in this paper could be readily incorporated into the CSR paradigm, and could be used as a basis for assessment of cultural sustainability at the micro level. Are the corporate values and behavioural norms adopted within the firm consistent with cultural respect, non-discrimination, freedom of expression, etc.? Does the company maintain positive cultural relations with its stakeholders? Are there strategies in place to support the arts in the community? These and other questions could be addressed by applying the principles of CSD to an assessment of corporate behaviour, for example by regarding the principles as a checklist against which to judge both general and specific aspects of the company's operations. Such assessments could become a standard part of systems of corporate governance, and could be monitored via quadruple-bottom-line reporting procedures.

7. Conclusions

In the Introduction to this paper we noted that before the concepts of sustainability and sustainable development can become operational in theoretical or empirical terms, they need to be rescued from the wilderness of vagueness and generality in which they are all too often lost, and given a precise interpretation. The purpose of this paper has been to provide such an interpretation in the context of their application to culture. We have argued for a specific concept of CSD, an argument that draws on the theoretical parallels between natural and cultural capital to provide a means for linking the concepts of ESD and CSD. We have gone on to suggest that the principles of CSD can provide a systematic framework within which to interpret the role of culture in development, and can serve as a practical basis for assessing whether or not cultural policies conform to various desirable properties.

With the SDGs now marginalised if not eliminated as a tool for recognising the links between cultural and economic development, an alternative mechanism is needed for guiding the possible application of CSD principles in the implementation of development policies, and for assessing their success or otherwise in particular policy contexts. We have suggested that a vehicle for this purpose is provided by the 2005 Cultural Diversity Convention, in particular through its sustainability provisions. It remains to be seen whether the optimism of the Convention's proponents or the pessimism of its critics will prevail in the future. But experience so far does suggest that countries striving to implement the Convention's various intentions have indeed been able to introduce a range of different policy strategies for integrating culture into development processes, and moreover that these policies can deliver outcomes that are consistent with the principles of CSD. Nevertheless, if these principles are to become more widely understood as encapsulating desirable properties of cultural development paths, more work will be needed to devise sharper assessment tools for monitoring their application.

To conclude, is there an answer to the question posed in the title of this paper? Differing opinions will doubtless persist, signs of a healthy critical discourse. But as a contribution to the debate, this paper has attempted to show that CSD is indeed a concept that has *both* theoretical substance *and* a potential for application to real policy problems.

Notes

1. See in particular Isar's paper in this volume.
2. This section and the next draw some material from several of the author's earlier writings, including Throsby (2010, Ch 12, 2012a).
3. See, for example, Caldwell (1984); Smith (1995); Drexhage and Murphy (2010).
4. Illustrations include applications to fisheries (Fletcher et al. 2005) and water quality (Harding 2006); the latter paper also contains a succinct account of ESD policy development in Australia.
5. The reports emanating from this process comprise a comprehensive collection of industry analyses and discussion of inter-sectoral issues in the application of ESD in Australian policy in the early 1990s – see ESD Working Group Chairs (1992); see also Emmery (1993); Productivity Commission (1999).
6. The industries considered in the Australian process were agriculture, fisheries, forestry, mining, manufacturing, energy production, energy use, transport and tourism. Note that this process pre-dated the emergence of the creative economy, so cultural or creative industries were not included.
7. See, for example, Environment Canada (2010).
8. Similarly the chapter discussing 'Culture and Sustainability' in the 1998 *World Culture Report* deals with cultural knowledge as a guide to environmental management and related issues; see Leach (1998).
9. See Throsby (1995, 1997, 1999).
10. For a thorough treatment of cultural capital, including a discussion of 'weak' and 'strong' sustainability, see Rizzo and Throsby (2006); see also Dalziel et al. (2009).
11. The latter are sometimes referred to as 'cultural ecosystems' in imitation of the parallel concept in ecology.
12. Members of such organisations do of course also enjoy a private benefit from their membership; it is not known what proportions of an organisation's membership revenues derive from public-good and/or private-good demand.
13. See contributions to Towse (1997); see also Frey (2011).
14. An economic analysis of the relationship between trade in movies and cultural diversity can be found in Shin (2015).
15. To implement such a proposal requires a valid means for assessment of cultural value; heritage evaluation is one area where some progress has been made in this direction, thanks to the fact that indicators of cultural significance are called for in the processing of listing decisions. On measurement aspects, see Throsby (2013).
16. See UN Department of Economic and Social Affairs (2013).
17. For examples of culture as a component of city development, see UNESCO (2013a) and Dessein et al. (2015).
18. See UN System Task Team on the Post-2015 UN Development Agenda (2012).
19. See respectively UNESCO (2013b); http://kebudayaan.kemdikbud.go.id/wcf2013/wp-content/uploads/sites/48/2013/11/Bali-Promise-English.pdf; and UNESCO (2014).
20. See, for example, Resolution 66/208 'Culture and Development' adopted by the General Assembly of the UN on 22 December 2011.
21. See http://www.un.org/sustainabledevelopment/sustainable-development-goals/.
22. For example in Sen (1998, 1999).
23. See, for example, contributions to De Beukelaer, Pyykkönen, and Singh (2015).
24. For a wide range of examples, see UNESCO's *Global Monitoring Report* (UNESCO 2015); for an account relating specifically to culture and sustainable development, see this Report's Ch. 8, 151–169.
25. See http://www.oecdbetterlifeindex.org/.
26. See, for example, Okpara and Idowu (2013); for a review of CSR in the context of developing economies, see Eweje (2014).

Acknowledgements

I am grateful for comments from two anonymous referees which enabled many improvements to this paper. Views expressed are entirely my own.

Disclosure statement

No potential conflict of interest was reported by the author.

References

Aga Khan Trust for Culture. 2005. *Al-Azhar Park, Cairo, and the Revitalisation of Darbal-Ahmar: Project Brief*. Geneva: Aga Khan Trust for Culture.

Alper, N. O., and G. H. Wassall. 2006. "Artists' Careers and Their Labor Markets." In *Handbook of the Economics of Art and Culture Vol 1*, edited by V. A. Ginsburgh and D. Throsby, 813–864. Amsterdam: Elsevier/North-Holland.

Attfield, R. 1998. "Environmental Ethics and Intergenerational Equity." *Inquiry* 41 (2): 207–222.

Bailey, C., S. Miles, and P. Stark. 2004. "Culture-led Urban Regeneration and the Revitalisation of Identities in Newcastle, Gateshead and the North East of England." *International Journal of Cultural Policy* 10 (1): 47–65.

Caldwell, L. K. 1984. "Political Aspects of Ecologically Sustainable Development." *Environmental Conservation* 11 (4): 299–308.

Carson, R. 1962. *Silent Spring*. Boston, MA: Houghton Mifflin.

Costantino, E., M. P. Marchello, and C. Mezzano. 2010. *Social Responsibility as a Driver for Local Sustainable Development*. (FEEM Working Paper No. 109.2010). Milan: Fondazione Eni Enrico Mattei.

Costanza, R. 1992. *Ecological Economics: The Science and Management of Sustainability*. New York: Columbia University Press.

Council of Europe. 2008. *White Paper on Intercultural Dialogue: Living Together as Equals in Dignity*. Strasbourg: Council of Europe.

Coyle, D. 2015. *GDP: A Brief but Affectionate History*. Princeton, NJ: Princeton University Press.

Dalziel, P., and C. Saunders with R. Fyfe, and B. Newton. 2009. Sustainable Development and Cultural Capital. *Official Statistics Research Series, 5*, November. Wellington: Statistics New Zealand.

De Beukelaer, C., M. Pyykkönen, and J. P. Singh, eds. 2015. *Globalization, Culture and Development: The UNESCO Convention on Cultural Diversity*. London: Palgrave Macmillan.

Dessein, J., K. Soini, G. Fairclough, and L. Horlings, eds. 2015. *Culture in, for and as Sustainable Development: Conclusions from the COST Action IS1007: Investigating Cultural Sustainability*. Jyväskylä: Jyväskylä University Press.

Drexhage, J., and D. Murphy. 2010. *Sustainable Development: From Brundtland to Rio 2012* (Background Paper prepared for consideration by the High Level Panel on Global Sustainability). New York: United Nations.

Ecologically Sustainable Development Working Group Chairs. 1992. *Intersectoral Issues Report*. Canberra: Australian Government Publishing Service.

Emmery, M. 1993. *An Overview of Ecologically Sustainable Development Processes in Australia 1990–1992*. Canberra: Parliament of the Commonwealth of Australia.

Environment Canada. 2010. *Planning for a Sustainable Future: A Federal Sustainable Development Strategy for Canada*. Gatineau: Sustainable Development Office, Environment Canada.

Eweje, G. 2014. *Corporate Social Responsibility and Sustainability: Emerging Trends in Developing Economies*. Bradford: Emerald Group.

Fletcher, W. J., J. Chesson, K. J. Sainsbury, T. J. Hundloe, and M. Fisher. 2005. "A Flexible and Practical Framework for Reporting on Ecologically Sustainable Development for Wild Capture Fisheries." *Fisheries Research* 71 (2): 175–183.

Frey, B. 2011. "Public Support." In *Handbook of Cultural Economics*. 2nd ed, edited by R. Towse, 370–377. Cheltenham: Edward Elgar.

Hahn, M. 2006. "A Clash of Cultures? The UNESCO Diversity Convention and International Trade Law." *Journal of International Economic Law* 9 (3): 515–552.

Hamilton, C., and D. Throsby, eds. 1997. *The ESD Process: Evaluating a Policy Experiment*. Canberra: Academy of the Social Sciences in Australia.

Harding, R. 2006. "Ecologically Sustainable Development: Origins, Implementation and Challenges." *Desalination* 187 (1–3): 229–239.

Harris, S., and D. Throsby. 1997. "The ESD Process: Background, Implementation and Aftermath." In *The ESD Process: Evaluating a Policy Experiment*, edited by C. Hamilton and D. Throsby, 1–19. Canberra: Academy of the Social Sciences in Australia.

Hartwig, J. 1977. "Intergenerational Equity and the Investing of Rents from Exhaustible Resources." *American Economic Review* 67: 972–974.

Hawkes, J. 2001. *The Fourth Pillar of Sustainability: Culture's Essential Role in Public Planning.* Melbourne: Common Ground Publishing for Cultural Development Network (Vic).

Hilson, G. 2002. "An Overview of Land Use Conflicts in Mining Communities." *Land Use Policy* 19 (1): 65–73.

Iapadre, P. L. 2013. "Cultural Products in the International Trading System." In *Handbook of the Economics of Art and Culture Vol 2*, edited by V. A. Ginsburgh and D. Throsby, 381–409. Amsterdam: Elsevier/North Holland.

Jansson, A.-M., M. Hammer, C. Folke, and R. Costanza, eds. 1994. *Investing in Natural Capital: The Ecological Economics Approach to Sustainability.* Washington, DC: Island Press.

Leach M. A. 1998. "Culture and Sustainability." In UNESCO, *World Culture Report 1998: Culture, Creativity and Markets*, 93–104. Paris: UNESCO.

Martin, A. 2003. *The Impact of Free Entry to Museums.* London: MORI House.

Meadows, D. H., D. L. Meadows, J. Randers, and W. W. Behrens III. 1972. *The Limits to Growth.* New York: Universe Books.

Menger, P.-M. 2014. *The Economics of Creativity: Art and Achievement under Uncertainty.* Cambridge, MA: Harvard University Press.

Merkel, C. M. 2015. "New Voices: Encouraging Media Diversity." In UNESCO, *Re-Shaping Cultural Policies: A Decade Promoting the Diversity of Cultural Expressions for Development*, 61–73. Paris: UNESCO.

Mishan, E. J. 1967. *The Costs of Economic Growth.* London: Staples Press.

Moon, J. 2007. "The Contribution of Corporate Social Responsibility to Sustainable Development." *Sustainable Development* 15 (5): 296–306.

Neumayer, E. 2013. *Weak versus Strong Sustainability: Exploring the Limits of Two Opposing Paradigms.* 4th ed. Cheltenham: Edward Elgar.

O'Connor, M. 2009. "Intergenerational Equity, Human Rights and Ethics Issues in Sustainable Development." In *Principles of Sustainable Development, Vol 1*, edited by G. Barbiroliyate, 316–335. Paris: UNESCO and the Encyclopaedia of Life Support Systems.

Okpara, J. O., and S. O. Idowu, eds. 2013. *Corporate Social Responsibility: Challenges, Opportunities and Strategies for 21st Century Leaders.* Berlin: Springer.

Payne, A. 2006. "Corporate Social Responsibility and Sustainable Development." *Journal of Public Affairs* 6 (3–4): 286–297.

Philipsen, D. 2015. *The Big Little Number: How GDP Came to Rule the World and What to Do about It.* Princeton, NJ: Princeton University Press.

Productivity Commission. 1999. *Implementation of Ecologically Sustainable Development by Commonwealth Departments and Agencies.* Canberra: Commonwealth of Australia Productivity Commission.

Rangel, A. 2003. "Forward and Backward Intergenerational Goods: Why is Social Security Good for the Environment?" *American Economic Review* 93 (3): 813–834.

Rentschler, R., A.-M. Hede, and T. R. White. 2007. "Museum Pricing: Challenges to Theory Development and Practice." *International Journal of Nonprofit and Voluntary Sector Marketing* 12 (2): 163–173.

Rizzo, I., and D. Throsby. 2006. "Cultural Heritage: Economic Analysis and Public Policy." In *Handbook of the Economics of Art and Culture Vol 1*, edited by V. A. Ginsburgh and D. Throsby, 984–1016. Amsterdam: Elsevier/North-Holland.

Sandler, T. 2009. "Intergenerational Public Goods: Transnational Considerations." *Scottish Journal of Political Economy* 56 (3): 353–370.

Sen, A. 1998. "Culture, Freedom and Independence." In UNESCO, *World Culture Report 1998: Culture, Creativity and Markets*, 317–321. Paris: UNESCO.

Sen, A. 1999. *Development as Freedom.* New York: Oxford University Press.

Shin, Yousun. 2015. "Cultural Diversity and International Trade in Cultural Products." Unpublished PhD thesis, Department of Economics, Macquarie University, Sydney.

Smith, S. L. 1995. "Ecologically Sustainable Development: Integrating Economics, Ecology, and Law." *Williamette Law Review* 31 (2): 261–306.

Solow, R. 1986. "On the Intergenerational Allocation of Natural Resources." *The Scandinavian Journal of Economics* 88: 141–149.

Stamatopoulou, E. 2007. *Cultural Rights in International Law: Article 27 of the Universal Declaration of Human Rights and beyond.* Leiden: Martinus Nijhoff.

Throsby, D. 1994. "Linking Culture and Development Models: Towards a Workable Concept of Culturally Sustainable Development." Paper Prepared for World Commission on Culture and Development, Paris: UNESCO.

Throsby, D. 1995. "Culture, Economics and Sustainability." *Journal of Cultural Economics* 19 (3): 199–206.

Throsby, D. 1997. "Sustainability and Culture Some Theoretical Issues." *International Journal of Cultural Policy* 4 (1): 7–19.

Throsby, D. 1999. "Cultural Capital." *Journal of Cultural Economics* 23 (1/2): 3–12.

Throsby, D. 2010. *The Economics of Cultural Policy.* Cambridge: Cambridge University Press.

Throsby, D. 2012a. "Article 13: Integration of Culture in Sustainable Development." In *The UNESCO Convention on the Protection and Promotion of the Diversity of Cultural Expressions: Explanatory Notes*, edited by S. von Schorlemer and P-T. Stoll, 361–370. Berlin: Springer-Verlag.

Throsby, D. 2012b. "Sustainable Development and the Convention on the Diversity of Cultural Expressions." In *The UNESCO Convention on the Diversity of Cultural Expressions: A Tale of Fragmentation in International Law*, edited by T. Kono and S. Van Uytsel, 353–361. Cambridge: Intersentia.

Throsby, D. 2013. "Assessment of Value in Heritage Regulation." In *Handbook on the Economics of Cultural Heritage*, edited by I. Rizzo and A. Mignosa, 456–469. Cheltenham: Edward Elgar.

Throsby, D., and K. Petetskaya. 2016. "Sustainability Concepts in Indigenous and Non-Indigenous Cultures." *International Journal of Cultural Property* 23 (2): 119–140.

Tisdell, C. 2003. *Ecological and Environmental Economics: Selected Issues and Policy Responses*. Cheltenham: Edward Elgar.

Towse, R., ed. 1997. *Cultural Economics: The Arts, the Heritage and the Media Industries, 2 Vols*. Cheltenham: Edward Elgar.

United Nations. 1997. "Earth Summit." In *UN Briefing Papers/the World Conferences: Developing Priorities for the 21st Century*, New York: United Nations.

UNCTAD (United Nations Conference on Trade and Development). 2008, 2010. *Creative Economy Report*. Geneva: UNCTAD.

United Nations Department of Economic and Social Affairs. 2013. "Towards Sustainable Cities." In *World Economic and Social Survey 2013: Sustainable Development Challenges*, Chap. III. New York: United Nations.

UNESCO (United Nations Educational, Scientific and Cultural Organisation). 1998. *Final Report of Intergovernmental Conference on Cultural Policies for Development: The Power of Culture, Stockholm, 30 March – 2 April*. Paris: UNESCO.

UNESCO (United Nations Educational, Scientific and Cultural Organisation). 2013a. *Widening Local Development Pathways: Creative Economy Report 2013*. Paris: UNESCO.

UNESCO (United Nations Educational, Scientific and Cultural Organisation). 2013b. *The Hangzhou Declaration: Placing Culture at the Heart of Sustainable Development Policies*. Paris: UNESCO.

UNESCO (United Nations Educational, Scientific and Cultural Organisation). 2014. *Florence Declaration. Third UNESCO World Forum on Culture and Cultural Industries: Culture, Creativity and Sustainable Development – Research, Innovation, Opportunities*. Paris: UNESCO.

UNESCO (United Nations Educational, Scientific and Cultural Organisation). 2015. *Reshaping Cultural Policies; a Decade Promoting the Diversity of Cultural Expressions for Development*. Paris: UNESCO.

United Nations System Task Team for the Post-2015 UN Development Agenda. 2012. *Realizing the Future We Want for All: Report to the Secretary-General*. New York: United Nations.

Vickery, J. 2007. *The Emergence of Culture-led Regeneration: A Policy Concept and Its Discontents*. (Centre for Cultural Policy Studies Research Paper No. 9). Coventry: University of Warwick.

WCCD (World Commission on Culture and Development). 1995. *Our Creative Diversity*. Paris: WCCD.

WCED (World Commission on Environment and Development). 1987. *Our Common Future*. Oxford: Oxford University Press.

'Culture', 'sustainable development' and cultural policy: a contrarian view

Yudhishthir Raj Isar

ABSTRACT

This essay offers a critical analysis of the 'culture and sustainable development' discourse, notably among cultural activists and in actually existing cultural policy. It interrogates the utility of the narrative, seeks to uncover the semantic manoeuvres it employs and challenges the conventional wisdom it represents. The essay first explores the itinerary of the ductile notion of 'sustainability', the ways in which it has been stretched far beyond the original intent of those who coined the term, and identifies the conceptual discontents that this semantic multiplication has entailed. It hypothesizes that precisely because the term 'sustainable' and its derivatives are so acceptable and malleable at the same time, they have been easy to yoke to the bandwagon of the many-faceted and totalizing process that is 'development', allowing many different actors to project their interests, hopes, and aspirations under this composite banner. The essay then analyses the campaign to make culture 'the fourth pillar of sustainability' under the banner of the movement called 'Agenda 21 for Culture'. It concludes with a plea for a return to the original ecological focus of the term 'sustainability' – notably as regards climate change – and outlines some cultural policy responses such a focus can and should generate.

A contrarian case

This essay offers a critical analysis of the discourse of 'culture and sustainable development', as it is deployed by cultural advocacy groups as well as by governments and international organizations. Around the twinning of 'culture' and 'sustainable development' a number of tropes have moved to centre-stage in public policy discourse over the last three decades. In the process they have generated discursive formations of the kind that several of my recent reflections have sought to unpack (Isar 2010, 2013). My purpose has been to interrogate the utility of these discourses, to uncover the semantic manoeuvres they use and, if necessary, to challenge the 'doxa', in Bourdieu's sense, that they represent.[1] To do so, I have combined the gaze of the anthropologist with the insights of cultural theory. In the present instance, my scrutiny has generated a contrarian view, one that goes against the contemporary grain.

The term 'sustainable development', as the Brundtland Commission coined it in 1987, had a clear ecological focus. It meant a process 'that meets the needs of the present without compromising the ability of future generations to meet their own needs'. It responded to an ambition formed for humankind in the context of *accelerated climate change* and severe *environmental* degradation. But since then, the notion has been greatly stretched beyond this original meaning. As a result of this semantic inflation, the policy prescriptions articulated around the term, notably as regards 'culture and sustainable development', have come to embrace practically every aspect of the human condition. In the process, the term itself has become a floating signifier.

Hence two questions arise. First, what is the utility of this hugely expansive reading of sustainability as a horizon for cultural policy? In other words, if it means so many different things, what is the specific *cultural policy* challenge that is being invoked? Second, if one believes, as I do, in the primacy of the original idea of sustainability, that is to say as a macro challenge of human values and mental maps with regard to the *natural environment*, then what purchase can actually existing cultural policy, in other words policy for the arts and heritage, actually have on these values and mental maps?

I shall attempt to address these questions below. In so doing, I shall briefly review how the *urtext* of sustainability has been superseded over the years in the international discourse, principally in the United Nations System, and has become a leading grand narrative of our time (along with themes such as 'peace', 'freedom', 'security' and, of course, 'development' itself (Kates, Parris, and Leiserowitz 2005). I shall also analyse, in a deconstructionist yet friendly spirit, how a significant international cultural actor, namely the Culture Committee of United Cities and Local Governments (UCLG), has pioneered the cause of 'culture as the fourth pillar of sustainable development'. This advocacy movement, which has become quite visible internationally, while vigorously conducted and with the best of intentions, nicely illustrates the problematic nature of the semantic entanglements that have been in play. But first, I shall explore the polysemy in more general current usage of the term 'sustainable' as well as different couplings of the terms 'culture' and 'development'. For these couplings set the stage for the problem as I see it.

The expediency of culture

Advocates of cultural policy for sustainable development are obliged to position themselves within the logic of the expediency of culture, a logic that sees cultural values, forms and expressions as resources to be invested and deployed in the service of various socio-political and economic ends (Yúdice 2003). It is very much in this way that the tropes of 'culture in sustainable development' are energetically voiced today by a considerable number of different groups ranging from indigenous activists and local associations, to national governments and intergovernmental organizations such as UNESCO, to hybrid activist bodies such as the UCLG and to nongovernmental organizations. But on closer observation, this particular axis of instrumentalization turns out to be rather more problematic than most of the others that are salient nowadays. Given the contemporary centrality of culture, in both substantial and epistemological terms (Hall 1997), it is easy to argue that cultural expression can be a tool of economic growth, employment, or social cohesion; or that it can provide inspiration for conflict resolution and peace-building; or that it is a potential fount of social energy and mobilization. For we can easily observe that jobs and the economic growth are created by the cultural and creative industries, or that community arts projects are generators of social capital. These domains of endeavour or aspiration are clearly demarcated ones, in which cultural expressions, goods and services have clearly demonstrated utility.

'Sustainable development' on the other hand, is a loose and constantly expanding concatenation of notions, some of which are rather abstract. Thus, when people make 'sustainable development' an issue of cultural policy nowadays they could be referring to very different things – the notion has become positively polysemic in the multiplicity of its understandings. Consequently, it has become analytically problematic. Indeed it is probably one of the most imprecise notions in the current public discourse.

For many years now, those championing the cause of according a more central place to cultural factors in public policy-making have been appending the adjective 'sustainable' to the notion of 'development'. While in both popular and specialized usage what is meant by 'development' is rarely, if ever, defined, the concept clearly connotes positive, transformative change, regardless of the specifics that its users actually wish to denote. For this reason it is the less problematic of the two terms; for this reason also, apart from the fact that there is not the space to do so here, I shall refrain from exploring different understandings of 'development' in this essay. Yet it is also clear that already by the early 1960s, the term 'development' had come to be seen as unsatisfactory, somehow wanting, when used on its own.

Disappointment with the economic growth led development model ushered in after the Second World War spawned a whole series of qualifiers – 'integrated development', 'endogenous development', 'human development' among others – of which 'sustainable development' appears to have become the most lasting and pervasive. That said, we should also recall how Wolfgang Sachs characterized the notion of 'development' itself as 'a perception which models reality, a myth which comforts societies, and a fantasy which unleashes passions' (2010, xvi). As he also observed, perceptions, myths and fantasies operate quite independently from empirical facts or rational conclusions. Instead, they appeal to our contemporary imaginary because they are 'pregnant with promise'. Just as, in this perspective, we would do well to question the credo of 'development', so also should we question the promises of 'sustainability'.

The etymology of the latter term is in fact even more complex and problematic than that of 'development', in particular when it is related to 'cultural policy' as commonly understood, notably by the editors and readers of this journal, as what governments (as well as other entities) envision and enact in terms of cultural affairs. Cultural policy, in other words, is the field of visions, goals, measures and mechanisms relating to 'the works and practices of intellectual, and especially artistic activity' (Williams 1988, 90). It concerns the arts (currently ennobled by the buzzword 'creativity') and heritage. The difficulty is that actually existing cultural policy, i.e. arts and heritage policy, is capable of having only limited purchase on the rather vast – and fundamentally cultural – challenge of sustainability in its original meaning (cf. Clammer 2015). As we shall argue below, there is a close link between the potential of cultural expression and the challenges of sustainability. But for the moment, the point is that the cultural in the broad anthropological sense far transcends the remit and capabilities of cultural policy, as it is commonly understood.

The pairing of 'culture' and 'development' is ambiguous as well. Is it 'cultural development', 'development for culture', 'culture for development', or 'culture in development'? Are we talking about cultural development as the flourishing of the arts and culture sector, e.g. the long-standing French understanding of the term, or as the flourishing of a way of life as a whole? In that case, for example, given that the state of Bhutan has begun to apply the notion of 'gross national happiness' instead of gross national product (GDP), is Bhutan's state policy actually the ultimate degree of advancement in envisioning 'cultural development'? Or are we returning to the 'cultural dimensions of development' usages established and propagated by UNESCO in the 1980s, which proved so difficult to pin down and act upon? Are we talking about development itself as a cultural project and thus would we want to assert, in line with the capabilities approach of Amartya Sen and Martha Nussbaum (Sen 1999; Nussbaum 2011), that culture is constitutive and foundational for development, rather than just a means towards it? Do we mean that culture as the bedrock of values and ideals on which a society dreams its dreams and charts its aspirations must be the basis upon which its own path or model of development is envisioned or defined? There are no clear answers to any of these questions.

But let us return now to the term 'sustainable'. Yoked to the concept of 'development', the word has become a politically correct qualifier, often unthinkingly used. In other words, as an element of discursive ritual. Indeed, the same can be said of the term's extension to other domains, across a wide array of economic, social or political processes. It has become a commonplace; its usage is often sheer cant, and a semantically muddled one as well. Thus it can refer to the maintainability of a broad societal process such as socio-economic development. Or to whether this or that project has the capacity to endure. Or to whether this or that expenditure can be afforded over the long term. Or to the financial viability of a project or institution. Or to the ways in which certain practices may be conducive to a better quality of life. To be sure, all of these understandings of sustainability have their usefulness – provided we say something specific and definable when we use the term in each of these different ways. Witness this architect's lament:

> The very word, emptied of meaning through overuse, increasingly dominates architectural design and discourse, and – frankly – it drives me crazy. People use it all the time without really knowing what they are talking about. I always ask: sustainable of what? Too often the word becomes appropriated as a band-aid, cure-all additive that can be applied as environmental/ecological veneer to an architectural project, like icing on a cake. But the word has become such an all-encompassing buzzword, a signifier onto which so many different aspirations and agendas have been projected, that it doesn't really mean anything anymore.[2]

The planetary destiny of a ductile term

The process whereby sustainable development has emerged over the last three decades as an 'all-encompassing buzzword' has been a planetary one, shaped mainly by processes of deliberation and definition carried out in, by and around the United Nations. The resulting terminology and discourse have been 'naturalized' by officials and politicians, public intellectuals, journalists and a range of activists in a number of fields, including many academics, everywhere in the world. The usage has in fact become a commonly shared vulgate in the contemporary *zeitgeist*.

It is worth recalling here that in every historical period, new ideas and new terms emerge in the intellectual landscape. Over the last 50 years or so, the pace of such lexical emergence has been rapid, producing a brisk turnover in ideas and intellectual fashions. A succession of dominant ideas have derived their impact from the apparent ease with which each one of them has seemed able to address complex issues. These key ideas have operated as organizers on several different levels; in particular they have focused political, organizational and media attention. The life of these sorts of terms usually goes through different phases – formation, dissemination, discursive adaptation and popularization. Then they reach a final stage of consolidation, becoming integral parts of the general vocabulary. In the process, they become truth-generating concepts. They don't always last long in this capacity, however; sooner or later, many of these catchwords are abandoned and forgotten. Some of them, however, prove their usefulness and continue to be of value well past their phase of consolidation.[3]

'Sustainable development' is such a term; it no doubt has decades of useful life ahead of it. Now one would have expected its itinerary so far to have been the object of scholarly scrutiny. Contrary to such expectations, however, the term has not been examined in any depth through the lenses of the history of ideas. For the purposes of this essay, I had hoped to be able to find at least one analysis carried out in the spirit of a Raymond Williams (1988) or of the *Begriffsgechichte* school of history writing, e.g. the work of Reinhart Koselleck. Such an analysis would have unpacked the origins of the notion, traced its path towards acceptance as well as its shifts in meaning in the light of contingent historical and sociocultural conditions and would have sought to explain how and why it has become paradigmatic. It would have told us how the term became a 'mobilizing metaphor' (Shore and Wright 1997) for different actors, and how and why it came to be understood by them in an extremely diverse and broad range of ways. As a UN document avows: 'the nearly universal adoption of sustainable development as a guiding principle, is, in part, due to its flexibility. It allows various stakeholders to adapt the concept to their own purposes. This strength, however, is also its liability because various interpretations have led to confusion and compromised implementation' (United Nations 2010, 9).[4]

A conceptual history reading would have sought to explain precisely how and why, in the late 1980s, the adjective 'sustainable' was so eagerly seized upon and internalized, replacing a raft of predecessor terms, such as 'integrated', 'endogenous' and the like (it should be noted that this happened before the notion of 'human development', based on the ideas of Sen and Nussbaum, was adopted by the United Nations Development Programme). Such an account would also have identified the key the agenda setters: whose views were co-opted by whom, at what juncture and in connection with what triggering events (Kingdon 1995). Unfortunately, no such dedicated analysis appears to exist. Carrying one out would have been beyond the scope of this essay. Rather than speculate without evidence, what I offer instead is a review of the process in broad brushstrokes, using and contextualizing information made available in several existing accounts.

That said, however, one might put forward a simple, perhaps simplistic hypothesis, which is that precisely because the term 'sustainable' and its derivatives are highly suggestive and malleable at the same time, they are the quintessential stuff of the 'motherhood statement' (defined by Wiktionary as 'a vague, "feel good" platitude, especially one made by a politician, that few people would disagree with')[5]. So much so that they were easily recruited to the cause of qualifying the extremely many-faceted and totalizing process that is 'development'. The word 'sustainable' is sexy, as it were, because it sounds so correct and comforting. Some speculate that it also served to address deep anxieties about the ecological depredations against which the theory and practice of sustainable development would be a bulwark. While this thesis is likely to be true as regards the ecological realm, in other fields it simply cannot hold. Anxieties alone cannot account for the malleability that 'allows programs of environment or development; places from local to global; and institutions of government, civil society, business and industry to each project their interests, hopes, and aspirations onto the banner of sustainable development' (Kates, Parris, and Leiserowitz 2005, 10).

The conceptual framework for the term evolved between 1972 and 1992 through a series of international conferences and initiatives. The UN Conference on the Human Environment, held in Stockholm in 1972, was the founding moment. Apart from the political momentum it created to pursue the goal of sustainability (widely sensed, but not yet formally defined), the Stockholm Conference led to the establishment of the United Nations Environment Programme (UNEP) as well as the creation of many national environmental protection agencies. The Stockholm recommendations were further elaborated in the ecological realm through the 1980 World Conservation Strategy developed jointly by the International Union for the Conservation of Nature, the World Wildlife Fund and the United Nations Environment Programme (UNEP). The term as already cited above was itself was popularised in *Our Common Future,* the report of the World Commission on Environment and Development (WCED) published in 1987, widely known as the 'Brundtland Report'. The report was endorsed by the United Nations General Assembly soon afterwards and by 1992 enough political salience had been given to it for political leaders to set out a large number of additional principles at the celebrated Rio Summit (or 'Earth Summit'), the UN Conference on Environment and Development.

The resulting 'Agenda 21: A Programme of Action for Sustainable Development' was a 700 page document representing a consensus reached by 178 States, whose 40 chapters in four sections swept an astonishingly huge range of themes and issues into a single maw. Section II, 'Conservation and Management of Resources for Development' targets the core environmental issues, such as atmospheric protection, combating deforestation, protecting fragile environments, conservation of biodiversity, control of pollution and the management of biotechnology and radioactive wastes. But Section I, on the other hand, entitled 'Social and Economic Dimensions' deals with combating poverty, especially in developing countries, changing consumption patterns, promoting health, achieving a more sustainable population, sustainable human settlements and decision-making for sustainable development (again the word itself, in three tautological reiterations). Section III, 'Strengthening the Role of Major Groups' concerns a wide range of stakeholders across all these fields, viz. children and youth, women, NGOs, local authorities, business and industry, and workers; and strengthening the role of indigenous peoples, their communities, and farmers. Section IV, 'Means of Implementation', similarly embraces issues ranging from the needed financial resources, to science and technology, building awareness through education and the creation of institutions – once again covering the entire gamut of issues that are relevant to the entire field of development. To be sure, the core Brundtland Report challenge of intergenerational equity focusing on the state of the environment calls for a holistic approach – it is more than obvious that all the issues involved are deeply interconnected. The point is, however, that the objectives and actions have been all stacked up as clusters or silos, without enough exploration of the details of the links and interactions among them. 'Sustainable development' has been generally used as an overarching category, with only limited unpacking of the relationships among the variables it packs together (Kuper 1999; see also below). Having become an over-extended term, it hampers rather than facilitates analytical purchase.

The international geopolitical climate, notably the global development agenda, pushed steadily during the 1990s towards the continuing extrapolation from the original core concept into the famous 'three pillars' of sustainable development – economic development, social equity and environmental protection – that crystallized at the 2002 Johannesburg World Summit on Sustainable Development. At no point was the breadth of this framework questioned. A reading of recent UN documents reveals a justifiable concern that the discourse has tended to view development in purely economic terms, but what is also striking is the deliberate strategic option of going well beyond the core ecological challenge. Thus the assertion that negotiations after Rio placed 'too much of an emphasis on the 'environment pillar' (United Nations 2010, 8). The same UN study notes with approval that the Johannesburg negotiations 'demonstrated a major shift in the perception of sustainable development – away from environmental issues toward social and economic development' (2010, 8). The study also notes that this shift, which was driven by the needs of developing countries and strongly influenced by the Millennium Development Goals (MDGs), is but one more example of how the term has been pulled in various directions. The endorsement, indeed encouragement, of the shift has been largely responsible for making the term so elusive and analytically inadequate.[6]

The 'fourth pillar of sustainability'

A similar semantic evolution has taken place in the cultural arena. In the early 2000s, the idea began to take shape that 'culture' was a dimension missing from the canonical trilogy of pillars. Why should it miss the chance to jump on the doctrinal, operational – and financial – bandwagon set in motion by the mobilizing metaphor sustainable development had become? The ambition of drafting a cultural complement to the original Agenda 21 emerged in 2002, largely inspired by the work of the Australian activist Jon Hawkes, who had already formulated the notion of culture as a 'fourth pillar'. In his essay *The Fourth Pillar of Sustainability. Culture's Central Role in Public Planning* (2001), Hawkes argued that 'the introduction of the concept of culture into the theoretical and operational frameworks of public affairs has an extraordinary range of potential benefits'. He recast the three pillars as 'social equity, environmental responsibility and economic viability' and plumped squarely for the same totalizing approach by recommending that 'for public planning to be more effective, its methodology should include an integrated framework of cultural evaluation along similar lines to those being developed for social, environmental and economic impact assessment' (Hawkes 2001, vii). His call did not fall on deaf ears. In September 2002, at a first World Public Meeting on Culture held during the World Social Forum in Porto Alegre, the idea was adopted to draw up a document elaborating guidelines for local cultural policies as a complement to Agenda 21. After nearly two years of drafting at conferences organized by the international cultural networks that encouraged its creation, an 'Agenda 21 for Culture' was approved in on May 2004 in Barcelona under the aegis of the international organization of city authorities known as United Cities and Local Governments (UCLG). The latter's Committee on Culture, responsible for drafting the document, has subsequently coordinated the worldwide movement that has emerged.

'Agenda 21 for Culture' contained 67 articles, focused on five main 'culture and…' subjects: human rights; governance; sustainability and territory; social inclusion; economy. Under each article it set out principles, undertakings and recommendations. It was thus cast entirely in the mould of the wider 'sustainable development' discourse, encompassing a broad range of topics other than that of environmental sustainability. Vigorously promoted by the Committee on Culture of the UCLG, 'Agenda 21 for Culture' has seen several adaptations and improvements since 2004, yet all the while increasing its breadth of coverage. A 2015 document entitled 'Culture 21: Actions', adopted at the UCLG's first 'Culture Summit' held in Bilbao, is currently the guiding template UCLG 2015. Interestingly, the Introduction invokes 'human development' rather than 'sustainable development' and foregrounds the notions of cultural development and cultural diversity (in the ambiguous sense of the 2005 UNESCO Convention; cf. Saouma and Isar 2015). The core 'Values' section of the text makes it clear that every conceivable issue related to the flourishing of the cultural sector is being addressed – everything from the long-standing concern with 'access to and participation in' cultural life to the promotion of the cultural and creative industries and to heritage conservation. Also targeted is the socio-political issue of cultural rights and citizenship, as well as cultural diversity. The commitments are enunciated cover a staggering range of domains: cultural rights; heritage, diversity and creativity; culture and education; culture and environment; culture and economy; culture, equality and social inclusion; culture, urban planning and public space; culture, information and knowledge and finally, governance of culture. In each case, challenges are set out and measures are envisaged in both lucid and extremely broad-ranging terms. This comprehensiveness is precisely where the rub lies, making the 'Agenda 21 for Culture' a blueprint for tackling the entire gamut of challenges in the contemporary human condition. The interactions between cultural factors and the *natural environment* are addressed only in a single chapter, albeit one that is very well conceived, and appropriately entitled 'Cultural factors as accelerators of environmental responsibility'.

Programmes so vast are highly elusive for analytical purposes. They include too much and are too diffuse either to separate analytically the 'twisted threads of human experience or to interpret the designs into which they are woven' (Keesing 1974, 73). In a 1995 contribution to the work of the World Commission on Culture and Development, the anthropologist Marshall Sahlins reminded us that

> A great deal of confusion arises in both academic and political discourse when culture in the humanistic sense is not distinguished from 'culture' in its anthropological senses, notably culture as the total and distinctive way of life of a people or society. From the latter point of view it is meaningless to talk of 'the relation between culture and the economy'; since the economy is part of a people's culture… Indeed the ambiguities in this phrase pose the great ideological issue confronted by the Commission: is 'culture' an aspect or a means of "development", the latter understood as material progress; or is 'culture" the end and aim of 'development': the latter understood as the flourishing of human existence in its several forms and as a whole? (World Commission on Culture and Development 1996, 21)

In effect, the way in which the notion of 'culture' floats between the two distinct understandings is at the heart of the problem. Cultural advocates and policy makers tend to speak out of both sides of their mouths, sometimes evoking culture as the arts and heritage, sometimes as entire ways of life or collective identities, generally but not exclusively as the possession of a nation state. The two different notions are also increasingly conflated. Thus, the idea that cultural expression must be 'protected' or 'promoted' in the name of preserving entire (national) ways of life is now enshrined in the 2005 UNESCO Convention on the Protection and Promotion of the Diversity of Cultural Expressions. The idea has been around for many years in fact: it has been a long-standing although not always explicit plank of cultural (including media) policy at the European level, as in the European Union's defence of European audio-visual culture as the expression and representation of the 'European way of life' (Schlesinger 2001). A problem arises, however, when the attainment of sustainability is contradicted by the values and 'design for living' attached to particular ways of life, for these are matters in which ministries and departments of culture have no purchase. Hence while advocating the necessary transformation of our ways of life is most certainly an issue of *public* policy, it transcends the competences of *cultural* policy as such.

Nevertheless, a number of municipalities belonging to UCLG have begun to put in place cross cutting local policies and mechanisms to implement the *Agenda 21 for Culture*. But it is extremely hard to find any national level frameworks of this kind. A scanning of the websites of ministries of culture across the world shows that there is no 'sustainable development' component in the cultural policy of any 'developing' country. As far as 'developed' countries are concerned, the references are extremely rare. In one case, France, there is a 2011 reference to a 'stratégie de développement durable' ('a sustainable development strategy') on the ministry of culture's website, but the page has no content; there is no strategy document, which is curious to say the least, given the country's hosting of the 2015 COP21. In the UK, however, the Department of Culture Media and Sport put out in late 2008 a *DCMS Sustainable Development Action Plan 2008–2011*. The stated aim of the Action Plan was 'to improve the quality of life for all through cultural and sporting activities, support the pursuit of excellence, and champion the tourism, creative and leisure industries' (DCMS 2008, 2), in other words to pursue purposes broader than the environmental and in keeping with the British government's foregrounding of the 'expediency' of culture. Yet the text itself did have a clear climate change focus (including a separate chapter on the topic). It also defined actions under a chapter entitled 'The Arts and Sustainable Development' designed to promote awareness of the ecological issues. Quebec's *Plan d'action développement durable 2013–2015* is a mixed bag: oriented principally towards education and awareness building, most of the 14 Actions in the Plan concerned topics such as heritage conservation and support to the arts and the condition of the artist, links between culture and education and cultural philanthropy. So, once again here, the term 'sustainable' serves as a proxy for a range of other purposes. Several other governments have enunciated sustainable development strategies, but these are defined and/or conducted under the authority of ministries or departments other than the cultural.

What is more, very few academic writers on sustainability refer to the cultural dimension. Margaret Robertson (2014), for example, does not. Neither 'culture' nor 'cultural' figures in the glossary of her authoritative book *Sustainability. Principles and Practice*. Nor does the term cultural policy. No work dealing with culture in sustainable development along the lines of the 'Agenda 21 for Culture' is cited in her bibliography. Her chapter 'Liveable cities' lists out a raft of issues that are cultural in the ways of life sense. These range from mixed use neighbourhoods to building community; they are not presented, however, as challenges for the city cultural department, but as issues for the urban planners – she refers to 'building durable social communities' rather than 'cultural' ones. To my mind, this is less a failure on the part of the author than a lack of reach on the part of the culture in sustainable development advocacy community, which has simply not succeeded in sharing its message as widely as it ought to have. Another complicating factor is that consultants and academic researchers tend to reproduce the established discourse of 'culture and sustainable development' as I have outlined it above, which means that science based knowledge production does not really advance our understanding.

One constructive academic response to the elision of sustainability as a cultural policy issue has been the work of the cultural economist David Throsby, who has elaborated the concept of 'culturally sustainable development'. He bases this concept on a parallel between natural and cultural capital, which, in its economic interpretation, he defines as assets that embody or give rise to cultural value in addition to whatever economic value they may possess. While natural capital includes natural resources, ecosystems and biodiversity, cultural capital is comprised of cultural resources, cultural networks and cultural diversity. Throsby therefore spells out principles for cultural sustainability that mirror what can be specified for ecologically or environmentally sustainable development. Thus *intergenerational equity* would require that development does not compromise the capacities of future generations to access cultural resources and meet their cultural needs; this in turn would require particular concern for protecting and enhancing a nation's tangible and intangible cultural capital. *Intragenerational equity* requires equity in access to cultural production, participation and enjoyment to all members of the community on a fair and non-discriminatory basis. Particular attention would need to be paid to the poorest members of society to ensure that development is consistent with the objectives of poverty alleviation. Thirdly, *cultural diversity*: just as ecologically sustainable development requires the protection of biodiversity, so also should account be taken of the value of cultural diversity to economic, social and cultural development (Throsby 2015).

But the prevailing culturalist discourse on culture and sustainable development does not take such a clearly delimited and actionable path. Instead, it lends weight to the polemical challenge issued some years ago by the literary critic Terry Eagleton, who critiqued the reification and objectification of culture as a determining force endowed with explanatory power, and exerting an impact on everything. As he put it,

> culture can be too close for comfort. This very intimacy is likely to grow morbid and obsessional unless it is set in an enlightened political context, one which can temper these immediacies with more abstract, but also in a way more generous, affiliations. We have seen how culture has assumed a new political importance. But has grown at the same time immodest and overweening. It is time, while acknowledging its significance, to put it back in its place. (Eagleton 2000, 131)

A concluding plea for a return to original intent

Putting culture back in its place in no wise means downplaying its true significance, but it does require us to acknowledge that significance in terms that are at once more realistic and more ambitious. So what might be the appropriate perspective in which to link culture and sustainable development? It will be no surprise that I root such a perspective in the original ecological concern of the Brundtland Commission. Furthermore, given the overriding and central importance today of the issue of climate change, it behoves us to narrow the focus even further, to cover

> the probable social and cultural consequences of significant shifts in climatic patterns as a result of global warming on different human populations, including the immense social suffering likely to result" and "the cultural factors that have contributed to the ecological crisis in the first place. (Clammer 2012, 144)

In other words, at the heart of the challenge are the myriad attitudes, behaviours and practices that together generate unsustainable development, together with the many cultural activities that are in reality ecologically dangerous or destructive (as discussed by Maxwell and Miller in this Special Issue).

Given these two main axes of concern, inquiry and action, the 'cultural' in question must surely be the broad anthropological concept that actually existing cultural policy cannot address. However, to foreground the 'ways of life' understanding for the purposes of sustainable development is in no wise to deny that the work of the arts and artists can powerfully illuminate the issue of climate change itself and transform hearts and minds in relation to it. A wide range of possibilities has been set out recently by John Clammer, who has argued for the 'close connects … between the arts and sustainability', notably in envisioning alternative viable futures and bringing about a 're-enchantment of the world' (2015, 43).[7]

Analogous roles can be imagined for arts and culture institutions. For example, museums, libraries and theatres, as artefacts that consume non-renewable energy resources, can and should organize their functions in ways that reduce their carbon footprint, plan their buildings and operations in ways that consume less non-renewable energy or ensure that their modes of operation contribute as minimally as possible to environmental pollution. Thus cultural institutions can and should take up the challenge of relating ordinary people to the wider environment within which they too may contribute to the development of sustainable cultural systems, just as they already do with regard to other issues such as racism, migrations, homelessness and the like. As regards museums in particular, climate change 'will present challenges that are difficult even to imagine at present' (Ballantyne and Uzzell 2011, 8), which may require the adoption not only of new technologies for different temperatures and humidity levels but also new skills in the workforce to manage the contents in different ways. Given the projected rise in sea levels in coastal areas, many museums may have to be relocated. Mass international tourism could well reach its peak levels soon, before beginning to decline, simply because the way in which people are traveling, in particular by air, consuming non-renewable energy and contributing to the shrinking of the ozone layer. And it is precisely because this possibility is so real, 'the position of museums as keepers of the past and the collective memory will become more important than ever as societies are forced to change and environments get transformed' (2011, 8).

Moreover, couldn't cultural institutions address climate change itself, rather than re-invent themselves in response to it? As Benjamin Morris has pointed out, the impacts of climate change on the environment in one region of the world (high-carbon emitting developed nations) can have far-reaching, and severe, impacts in distant, seemingly unconnected regions (low-emitting, developing nations). Therefore 'the imbalance of the burden between polluter and sufferer has served, paradoxically, to reconnect those agents' (Morris 2011, 132). Morris in turn cites Smith, Clark, and Yusoff, who argue that we can no longer reflect on global social processes and act as global citizens (whether individually or institutionally),

> without also considering pressing global ecological issues – most notably climate change and biodiversity loss. The coincidence of economic and cultural globalization with the maturing of global environmental change science is carrying a whole body of academic, political and media practitioners into new and unfamiliar terrain where it is necessary to grapple simultaneously with the dynamics of the earth's atmosphere, hydrosphere, lithosphere, cryosphere, and biosphere (air, water, rock, ice and life) and with ongoing transformations in a globalising economy and cultural system. (cited in Morris 2011, 133)

Morris reminds us also that climate change is not merely a global process acting on the environment, but that it is also one that acts on the societies that govern and maintain that environment. At the present time, both the climate and our relations with it are in a state of flux. Both require a new and creative spirit of conservation and renewal. The environment as a form of heritage requires permanent reassessment of the societal values, norms, and expectations attached to it: 'hence stemming the tide of its exploitation and degradation requires a change in the way that the heritage is not just used, but how it is conceived, by the purpose sought for the natural world' (2011, 133).

The worst negative consequences of climate change will strike the poor first and most intensely, for they are the most vulnerable to the range of natural 'bads' that are already unfolding and will do with increasingly destructive force (Clammer 2012). This bring us back to the original Brundtland Commission stress on the essential needs of the world's poor, to which overriding priority should be given; and the idea of limitations imposed by the state of technology and social organization on the environment's ability to meet present and future needs. The other dimension of the interaction between culture and climate relates to the cultural factors that have promoted the climate change in the first place. Pointing out how easily we nowadays blame corporations and industrialism, Clammer also reminds us that 'we are all complicit with this by way of our own patterns of consumption, greed and movement' (2012, 146). These include unlimited wants, addiction to travel, the car culture in our cities and country-side, our inability to recycle significantly, our addiction to plastics and 'the widespread failure to adopt event those environmentally friendly technologies that already exists… What is frightening is our path-dependent relationship to these practices' (2012, 147). Despite all we now know, few people are doing anything to avert the crisis.

Hence the urgent priority is our everyday cultural practices, many of them deeply embedded in the contemporary habitus. For it is these practices that contribute to the production not only of climate change, but also to the production of climate or environmental injustice. Exploring the opposite, i.e. environmental justice, is beyond the scope of this essay, but it is clear that achieving it requires 'not only a transformation of our cultural stories and cultural myths … but also of our institutions, including some of the most sacred in a secular society such as the law' (Clammer 2012, 161).

This means calling into question much that is taken for granted in our existing ways of life, of com-bating the exclusions and oppressions built into them. As a cultural challenge, this is tantamount to radically transforming those ways of life, or of imagining entirely new ones that can bring us closer to true sustainability, moving us closer also for that purpose 'towards what Derrida called 'the enlighten-ment to come', where reason and the rules that and categories that define current 'logics' are overturned' (Bussey 2014, 219). Promoting such imaginings through cultural expression ought to be at the heart of any cultural policy, but as we have seen, still very rarely is.

Notes

1. Ideas that are taken for granted in any particular society, the experience by which 'the natural and social world appears as self-evident' in that society (Bourdieu 1977, 164).
2. Progressive Reactionary Blog, 3 January 2009: http://progressivereactionary.blogspot.in/ (accessed 28 September, 2015).
3. I owe this insight indirectly to the philosopher Susanne Langer, as it was used by Hans-Rudolf Wicker in his chapter 'From Complex Culture to Cultural Complexity' in P. Werbner and T. Modood eds. *Debating Cultural Hybridity*. London: Zed Books, 2000.
4. Dozens, if not hundreds of alternative definitions have been offered. There have also been a range of controversies. Opponents of the concept (mainly in North America) consider that it is 'a top-down attempt by the United Nations to dictate how the people of the world should live their lives – and thus as a threat to individual freedoms and property rights' (Kates, Parris, and Leiserowitz 2005, 18). Others see the discourse as little more than rhetoric or lip service, since development remains driven by the interests of business and finance under the neo-liberal capitalist dispensation. The debate is valid to be sure, but this is not to place to explore them.
5. See http://www.yourdictionary.com/motherhood-statement (accessed 25 September 2015).
6. It is heartening to note in this regard that today, the United Nations preference for the excessively broad concept of 'sustainable development' is in retreat, notably with the recent adoption of the 'Sustainable Development Goals 2030' (SDGs). Ten of the 17 SDGs relate in some way to climate change, including one promising urgent action to combat global warming and its impacts, and others on ending hunger and providing water for all.
7. The present text was completed long before the publication in September 2016 of *The Great Derangement. Climate Change and the Unthinkable* by the novelist Amitav Ghosh, a masterful essay that offers powerful new perspectives on the economic, political and historical dimensions of climate change and the fundamentally cultural challenge that it represents. Indeed the book should be required reading on the topic. Ghosh's analysis eloquently confirms the author's vision of the cultural challenge, yet by homing in on how scantily it has been taken up in literary fiction today, it cautions us not to expect too much from at least some categories of creative artist…

Disclosure statement

No potential conflict of interest was reported by the author.

References

Ballantyne, R., and D. Uzzell. 2011. "Looking Back and Looking Forward: The Rise of the Visitor-centered Museum." *Curator* 54 (1): 1–8.

Bourdieu, P. 1977. *Outline of a Theory of Practice*. Cambridge: Cambridge University Press.

Bussey, M. 2014. "The Poetics of Possibility and Critical Spirituality." In *Meeting Rivers. Reflections on Culture, Religion and Ecology*, edited by Siddhartha. Bangalore: Meeting Rivers, Pipal Tree, Fireflies Ashram.

Clammer, J. 2012. *Culture, Development and Social Theory. Towards an Integrated Social Development*. London: Zed Books.

Clammer, J. 2015. *Art, Culture and International Development: Humanizing Social Transformation (Rethinking Development)*. London: Routledge.

Eagleton, T. 2000. *The Idea of Culture*. Oxford: Blackwell.

Ghosh, A. 2016. *The Great Derangement. Climate Change and the Unthinkable*. Gurgaon: Penguin Books India.

Hall, S. 1997. "The Centrality of Culture: Notes on the Cultural Revolutions of Our Time." In *Media and Cultural Regulation*, edited by Kenneth Thompson, 208–238. Milton Keynes: Open University Press.

Hawkes, J. 2001. *The fourth pillar of sustainability. Culture's essential role in public planning*. Melbourne: Common Ground Publishing.

Isar, Y. R. 2010. "Cultural Diplomacy: An Overplayed Hand?" *Public Diplomacy* (3), Winter.

Isar, Y. R. 2013. "Beware of Vaulting Ambitions." In *Culture and Conflict. Challenges for Europe's Foreign Policy (Culture Report. EUNIC Yearbook 2012/2013)*, 192–200. Stuttgart: EUNIC.

Kates, R. W., T. M. Parris, and A. A. Leiserowitz. 2005. "Editorial: What is Sustainable Development? Goals, Indicators, Values and Practice." *Environment. Science and Policy for Sustainable Development* 47 (3): 8–21.

Keesing, R., 1974. "Theories of Culture." *Annual Review of Anthropology* 3: 73–97.

Kingdon, J. 1995. *Agendas, Alternatives and Public Policies*. New York: Harper Collins.

Kuper, A. 1999. *Culture: The Anthropologist's Account*. Cambridge, MA: Harvard University Press.

Morris, B. 2011. "Not Just a Place: Cultural Heritage and the Environment." In *Heritage, Memory and Identity, the Cultures and Globalization Series, 4*, edited by Helmut K. Anheier and Yudhishthir R. Isar, 124–135. London: Sage.

Nussbaum, M. 2011. *Creating Capabilities: The Human Development Approach*. Cambridge, MA: Belknap Press of Harvard University Press.

Robertson, M. 2014. *Sustainability. Principles and Practice*. New York: Routledge.

Sachs, W. 2010. "Introduction." In *The Development Dictionary: A Guide to Knowledge as Power*, edited by W. Sachs, 2nd ed., xv–xx. London: Zed Books.

Saouma, G., and Y.R. Isar. 2015. 'Cultural Diversity at UNESCO: the Trajectory Seen Critically' In *Globalization, Culture and Development. The UNESCO Convention on cultural diversity*, edited by C. De Beukelaer, M. Pyykkonen and J.P. Singh. Basingstoke: Palgrave Macmillan.

Schlesinger, P. 2001. "From Cultural Protection to Political Culture? Media Policy and the European Union." In *Constructing Europe's Identity. The External Dimension*, edited by L.-E. Cedermann, 91–114. Boulder: Lynne Riener.

Sen, A. 1999. *Development as Freedom*. Oxford: Oxford University Press.

Shore, C., and S. Wright, eds. 1997. *Anthropology of policy. Critical perspectives on governance and power*. London: Routledge.

Throsby, D. 2015. "Culture in Sustainable Development." In *Re|Shaping Cultural Policies. 2005 Convention Global Report*, edited by Y.R. Isar, 151–169. Paris: UNESCO Publishing.

UCLG (United Cities and Local Governments). 2004. *Agenda 21 for Culture*. Accessed September 19, 2015. http://www.agenda21culture.net/index.php/docman/agenda21/212-ag21en/file

UCLG (United Cities and Local Governments). 2015. *Culture 2: Actions. Commitments on the Role of Culture in Sustainable Cities*. Accessed September 23, 2015. http://www.agenda21culture.net/index.php/newa21c/new-a21c

United Nations. 2010. *Sustainable Development: From Brundtland to Rio 2012*. (Background Paper prepared for consideration by the High Level Panel on Global Sustainability at its first meeting, 19 September 2010).

Williams, R. 1988. *Keywords: A Vocabulary of Culture and Society*. London: Fontana.

World Commission on Culture and Development. 1996. *Our Creative Diversity*. Paris: UNESCO Publishing.

World Commission on Environment and Development. 1987. *Our Common Future*. Oxford: Oxford University Press.

Yúdice, G. 2003. *The Expediency of Culture. Uses of Culture in the Global Era*. Durham: Duke University Press.

Cultural rights and their contribution to sustainable development: implications for cultural policy

Jordi Baltà Portolés and Milena Dragićevic Šešić

ABSTRACT

This article aims to analyse the meaning and implications of cultural rights for cultural policies concerned with sustainable development. Although references to both cultural rights and sustainable development have become widespread within cultural policy documents in recent decades, the actual conceptual and operational implications often remain vague, as an ambitious discourse that may conceal a poverty of resources and capacities. As a result, the ideal horizon suggested by cultural rights and sustainable development may not always be achieved in practice, nor are the mechanisms to achieve it always well known. In this respect, the article aims to dissect the actual requirements posed by cultural rights and sustainable development, including their different notions and areas of synergy and intersections, in order to shed light on relevant cultural policy approaches. To this end, a range of examples taken from a variety of contexts will also be examined as areas of expressed needs or areas of possible solutions.

Introduction

This article aims to analyse the meaning and implications of cultural rights for cultural policies concerned with sustainable development. Although references to both cultural rights and sustainable development have become widespread within cultural policy documents in recent decades, the actual conceptual and operational implications often remain vague, as an ambitious discourse that may conceal a poverty of resources and capacities. As a result, the ideal horizon suggested by cultural rights and sustainable development may not always be achieved in practice, nor are the mechanisms to achieve it always well known. In this respect, the article aims to dissect the actual requirements posed by cultural rights and sustainable development, including their different notions and areas of synergy and intersections, in order to shed light on relevant cultural policy approaches. To this end, a range of examples taken from a variety of contexts will also be examined as areas of expressed needs or areas of possible solutions.

The main methodological approach will consist of 'establishing relations' (cross-analysis) between relevant international legal acts (legally-binding international agreements) of the UN, UNESCO, the Council of Europe (CoE) and the EU, and of national and local cultural policy strategies and policy instruments enabling the implementation of human rights and cultural rights principles. The authors' standpoint is that cultural rights, in order to be fully exercised, have to be taken into account in cultural policy-making on all levels, including legal instruments for their protection and implementation. Cultural policies should be based on cultural rights, enabling the arts and culture sector 'to look for concrete implications in the relation between cultural practices and social cohesion and inclusion' (Laaksonen 2005, 1) and, more broadly, ensuring that everyone has opportunities to access and participate in cultural life. However, in many cases, especially when it comes to national cultural policies (state level), this is not made effective. Therefore, 'strengthening legal instruments and policies is an important necessary step' (1), which can foster the sense of responsibility of the cultural sector towards the community and towards sustainable development.

Cultural rights and sustainable development: background

In recent decades, cultural rights have become an oft-cited rationale for cultural policies. In a context where rights-based and capacity-based approaches to several fields of policy-making have gained increasing attention, most notably in development contexts (Sen 2000; Nussbaum 2011), cultural rights have in some contexts come to replace or complement other cultural policy rationales, including those concerned with the economic or social impacts of culture (Delgado 2001). In so doing, they have often taken recourse to ideas which had been raised decades earlier, including the democratisation of culture and cultural democracy – indeed, universal access to and participation in culture for everyone, including in decision-making, stand among the main components of rights-based approaches to cultural policy, as shall be seen.

The affirmation of human rights as a core component of human dignity, which should inspire public policies universally, may be seen as one of the major legacies of the twentieth century – yet whilst the international community provided itself with a set of major human rights standards, actual policies have continued to fall short. It could also be argued that until the turn of the millennium, cultural rights did not have a visible place on this stage – their actual policy implications had seldom been examined and only limited monitoring mechanisms existed within civil society or in public organisations (mostly connected to collective cultural rights in relation to the use of mother tongue in public life, education, etc.) (Delgado 2001; Donders 2004). In a context where economic, social, and cultural rights have generally been less attended to than civil and political rights, cultural rights have been particularly neglected, and sometimes been termed the 'cinderella' of human rights, partly as a result of their unclear content and scope (see e.g. Donders 2004) and the visible discrepancies between existing standards and actual practice (Hristova 2006).

In recent years, several efforts have been made to clarify the implications of cultural rights. One major initiative was the Fribourg Declaration on Cultural Rights, adopted in 2007 by an independent working group, which had originally been commissioned by UNESCO in the late 1990s but was not formally endorsed by the organisation (Fribourg Group 2007). The Declaration emphasises that cultural rights, rather than applying particularly to minorities, are universal, and that in order to overcome the existing dispersion in several human rights instruments, 'it is important to group these rights together in order to ensure their visibility and coherence and to encourage their full realization'. (Fribourg Group 2007, 3, 4). Indeed, as other authors have also argued, cultural rights encompass and are closely linked to other human rights, such as freedom of religion, freedom of expression, freedom of assembly and association, and the right to education (Donders 2015, 117, 118).

Further attempts to define the scope of cultural rights and how they relate to other human rights have been made by the United Nations Independent Expert in the Field of Cultural Rights (currently the UN Special Rapporteur in the Field of Cultural Rights) upon taking office in 2010 (UN Independent Expert in the Field of Cultural Rights 2010). The setting-up of this post within the UN human rights environment, as well as the adoption of relevant documents in the field of cultural rights, including the General Comment on the Right to Take Part in Cultural Life (UN Committee on Economic, Social and Cultural Rights 2009), attest to the increasing attention paid to cultural aspects within the institutional context of human rights. Moreover, this shows the recognition of the fact that 'cultural rights are pivotal to the recognition and respect of human dignity, as they protect the development and expression of various world visions – individual and collective – and encompass important freedoms relating to matters of identity.' (UN Independent Expert in the Field of Cultural Rights 2010, 3, 4). Overall, therefore, initiatives such as the Fribourg Declaration on Cultural Rights and the work by the UN Special Rapporteur in the Field of Cultural Rights provide an increasingly clear framework for the implications of cultural rights, on which cultural policies can be based.

The progressive exploration of the links between cultural rights and broader issues related to human dignity may be seen as an analogous and sometimes interwoven process to that which has placed cultural rights and other cultural aspects within contemporary approaches to sustainable development. Sustainable development has become a core component of international policy discussions since the late 1980s, notably upon the publication of the UN-commissioned *Our Common Future* report, which famously defined it as 'development that meets the needs of the present without compromising the ability of future generations to meet their own needs' (World Commission on Environment and Development 1987). Recently, the adoption of the global 2030 Agenda for Sustainable Development has confirmed the central place of the term in global agenda-setting and policy-making (UN General Assembly 2015).

However, the prevalence of references to sustainable development and related terms (e.g. sustainability) in international debates has also led to different meanings, often being used interchangeably despite their visible differences. In addition to the aforementioned meaning of sustainable development as that development which guarantees equal opportunities for future generations, the more functional and somehow narrower term 'sustainability' is often used to refer to the durability of structures and processes, and regularly applied to the ability of organisations and projects, in whichever field, to overcome difficulties and become long-lasting. In this respect, the combination of culture, cultural rights, sustainability and sustainable development has also been used to describe a wide range of situations and meanings, as explained hereafter:

(1) The functional, operational term 'sustainability', when applied to cultural processes, often implies the ability of cultural organisations and projects to become long-lasting. In this context, 'cultural sustainability', or 'the sustainability of a cultural organisation/project', has a limited, operational scope, rather than the broader societal and political implications of other uses of 'sustainability' and 'sustainable development'. The term is often used to highlight the ability of certain processes to outlast their initial funding period, including projects which receive public or private funding in their start-up phase and manage to generate or raise other resources upon its ending. This usage may only have an indirect relation to cultural rights – the ability of certain processes and organisations to foster cultural rights through the active involvement of different groups of people in their activities may contribute to their ability to strengthen their constituency and become sustainable, although this should be complemented with a variety of other practices.

(2) A somehow related, but broader understanding of 'cultural sustainability' refers to the ability of cultural processes to reinforce one another and contribute to each other's durability, thus contributing to the sustainability of what is often referred to as 'cultural ecosystems' or 'cultural ecology' – another environmental analogy that serves to stress the interconnectedness between different processes and agents in the cultural sector: 'To define the cultural field as an "ecology" means being attentive to the diversity and richness of the elements that constitute culture in any given social formation and, importantly, the relations between the elements (and the relative robustness and health of those relations) rather than a rigid separation and demarcation of, for example, the publicly funded and community sectors from the commercial sector.' (Mercer 2002, 62; see also Holden 2015). In this context, cultural sustainability depends on the continuity of and mutual reinforcement between different elements of the ecosystem. The emphasis is often placed on *financial* sustainability (Smiers 2003; Miralles 2009; Vellani 2014). From a perspective of cultural rights, the financial viability of certain cultural expressions should be considered, and protection and support measures may be necessary. However, this is again a tenuous link, since the focus of cultural sustainability when approached from

an 'ecosystemic' perspective lies on cultural organisations and expressions, rather than on individuals and their rights.

Whereas the previous notions referred mainly to the durability of structures (i.e. the narrower approach to sustainability), other approaches are based on sustainable development at a societal level (i.e. the broader approach), as explained below. As several authors have noted (Abelló Vives, Aleán Pico, and Berman Arévalo 2010; Dessein et al. 2015), different perspectives may be applied to explain this relationship. The most relevant among them are presented hereafter:

(3) Several authors and institutions have increasingly argued that the standard sustainable development paradigm adhered to by the international community over the past two decades, which combines environmental, economic and social aspects, should be completed with cultural aspects as a fourth 'pillar' or 'dimension'. In an influential pamphlet published in 2001, Jon Hawkes argued that the notion of sustainability (used as an equivalent to sustainable development in that context) and, more broadly, visions of the future were strongly informed by cultural values: 'In its simplest form, the concept of sustainability embodies a desire that future generations inherit a world at least as bountiful as the one we inhabit. However, how to get there … will always be the subject of constant debate. This debate is about values; it is a cultural debate.' (Hawkes 2001, 11) Hawkes identified cultural vitality as 'the fourth pillar of sustainability'. This approach, which contends that cultural aspects are interrelated with, but not secondary to, other dimensions of sustainable development, has provided inspiration to a number of initiatives, including the Agenda 21 for culture promoted by United Cities and Local Governments (UCLG), which fosters local cultural policies concerned with sustainable development and provides a link with cultural rights (UCLG 2004, 2015). In a broader sense, this understanding of culture as a central aspect of sustainable development could be linked to approaches in human development studies (Fukuda-Parr 2004; Sen 2004; Nussbaum 2011), which argue that cultural liberty is one of the intrinsic freedoms which development strategies should strive to achieve – making culture thus an *ends* of development. In this respect, the affirmation of culture as a pillar, dimension, or end of sustainable development may be seen as a reaction to other approaches which, often placing emphasis on *development* rather than on its *sustainable* nature, have stressed culture as a *means* or *resource* for the achievement of economic growth and other development goals (for a summary of approaches, see Abelló Vives, Aleán Pico, and Berman Arévalo 2010).

(4) Another perspective connecting culture and development sees cultural factors as the context in which development can take place, placing it as the foundation for economic, social or environmental development. Several approaches, including those that accept the universal, unquestionable nature of development and others that consider that mainstream approaches to development should be contested, exist (Abelló Vives, Aleán Pico, and Berman Arévalo 2010; Escobar 2011). In a somehow related vein, some analyses have described culture's potential 'mediating role' among the different dimensions of sustainable development (Dessein et al. 2015). This perspective highlights the inevitable tensions that may arise between different dimensions of sustainable development and sees culture as a *driver* for sustainability, helping to bridge differences and alleviate tensions. Whilst no explicit references are made to cultural rights in this context, it could be argued that the individual and collective ability to participate in the shaping of visions of the future and the negotiation of conflicts arising in approaches to sustainable development are essential in this context, and this is part of cultural rights.

(5) Finally, some authors have argued that culture embodies a potential for societal transformation, by taking an evolutionary, holistic and transformative role which provides a new paradigm to sustainable development. In this context, culture '… offers an ideal of doing things well, of culture as cultivation and sustaining life … This makes it possible to think of sustainability and sustainable development as processes, ongoing and in-the-making, not

as fixed states.' (Dessein et al. 2015, 32; Horlings 2016). Here, active community participation in social and political decision-making *and* eco-cultural practices which serve to foster a new understanding of the human place in the world are mentioned as relevant examples. Again, no explicit references to the notion of cultural rights are generally made in this context. However, by combining participation in decision-making and active engagement in experiences which involve transforming urban and rural landscapes and fostering new relationships with the natural and human environment, some connections may be established with elements in cultural rights, including the right to take part in cultural life (designing and implementing cultural and creative projects, taking part in decision-making on communities' cultural future, etc.).

Although the connection with cultural rights is not always made explicit in analyses regarding the relationship between culture and sustainable development, the observation above shows that some associations can clearly be made. Cultural rights become visible particularly in approaches focusing on sustainable development applied to individuals and communities, rather than to the sustainability of organisations and processes, as well as in those approaches which more directly address the political and policy implications of the relation between culture and sustainable development. On this basis, the next section will examine the implications of cultural rights for cultural policies from the perspective of sustainable development.

Cultural policies inspired by cultural rights

As mentioned above, the discourse on cultural rights has increasingly entered discussions and approaches in the field of cultural policies, but the exact operational implications are not always made clear. On the basis of the previous exploration of the implications for cultural rights from a perspective concerned with sustainable development and cultural sustainability, we present here five specific areas for action.

Access to and participation in cultural activities

With the right to freely take part in cultural life affirmed as a cultural right in several international documents (e.g. Universal Declaration on Human Rights, International Covenant on Economic, Social and Cultural Rights), the most evident requirement for rights-based approaches to cultural policy involves ensuring that measures are adopted to facilitate universal access to and opportunities to engage in cultural facilities, services and activities. Beyond the availability of venues, resources and activities, particular emphasis should be placed on the ability of everyone to actively engage in creative processes, including individual and collective creation (or 'co-creation') of expressions, symbols, and narratives and the presentation of a wide range of individual and collective memories and heritages. The need for this participation to be *free* involves that no one should be forced to take part in cultural activities and processes against their will. Access to and participation in cultural life may be seen as a central aim of all rights-based cultural policies. In order to make these *core* rights effective, a range of measures and *instruments* will be necessary, including participation in decision-making and management, decentralisation, and an analysis of the obstacles and factors which hinder the exercise of cultural rights. Several of these *instrumental* approaches are outlined below.

Participation in policy decision-making and management

The right to take part in cultural life includes the right to contribute to *shaping cultural life*. From a policy perspective, this involves the possibility to take part in decision-making processes as regards priority setting and resource allocation. A wide range of approaches can be adopted in this respect, from participation in elections to more active engagement in cultural councils and deliberation bodies and individual or collective participation in the management of cultural venues and facilities. The latter options are particularly suitable in local contexts (e.g. cities, towns, neighbourhoods), which allow for innovation in forms of engagement in public affairs (Pascual i Ruiz 2007). Participation in deliberation, decision-making and management is seen to increase the ownership of cultural processes and to be facilitated by and in turn contribute to strengthening civil society, including community groups, NGOs and professional associations. Furthermore, giving everyone the opportunity to express their needs can be seen as a deep transformation in traditional approaches to cultural policy wherein needs and priorities were defined by public decision-makers and managers (Jiménez 2014). This may be reinforced in practices such as those of participatory budgeting, which, originally established in Brazilian and other Latin American cities, has also been applied elsewhere and led to the setting-up of new cultural venues and programmes (see e.g. De Oliveira, Avelar, and Oliveira Junior 2014, as regards the establishment of decentralised cultural centres in Belo Horizonte, Brazil). Of course, principles of transparency, accountability, and equal representation should be applied in this context, in order to prevent only some voices from being heard and attended to, as well as to guarantee a connection between policy-making and actual management and delivery.

Addressing the obstacles that prevent participation in cultural life

Whether at the level of access to and participation in cultural activities or participation in decision-making, cultural rights are universal– and this requires being aware of obstacles which may hinder effective participation. Over the years, studies conducted in several contexts have suggested that gender, age, educational level, ethnicity, social class and spatial segregation may influence trends in cultural participation, and surveys have indicated that those who attend less often refer to issues such as price, distance, lack of transport, timing, or disability as hindrances to active participation in arts activities (see e.g. Holden 2010; TNS Opinion & Social 2013; Hargreaves, May, and Goulding 2015a, 2015b). In this respect, rights-based cultural policies should analyse obstacles which prevent participation and adopt effective measures to address them (Koivunen and Marsio 2007; Dragićević Šešić and Stojković 2012, 45–47). Relevant steps in this area may include improved communication of existing activities (including using a diverse range of languages and channels), outreach work, revised pricing strategies, partnerships with educational, social, and transport organisations, revised programming to cater to a diversity of interests and research on participation trends, enablers, and obstacles. Broadening opportunities for participation in decision-making and governance may also enhance transparency and ownership of cultural policies and act as an enabler for further participation among groups that have traditionally been reluctant to attend.

Protection of minorities and threatened identities and expressions

The rights to choose and have one's cultural identity respected and to know and have one's own culture and those that make up the common heritage of humanity respected have been identified as cultural rights (Fribourg Group 2007). The UN Special Rapporteur on Cultural Rights has also claimed that '… the respect, protection and promotion of cultural diversity are essential for ensuring the full respect of cultural rights' and that 'cultural diversity in a society can provide people … with the opportunity to enjoy a wider range of cultural choices.' (UN Independent Expert in the Field of Cultural Rights 2010, 11). Therefore, the protection of diverse identities and cultural expressions, and particularly those which represent minorities whose sustainability may be threatened, deserves particular attention in cultural policy. This is also in line with international cultural standards, including the UNESCO Universal Declaration on Cultural Diversity (UNESCO 2001) and the UNESCO Convention on the Protection and Promotion of the Diversity of Cultural Expressions (UNESCO 2005). Of course, measures adopted to protect minority identities and expressions should in no way prevent individuals and communities from freely defining their identities and cultural practices of choice, nor prevent the ability of cultural expressions to evolve.

Protection of cultural resources, rights and activities which may be put at risk by policies in other areas

Cultural resources, such as heritage, including 'dissonant heritage' (Kisić 2016) or the heritage of others; artistic research related to controversial or conflict areas, mostly addressing issues of religion; cultural services (such as cinemas or bookshops) that cannot be competitive on the global market or have become obsolete in the face of free trade agreements: these are only a few examples of cultural assets threatened by policies of other governmental and international organisations. Sometimes, even the same conventions have opposite, contradictory paragraphs, as in the case of the European Convention of Human Rights, where the relationship between *Freedom of Religion* (Article 9) and *Freedom of Expression* (Article 10) might be understood differently. This controversy is reinforced by the number of UN resolutions against defamation of religions between 1999 and 2011. Thus protection of freedom of speech is endangered by both policies of 'political correctness', and by UN resolutions (Human Rights Council 2008) in which defamation of religion is considered a criminal act, stimulating governments to create 'blasphemy laws', and different public authorities to use those resolutions against its political opponents in the arts and media.

Examples coming from Egypt and a few other countries with a Muslim majority show to what extent UN resolutions in this area might be used in judiciary systems to imprison those who dare to express any sort of critical statement.

> 'This new, censorious right' clashes squarely with the freedom of expression and freedom of information aspects of the Universal Declaration of Human Rights. ... [For] the first time in its history, the United Nations equated criticism of religion with racism, and raised 'respect' for a philosophical system-religion- to the level of a 'soft law' under inter-national law. (...) These resolutions targeted alleged defamatory speech, not discriminatory actions taken against the people – usually religious minorities – on the basis of their religious beliefs. (Eko 2012, 118)

The persecution of the Rohingya and other religious minorities was not stopped using international resolutions; instead, these were used to prevent free, dissident speech in numerous countries around the globe (Egypt, Pakistan, Turkey, etc.).

There are other forms of intolerance regarding artistic freedom of expression, always calling upon some other public policies in support. Artistic provocations of social values as well as of the public's feeling of justice/injustice like Marcus Harvey's *Myra* project within the exhibition *Sensation* in London in 1997 (Molyneux 1998) are endangering artistic positions in society and the positions of cultural organisations acting as producers, unless those projects are supported by powerful organisations or persons (Saatchi, Manifesta, etc.) or by cultural policies standing firmly behind the freedom of artistic expression as a value.

As Joost Smiers (2003, 199) declared:

> Public authorities should protect what comes into being and what cannot count immediately on the approval of huge crowds. The protection of what only some people want to see, hear, read or experience, belongs to the process of guaranteeing the continuity of cultures (...). Communication freedom is an essential value for society, so governments should not only refrain from interventions in cultural and artistic processes, they have the duty to create the conditions in which citizens can communicate with each other freely, including through the arts.

Policy strategies and instruments enabling cultural rights

Following the reflection on the implications of cultural rights for cultural policies, this section examines a set of examples and trends, in order to analyse to what extent the horizon of cultural rights is being implemented in practice.

International conventions and resolutions as drivers for policies and practices

Alongside the policies and instruments created in response to civil society advocacy, one major driver for developments in this area has been the ratification of international conventions, resolutions and charters (e.g. those developed by the Council of Europe, the United Nations or UNESCO).

Besides the European Convention on Human Rights, Member States of the Council of Europe are bound, among other regulations, to develop their public policies in relation to other rights-related texts, including the European Social Charter, the European Convention for the Prevention of Torture and Inhuman or Degrading Treatment or Punishment, the European Framework Convention for the Protection of National Minorities, the European Charter for Regional or Minority Languages and the Framework Convention on the Value of Cultural Heritage for Society (Faro Convention).

The Faro Convention (Council of Europe 2005) brings together two important concepts: that of universal cultural rights and that of sustainability. Seeing heritage as a community resource, potential and responsibility, it emphasises ways in which heritage is sustaining societies and communities, thus linking with the broader notions of sustainable development examined earlier. The Convention takes into account the largest possible definition of heritage 'central to everyday, ordinary real life, local as well as universal. It sees heritage (…) as continuing process of creating, constructing, using and modifying heritage' (Fairclough et al. 2014, 11). It aims to make a community sustainable, developing a shared life without conflicts and interruptions. Thus, within the implementation of the Convention, heritage, whether shared or distinctive, is accepted as both a right and a responsibility, integrated within a common collective culture of memory and everyday practices.

The UNESCO Convention on the Protection and Promotion of the Diversity of Cultural Expressions (2005) was developed as a response to challenges posed by economic globalisation and market liberalisation, including the uneven concentration of cultural production and consumption. The Convention's basic aim is to foster creativity, and to balance the economic and cultural aspects of development, and specifically sustainable development. It is based on eight key principles, starting with respect for human rights and fundamental freedoms (UNESCO 2015, 171–201), defending states' cultural sovereignty, guaranteeing equal dignity and respect for all cultures, and equitable access to cultural expressions from around the world.

These Conventions directly contribute to the development of adequate cultural and other public policy strategies and measures aiming to create conditions for the exercise of cultural rights in order to guarantee long-term sustainable development, as society and each of its minority or marginal groups would benefit from public policies that reflect their individual and collective rights, even if the link with cultural rights tends to be implicitly rather than explicitly made.

Comparative analysis of policy instruments (Slovenia and Denmark 2000–2014)

According to the Compendium, which since 2005 collects and reviews policies inspired by cultural rights, those rights are seen as part of human rights relating mainly to: 'freedom of expression; right to and responsibility for cultural heritage; right to free practice of art and culture and to creative work; right to protect the intellectual and material benefits accruing from scientific, literary and artistic production; right to participate in cultural life and right to equally accessible and available cultural, library, and information and leisure services; right to choose one's own culture; right to the development and protection of culture; respect for culture and its autonomy and for cultural identity' (ERICarts and Council of Europe, Compendium, http://www.culturalpolicies.net/web/ethics-human-rights.php).

As Compendium authors collect and present policy data and information about planned and implemented policy instruments and initiatives related to different national and international human and cultural rights instruments, relevant information about various aspects of human and cultural rights can be found throughout country profiles. Thus, we will 'test' two countries – Slovenia and Denmark, to see to what extent those policies might be considered as rights-based policies in the five domains that have been introduced earlier. The two countries, Denmark and Slovenia, represent respectively the 'northern' and 'western' point of view, on the one hand, and Central European policy traditions belonging to new democracies, but also to 'southern', Mediterranean identity, on the other. These two countries have also been selected because their policies, as shown below, may be representative of cultural policies which on the one hand promote accessibility while on the other may limit opportunities to take part in cultural life for certain groups.

Access to and participation in cultural activities

In Slovenia, the Act Regulating the Realisation of the Public Interest in the Field of Culture (2002) demands accessibility related to all art and media fields. This demand directly connects to cultural rights – the right of citizens to participate in and share national cultural values. Article 8 of this Law states the basic principles of public interest in culture, involving the need to ensure conditions for the accessibility of cultural assets. Article 65 defines state responsibilities, including funding public cultural programmes to cover all the national territory.

Furthermore, the State shall also fund those cultural programmes or projects aimed at the following: '(…) the *autochthonous* (italics by authors of the text) Italian and Hungarian minorities and the Roma community; the cultural integration of minority communities and immigrants if their cultural programmes/projects exceed the local level'. This means that collective cultural rights are applied only to *autochthonous* cultural minorities (defined in articles 5 and 64 of the Slovenian Constitution), while other 'new minorities' (e.g. Bosnians, Serbs, Croats) are treated as individuals and social groups, without particularly guaranteed collective cultural rights (Republic of Slovenia, 1991). Article 8 (which refers to the universal right to creativity and access to culture free from ethnic discrimination) and article 65 (that specifies that additional funds shall be made available to minority and migrant groups to implement their own programmes and projects) may apply to them. In the annual budget there are items related to cultural activities for ethnic minorities (Italians, Hungarians, Roma), as well as for the development of technical infrastructure and broadcasting for people with disabilities, and for social inclusion purposes.

As the latter group includes all 'other' minorities, migrants and disadvantaged groups, this clearly indicates the different status and different 'access to cultural rights' of different minority groups (even those that might represent third- or fourth-generation Slovenian citizens). This shows that 'old minorities' are seen as those who, sharing one same history (Austro-Hungarian citizens) might be sharing the same values and life-styles as the autochthonous population (with the exception of the Roma population, which continues to be treated differently from both old and new minorities). This means that old minorities are not perceived as a 'sustainability threat', while new migrants still provoke suspicions of being 'the Other', someone different.

In Denmark, since the creation of the Ministry of Culture in 1961, its welfare-based cultural policy focuses on the 'egalitarian dimension of culture for all' (Duelund, Valtysson, and Bohlbro 2012, 45). Social and political consensus exists around this. However, accessibility as a priority was questioned with political changes in 2001 (under the VKO conservative government), when new priorities were defined, such as the revitalisation of the national dimension, the stimulation of the creative industries and links between art and business. The working programme presented in 2010, *Denmark 2020 – knowledge, economic growth, wealth, welfare*, had a small paragraph on cultural policy related to political rights and freedom of expression, and to integration policies (immigrants' duty 'towards the mainstream', to accept values, the cultural canon and the canon of democracy) (Duelund, Valtysson, and Bohlbro 2012).

The new Slovenian National Programme for Culture has the following objectives (Čopič and Srakar 2015, 9): to ensure access to cultural goods and services; to encourage and promote cultural education in schools, etc., with the three leading principles of excellence, diversity and accessibility. However, a predominant new discourse focusing on the creative industries, the art market and employment in the cultural sector may be seen to contradict these principles, and a thorough analysis of the sectorial policies clearly identifies that cultural rights policies and their instruments are less important than those strengthening entrepreneurial capacities in the arts. The main objectives in the domain of cultural rights as related to minorities are identified as a 'higher level of sectoral and regional cultural integration of minorities; and diverse cultural activities of multiple members of vulnerable groups' (27). Accessibility is guaranteed through measures including 'education of audiences', 'raising media literacy' and the use of digital cultural content, 'paying particular attention to the content tailored to young people, cultural minorities and other vulnerable groups' (25–30). It is obvious that neither the new discourse nor new measures to stimulate creative industries, art market, and entrepreneurialism are applied to minority groups.

Participation in policy decision-making and government

The right to contribute to shaping cultural life is probably one of the least implemented in practice, as cultural and other public policies do not often establish adequate instruments enabling everyone to fully enjoy this right. During the period of self-governing Socialism in Yugoslavia, this right was guaranteed by laws and legal acts which demanded that self-governing communities of interest should be created in each field of public interest (such as education, culture, health, etc.). Councils of self-governing communities of interest were created at all levels (municipality, city, region and republic), including representatives of 'all concerned', 'producers', and 'users' of services. They were supposed to discuss programmes and budgets for culture, artistic activities, heritage protection etc. Representatives of 'users', often involving factory workers but also students, employees in services etc., were supposed to express their needs and interests to cultural professionals who were autonomous in creating their programmes. Besides, cultural institutions were obliged to 'offer in public debate' their yearly plans and reports. However, the system did not function autonomously, as one single political party controlled the dialogue behind the scenes.

More recently, several cities have established local councils for culture and other participatory tools (participatory budgeting on cultural matters), which allow citizens and cultural actors to influence policy design, implementation, and evaluation, through concerted dialogue with public authorities and other local stakeholders. Instruments such as the Agenda 21 for culture have contributed to developments in this field.

Cultural policy in Denmark has been led since 2003 by the Danish Arts Agency, Heritage Agency & Danish Agency for Libraries and Media – arm's length bodies that in 2012 merged to create the Danish Agency for Culture. At the same time territorial reform diminished the number of municipalities and counties, recognising rights to all territorial units to lead cultural policy.

It would be expected that in both Denmark and Slovenia more democratic dialogue and participatory processes of policy-making would have been established. However, as stated in the Compendium profiles, interactions are only happening between 'cultural administration, Government, Parliament, the arm's length bodies, local governments, cultural institutions, NGOs, individual artists and their associations' (Čopič and Srakar 2015, 14) Thus, neither citizens nor communities are seen as agencies in those processes, as the bureaucratic instrumentalisation of culture (Čopič 2014) and 'democratic elitism' (Gray 2012, 507) prevail in policy-making at all levels in spite of the proclaimed right of all to participate in policy-making.

Addressing the obstacles that prevent participation in cultural life

Usually, policies and actions in this area should aim to remove physical (e.g. 'design for all'), financial (ticketing policy and gratuity), geographic, spatial, psychological (fear and discomfort, unease in culture), and mostly culture-based barriers, including linguistic or ideological barriers. These policies, developed within the concept of culture 'as a public service', had to respond to increasing social inequalities, 'ensuring the effectiveness of the service. Such concern may even be more urgent in light of the agenda of social justice. … [Increasing] cultural participation also means tackling inequalities in the distribution of resources' (OMC 2012, 10).

Most of the instruments analysed focus on social barriers and cohesion-related aspects, since social integration is seen as the main objective. In both Danish and Slovenian policies (if possibly less in the latter), special attention is given to immigrant communities, as it is understood that their different background may prevent them from fully enjoying the cultural rights of European citizens. Integration and education are seen as key tasks, implemented under a slogan: 'There must be an end to parallel societies'. Even the Danish Cultural Canon, however controversial, was seen as a tool offering the immigrant community necessary knowledge and values to understand the society in which they lived. (The Canon, however, does not offer Danish citizens an understanding of the key values of immigrant communities, that are now an important part of the Danish social fabric).

At the same time many policy measures are related to the education of children and young people, and other 'vulnerable groups': low skills and competences were seen in both countries as major obstacles preventing participation. Tasks related to raising cultural competence of children and youth are more explicit than any other, including measures such as *the Year of Art and Culture* (2006/2007) in Slovenian schools, Cultural bazaars that promote arts and cultural education; 'Cultural days', implemented as part of schools' extra-curricular programmes that raise interest for the arts among pupils, or a longitudinal action that is enhancing reading habits: *The Reading Badge* (OMC 2012, 40; Čopič and Srakar 2015), or a specific priority within the Danish Arts Council Action Plan (2011–2015) – 'maintaining a strong focus on children and adolescents and their encounter with art and artistic tools' (Duelund, Valtysson, and Bohlbro 2012, 37). In the same line, the Educational Plan for Danish Museums (part of the 2006 governmental programme 'Culture for all') aimed to complement the formal education of children and youth, bringing them closer to Danish heritage and values. Programmes linked to the removal of other barriers, such as geographical ones, are rare and mostly operated by NGOs, but supported by Ministry funds, such as the project 'The Concert Visits You' developed by Jeunesses Musicales Slovenia.

All these programmes are aiming to contribute to the long-term social sustainability of Danish and Slovenian societies, as the prevailing opinion demands integration, 'sharing culture', and not culturally complex and differentiated communities.

Protection of minority and threatened identities and expressions
Although the EU report regarding access to and participation in culture (OMC 2012, 14) states that 'Among the excluded – or self-excluded – ethnic cultural minorities represent special and often statistically significant groups, and pose distinctive challenges: migrant communities and the Roma population', no single example of a cultural policy measure or an initiative regarding the Roma population in Slovenia could be found.

In Denmark, in the Arts Council's Action Plan (2007–2011) the only relevant line within the priority list was 'including more artists with a non-Danish ethnic background' – this may however not refer to the protection of the specificity of their cultural expressions, but enable those who accepted Danish values and cultural practices to be more integrated within the Danish cultural system. In the last Action Plan (2011–2015), ensuring diversity by 'allowing artists to develop their practice, regardless of social and cultural background' (Duelund, Valtysson, and Bohlbro 2012, 37.) does not mean enhancing diversity of practices and expressions, but suggests the inclusion of artists with a migrant background in mainstream cultural production, in order to reinforce social unity and its sustainability (no policy measures were adopted to stimulate intercultural dialogue and encourage Danish citizens to understand migrants' values, fears and creative practices).

Protection of cultural resources and activities which may be put at risk by policies in other areas
Over the last decade, freedom of expression became a major issue in Europe, that could be put at risk by other policies or pressures (foreign policies, security issues, etc.). In Denmark, the scandal around the Mohammed Cartoons (the journal Jyllands-Posten published 12 caricatures of Mohammed in 2005) showed to what extent society was culturally divided, but also that Danish society was more ready to protect freedom of expression than to conform to the economic and political demands – as the boycott of Danish goods in Arab countries threatened to endanger export results. However, in other European countries the protection of fundamental freedoms was often threatened by other policies (or due to international pressure), and cultural policy actors have not yet succeeded in finding the right answers to this, endangering often not only the own sustainability of cultural or media organisations, but also social and community sustainability.

Conflicts around defamation of religion vs. freedom of expression have shown to what extent the sustainability of cultural organisations and communities might be endangered. The happenings around *Behzti* (Grillo 2007) destabilised both city theatre and cultural operators within minority communities, and artistic practice as an agent of sustainability was questioned (the Birmingham Repertory Theatre's new programming policy of inclusiveness was postponed and thus its new mission and values of the theatre were shaken). In that sense it is clear that cultural policies that are 'controlling' rights and freedom of expression (even if 'justified' by UN resolutions), endanger not only the long-term sustainability of the cultural sector, but also that of communities who after those events feel divided and polarised.

Conclusions

The integration of cultural rights in cultural policies and in sustainable development strategies has traditionally been hampered by a limited understanding of the concepts of cultural rights and the vagueness of their policy implications. Although enshrined in a number of international law documents for over half a century, it is only in recent years that the meaning of cultural rights for a 'horizon' of human dignity and sustainable development has been explored in detail, as attested by developments at UN level and an increasing interest from policy-making (at national and particularly local level) and academic circles. Overall, these developments, while incomplete, may contribute to placing cultural rights on a more equal position with other human rights, exploring the interconnections with other rights and further recognising the relevance for sustainable development. In a rights-based approach to cultural policies, particular attention should be paid to the core, *substantial* right of everyone to access and participate in cultural life. This will involve, in turn, a set of *instrumental* measures, including the existence of forums or spaces for participation in decision-making and management, the decentralisation of cultural resources and the identification of obstacles and factors which hinder participation in cultural life.

The exploration also shows that policies and measures relevant to cultural rights and sustainable development had been implemented earlier, but had not always been phrased in a rights-based discourse or in relation to sustainable development. Increasing awareness in recent years may, nevertheless, contribute to making these links more explicit and may also help to prevent or, failing that, condemn abuses and violations of cultural rights, which have traditionally been widespread.

In a context where cultural (collective and individual) rights have often been seen as secondary to other human rights, and their implications perceived as unclear, frictions with other human rights often lead to the neglect of cultural rights. One area where this becomes visible is that of freedom of artistic expression, which has often been curtailed in the light of perceived threats to certain interest groups or in the name of public interest – even if the latter did not necessarily amount to a defense of human rights. Cultural policymakers and managers may need to pay particular attention to these issues and be increasingly aware of the implications of and threats to cultural rights, including their duty to ensure that the cultural rights of artists and citizens, even when representing a minority, should be seen as essential for a broader horizon of sustainable development in their communities.

Cultural rights comprise a range of forms of engagement and, when transferred to the policy realm, involve a variety of contexts in which public authorities should protect, respect and fulfill cultural rights, through diverse means and methodologies. Indeed, it could be argued that the ideal horizon provided by cultural rights, and its ultimate contribution to sustainable development, can only be achieved when instances of participation and engagement happen at all stages of policy development (design, implementation and evaluation) and in active programme management, and when opportunities are provided to as many people as possible, through individual and collective participation, to be part of this process. The latter involves paying attention to vulnerable or disadvantaged groups, including ethnic and linguistic minorities. In practice, whilst progress has been visible in some areas (e.g. physical accessibility of cultural venues), much remains to be done at other stages (e.g. active participation in policy design and evaluation, recognition of the manifold obstacles that prevent effective participation, equal attention to all disadvantaged groups, etc.), as previous observations have shown. In addition, it is necessary to continue to raise awareness and develop suitable policies to recognise that, cultural rights being universal, they should apply to everyone, rather than only to specific groups.

Different levels of government should also consider the implications that cultural rights have on the areas of competence in which they are most active – whilst some rights need to be enshrined in national legislation and rights frameworks, it is often at a local and regional level where actual fulfillment of rights will take place (Hristova, Šešić, and Duxbury 2015). The further exploration of implications for governance should also comprise recognition of the importance of civil society organisations, including

NGOs active in the field of culture, artists, and culture professionals' groupings, etc., which may play a role in awareness-raising, advocacy, policy debate, programme initiatives, and delivery.

A range of definitions of sustainable development and its implications for culture continue to exist, and this has led to a wide range of arguments on policies and programmes being implemented in the name of sustainable development whilst being guided by rather different values and aims. From the perspective of universal cultural rights, it is sustainable development applied to individuals and communities that should prevail. In addition, sustainable development being a combination of different dimensions, policies in this field should increasingly explore the connectedness with other areas of development, including economic development, social inclusion and environmental sustainability, through appropriate governance frameworks.

Furthermore, attention should also be paid to the sustainability of diverse cultural ecosystems as well, including the need for cultural organisations and projects to become sustainable. It is to be understood that broadening, diversifying and ensuring the engagement of audiences, i.e. providing opportunities to fulfill their cultural rights, can also be a source of sustainability for cultural organisations, by contributing both to their cultural connectedness and to their financial continuity (see e.g. OMC 2012, 3; Tomka 2013, on how funding programmes such as the European Commission's Creative Europe programme are increasingly placing emphasis on accessibility of culture on the basis of cultural rights and for institutional sustainability).

Disclosure statement

No potential conflict of interest was reported by the authors.

References

Abelló Vives, A., A. Aleán Pico, and E. Berman Arévalo. 2010. "Cultura y desarrollo: intersecciones vigentes desde una revisión conceptual reflexiva." In *Cultura y desarrollo. Un compromiso para la libertad y el bienestar*, edited by A. Martinell Sempere, 75–90. Madrid and Tres Cantos: Fundación Carolina/Siglo XXI. Accessed 13 November 2015. http://catedraunesco.com/resources/uploads/culturaydesarrollo_amartinell.pdf.

Čopič, V. 2014. "Birokratska instrumentalizacija kulture." In *Menadžment dramskih umetnosti i medija – izazovi XXI veka: Proceedings from International Conference, [10–11 December 2013]*, edited by M. Nikolić, 181–193. Belgrade: Faculty of Drama Arts.

Čopič, V., and A. Srakar. 2015. "Country Profile: Slovenia." In *Compendium of Cultural Policies and Trends in Europe*, edited by Council of Europe/ERICarts. 16th ed. http://www.culturalpolicies.net.

Council of Europe. 2005. *Framework Convention on the Value of Cultural Heritage for Society (The Faro Convention)*. http://www.coe.int/t/dg4/cultureheritage/heritage/Identities/default_en.asp.

De Oliveira, L. J., J. Avelar, and J. Oliveira Junior. 2014. "Belo Horizonte: Network of Regional Cultural Centres." In *A Good Practice Case Study of the Agenda 21 for Culture*. Barcelona: UCLG. http://agenda21culture.net/images/a21c/bones_practiques/pdf/pilot_BH-ENG.pdf.

Delgado, E. 2001. "Planificación cultural contra espacio público." *Karis* 11: 49–62.

Dessein, J., K. Soini, G. Fairclough, and L. Horlings, eds. 2015. *Culture in, for and as Sustainable Development. Conclusions from the COST Action IS 1007 Investigating Cultural Sustainability*. Jyväskylä: University of Jyväskylä. http://www.culturalsustainability.eu/conclusions.pdf.

Donders, Y. 2004. "The Legal Framework to the Right to Take Part in Cultural Life." Background Document for the International Congress Cultural Rights and Human Development, Barcelona, 24–27 August.

Donders, Y. 2015. "Cultural Human Rights and the UNESCO Convention: More than Meets the Eye?". In *Globalization, Culture, and Development. The UNESCO Convention on Cultural Diversity*, edited by C. De Beukelaer, M. Pyykkönen, and J. P. Singh, 117–131. Basingstoke: Palgrave.

Dragićević Šešić, M., and B. Stojković. 2012. *Culture: management, animation, marketing*. Belgrade: CLIO.

Duelund, Peter, B. Valtysson, and L. Bohlbro. 2012. "Country Profile: Denmark". In *Compendium of Cultural Policies and Trends in Europe*, edited by Council of Europe/ERICarts. 13th ed. http://www.culturalpolicies.net.

Eko, L. S. 2012. *New Media, Old Regimes: Case Studies in Comparative Communication Law and Policy*. Lanham: Lexington.

ERICarts and Council of Europe. 2005. "Intercultural Dialogue, Cultural Policies and the *Compendium*. Proposed indicators to collect information within the *Compendium* framework," draft for discussion. http://www.ericarts.org/web/files/131/en/intercultural_dialogue_johnfoote.pdf.

ERICarts and Council of Europe. *Compendium, Cultural Policies and Trends in Europe*. Accessed 10 November 2015. http://www.culturalpolicies.net/web/ethics-human-rights.php.

Escobar, A. 2011. *Encountering Development: The Making and Unmaking of the Third World*. New ed. Princeton: Princeton University Press.

Fairclough, G., M. Dragićevic Šešić, L. Rogač-Mijatovič, E. Auclair, and K. Soini. 2014. "The Faro Convention, a New Paradigm for Socially – And Culturally – Sustainable Heritage Action?" *Kultura/Culture* 8: 9–19.

Fribourg Group. 2007. *Cultural Rights. Fribourg Declaration*. Fribourg: Institut interdisciplinaire d'éthique et des droits de l'homme. http://www.unifr.ch/iiedh/assets/files/Declarations/declaration-eng4.pdf.

Fukuda-Parr, S., dir. 2004. *Human Development Report 2004. Cultural Liberty in Today's Diverse World*. New York: UNDP. http://hdr.undp.org/sites/default/files/reports/265/hdr_2004_complete.pdf.

Gray, C. 2012. "Democratic Cultural Policy: Democratic forms and Policy Consequences." *International Journal of Cultural Policy* 18 (5): 505–518.

Grillo, R. D 2007. "Licence to Offend? The Behzti Affair." *Ethnicities* 7 (1): 5–29. http://etn.sagepub.com/content/7/1/5.full.pdf+html.

Hargreaves, J., M. May, and N. Goulding. 2015a. *Taking Part, Focus On: Art forms. Statistical Release*. London: Department for Culture, Media & Sport. https://www.gov.uk/government/uploads/system/uploads/attachment_data/file/413046/Y9_Arts_Short_Story.pdf.

Hargreaves, J., M. Madeleine , and N. Goulding. 2015b. *Taking Part, Focus On: Barriers to Participation. Statistical Release*. London: Department for Culture, Media & Sport. https://www.gov.uk/government/uploads/system/uploads/attachment_data/file/413048/Yr9_Barriers_to_participation_Short_Story.pdf.

Hawkes, J. 2001. *The Fourth Pillar of Sustainability: Culture's Essential Role in Public Planning*. Melbourne: Cultural Development Network (Vic). http://www.culturaldevelopment.net.au/community/Downloads/HawkesJon%282001%29TheFourthPillarOfSustainability.pdf.

Holden, J. 2010. *Culture and Class*. London: Counterpoint/British Council. http://www.bluedrum.ie/documents/CultureAndClassStandard.pdf.

Holden, J. 2015. *The Ecology of Culture. A Report commissioned by the Arts and Humanities Research Council's Cultural Value Project*. Swindon: Arts and Humanities Research Council. http://www.ahrc.ac.uk/documents/project-reports-and-reviews/the-ecology-of-culture/.

Horlings, L. 2016. "The Worldview and Symbolic Dimension in Territorialisation. How Human Values Play a Role in a Dutch Neighbourhood". In *Cultural Sustainability and Regional Development. Theories and Practices of Territorialisation*, edited by J. Dessein, E. Battaglini, and L. Horlings, 43–58. Abingdon: Routledge.

Hristova, S. 2006. "Cultural Rights in European Context." In *Trajectories of Contemporary Sociology in Bulgaria, XVI ISA World Congress, Quarterly Journal of the Institute of Sociology*, edited by Several Authors, 120–130. Sofia: Bulgarian Academy of Science.

Hristova, S., M. Dragićević Šešić, and N. Duxbury, eds. 2015. *Culture and Sustainability in European Cities: Imagining Europolis*. London: Routledge.

Human Rights Council. 2008. *Combating Defamation of Religions*. Resolution 7/19. http://ap.ohchr.org/documents/E/HRC/resolutions/A_HRC_RES_7_19.pdf.

Jiménez, L. 2014. "Derechos culturales [Cultural Rights]." Transcript of keynote speech made at the Encuentro de Cultura San Luis Potosí 2013. San Luis Potosí: Secretaría de Cultura del Gobierno del Estado de San Luis Potosí.

Kisić, V. 2016. *Governing Heritage Dissonance: Promises and Realities of Cultural Policies*. Amsterdam: European Cultural Foundation.

Koivunen, H., and L. Marsio. 2007. *Fair Culture? Ethical Dimension of Cultural Policy and Cultural Rights*. Helsinki: Ministry of Education.

Laaksonen, A. 2005. "Measuring Cultural Exclusion through Participation in Cultural Life." Third Global Forum on Human Development: Defining and Measuring Cultural Exclusion, 17–19 January 2005, Paris.

Mercer, C. 2002. *Towards Cultural Citizenship: Tools for Cultural Policy and Development*. Hedesmora: Bank of Sweden Tercentenary Foundation and Gidlunds Forlag.

Miralles, E. 2009. "Cultura, cooperación descentralizada y desarrollo local". In *Anuario de la cooperación descentralizada*, nº4. Montevideo: Observatorio de Cooperación Descentralizada UE-Al. http://observ-ocd.org/es/anuario-de-la-cooperacion-descentralizada-ano-2008.

Molyneux, J. 1998. "STATE OF THE ART: A Review of the 'Sensation' Exhibition at the Royal Academy of Arts, September–December 1997." *International Socialism* 79. http://pubs.socialistreviewindex.org.uk/isj79/molyneux.htm.

Nussbaum, M. C. 2011. *Creating Capabilities. The Human Development Approach*. Cambridge: Belknap Press of Harvard University Press.

OMC. 2012. *Policies and Good Practices in the Public Arts and in Cultural Institutions to Promote Better Access to and Wider Participation in Culture*. Brussels: European Commission.

Pascual i Ruiz, J. 2007. "On Citizen Participation in Local Cultural Policy Development for European Cities". In *Guide to Citizen Participation in Local Cultural Policy Development for European Cities*, edited by H. Weeda, 10–39. Barcelona: Interarts Foundation, ECUMEST Association and European Cultural Foundation. http://www.ecumest.ro/pdf/Guide_to_Citizen_Participation_EN_web.pdf.

Republic of Slovenia. 1991. *Constitution of the Republic of Slovenia*. http://www.us-rs.si/o-sodiscu/pravna-podlaga/ustava/.

Sen, A. 2000. *Development as Freedom*. New York: Anchor Books.

Sen, A. 2004. "How Does Culture Matter?" In *Culture and Public Action*, edited by V. Rao and M. Walton, 37–58. Stanford: Stanford University Press/World Bank.

Smiers, J. 2003. *Arts under pressure*. London: Zed books.

TNS Opinion & Social. 2013. "Cultural Access and Participation. Report." In *Special Eurobarometer*, 399. Brussels: European Commission. http://ec.europa.eu/public_opinion/archives/ebs/ebs_399_en.pdf.

Tomka, G. 2013. "Reconceptualizing Cultural Participation in Europe: Grey Literature Review." *Cultural Trends* 22 (3–4): 259–264.

UCLG (United Cities and Local Governments). 2004. *Agenda 21 for Culture. An Undertaking by Cities and Local Governments for Cultural Development*. Barcelona: UCLG/City of Barcelona. http://agenda21culture.net/index.php/docman/agenda21/212-ag21en/file.

UCLG (United Cities and Local Governments). 2015. *Culture 21: Actions. Commitments on the Role of Culture in Sustainable Cities*. Barcelona: UCLG. http://agenda21culture.net/images/a21c/nueva-A21C/C21A/C21_2015web_en.pdf.

UN Committee on Economic, Social and Cultural Rights. 2009. *Right of Everyone to Take Part in Cultural Life (art. 15, para. 1(a), of the International Covenant on Economic, Social and Cultural Rights)*. Geneva: Committee on Economic, Social and Cultural Rights. General Comment nº21, E/C.12/GC/21. http://www2.ohchr.org/english/bodies/cescr/docs/gc/E-C-12-GC-21.doc.

UN General Assembly. 2015. *Transforming Our World: the 2030 Agenda for Sustainable Development*. New York: UN General Assembly. A/RES/70/1. http://www.un.org/ga/search/view_doc.asp?symbol=A/RES/70/1&Lang=E.

UN Independent Expert in the Field of Cultural Rights. 2010. *Report of the Independent Expert in the Field of Cultural Rights, Ms. Farida Shaheed, Submitted Pursuant to Resolution 10/23 of the Human Rights Council*. Geneva: Human Rights Council. A/HRC/14/36. http://daccess-dds-ny.un.org/doc/UNDOC/GEN/G10/124/40/PDF/G1012440.pdf?OpenElement.

UNESCO. 2001. *Universal Declaration on Cultural Diversity*. http://portal.unesco.org/en/ev.php-URL_ID=13179&URL_DO=DO_TOPIC&URL_SECTION=201.html.

UNESCO. 2005. *Convention on the Protection and Promotion of the Diversity of Cultural Expressions*. http://en.unesco.org/creativity/convention/2005-convention/2005-convention-text.

UNESCO. 2015. *Re/ Shaping Cultural Policies, A Decade Promoting the Diversity of Cultural Expressions for Development, 2005 Convention Report*. Paris: UNESCO.

Vellani, A. 2014. "Success Failure and Cultural Entrepreneurship". In *Enabling Crossovers. Good Practices in the Creative Industries*, 27–32. Singapore: Asia-Europe Foundation. Accessed 13 November 2015. http://www.asef.org/images/stories/publications/ebooks/ASEF_Publication_EnablingCrossovers.pdf

World Commission on Environment and Development. 1987. *Our Common Future*. Oxford: Oxford University Press.

Greening cultural policy

Richard Maxwell and Toby Miller

ABSTRACT

This article focuses on greening cultural policy within a sustainable development context. We examine shortcomings of major public-policy responses to the ecological crisis, linking this to the ambivalent philosophical heritage of anthropocentric worldviews that underpin ideas about the relation of culture to non-human nature. This ambivalence is reflected by weak environmentalism in the cultural policy arena, exemplified by surprisingly non-green cultural platforms espoused by green political parties. Green thinking is further hampered by the widespread adoption of digitisation within cultural organizations, which we contextualise in the broader political economy of digital capitalism and the attendant myth that high-tech culture is a low emissions business. Green cultural policy necessitates intensive self-examination of cultural institutions' environmental impact, at the same time these institutions deploy art, education, entertainment, sports, and news to raise awareness of ecological crisis and alternative models of economic activity. We cite the efforts of activist artists' resistance against fossil fuel corporations' sponsorship of arts and cultural organizations as a welcome provocation for greening cultural policy within cultural organizations and green political parties alike.

Introduction

This chapter is in keeping with work we have done over the past twenty-five years that sidesteps the customary separation of plastic or hanging art and performance from screen drama, sports, or news (Miller 1993; Maxwell 1995; Lewis and Miller 2002; Miller and Yúdice 2002; Maxwell and Miller 2012). We also disobey the norms that situate policy in a separate, fetishized category, apart from their incarnation in programs and organizations. For us, the actual conduct of institutions – whether Hollywood studios, journalists' unions, or museums of fine art – is as relevant a form of cultural policy as, for example, a set of cultural principles adopted by governments. Once we situate these forms of cultural policy in the context of the ecological crisis, the need for green cultural practices and policy should become self-evident.

After a synopsis of today's major public-policy responses to the ecological crisis, we examine the ambivalent philosophical heritage of anthropocentric and eco-centric worldviews that underpin ideas about the relation of culture to non-human nature. This sets the stage for a look at the contradictory manner in which environmental issues are discussed in the cultural policy arena, exemplified by cultural platforms espoused by green political organizations. We then describe how a variety of industries in the cultural sector have confronted – or need to confront – their environmental impact. The last two sections suggest key areas where cultural organizations and green political parties might begin to green cultural policy. We focus our discussion successively on the digitisation of cultural organizations, contextualized in the broader political economy of digital capitalism, and on activist art resistance against the complicity of cultural institutions with the extractive industries.

The wider problem

Since the 2009 United Nations Climate Change Conference (UNCCC), carbon emissions have risen 10% worldwide. That figure is a disheartening reminder that the 195 (potential) signatory nations to the 2015 Paris Agreement on Climate Change may have set their benchmarks well below the recommendations of the Intergovernmental Panel on Climate Change (IPCC): the reduction of 20 billion tons of carbon emissions within twenty years and seven billion tons by 2050. These are the panel's most minimal estimates of what should be done. And while the outcome of the 2015 Paris UNCCC cannot yet be fully assessed, the world's most powerful politicians and bureaucrats have already failed to direct their economies toward a sustainable future. That calls into question not just their will to act on global warming, but their very capacity to reason with the scientific consensus about it (Pollin 2015).

Part of the problem is that ideas of sustainability have become thoroughly muddled by political and economic ideologies of growth. Despite the scientific consensus that 'warming of the climate system is unequivocal' (Intergovernmental Panel on Climate Change 2007, 72), the twenty leading economic powers frequently treat climate change and other ecological hazards as one-more variable of international relations, ignoring decades-old warnings about the fast-closing circle of remedies for environmental ills (Commoner 1971). This is one of the most volatile contradictions of our time: whereas the interpretation of economic, social, and cultural needs is fraught with political conflict and requires negotiations at multiple scales of global governance, the 'scientific prerequisites for ecological sustainability' are not a matter of political debate over values or priorities: 'nature does not conduct consensus talks' (Schauer 2003, 3–6). Building in ambit claims or indulging in game theory may work in human negotiation, but not climate change.

And yet meeting upon meeting of peak councils of labour, capital, and the state inexorably depart from the lessons of science and towards immediate self-interest. In the terminology of ecological ethics, we might say that a dominant anthropocentric aspiration insists on managing environmental risks in ways that prioritise established human interests. This dominant paradigm is opposed by an eco-centric, inter-generational interest in future lives and ecosystems. The former emphasises the overarching legitimacy of human interests, the latter the necessity of preserving Earth's complexity.

Public policy responded better in the past than today to calls for absolute pre- and proscriptions based on evidence of ecological decline – consider US clean-air-and-water policies of the 1970s – or the use of a precautionary principle in the development of new technology or production practices rather than their enthusiastic application followed by cost-benefit analysis after the fact/disaster.

We are all familiar with the discourse of costs and benefits as a common-or-garden orthodoxy of mainstream policy analysis that weighs up the positive and negative aspects of actions, based in large part on what they have produced already in related or identical contexts. By contrast, the precautionary principle holds that 'our knowledge of the effects of our actions is always exceeded by our ignorance.' It lays the burden of proof of value and safety on those who would introduce potentially toxic substances or dangerous practices into the environment in circumstances where there is no scientific consensus about the consequences of such actions (Curry 2006, 48).

We have a scientific consensus and clear mandates for policies that promote sustainable development, that is, the efficient use and equitable distribution of natural resources for long-term, intergenerational socioeconomic wellbeing. Ideally, the term denotes a standard that 'rules out all practices except those that are indefinitely sustainable' by the Earth's ecosystems (Curry 2006, 48). The virtues of sustainable development are that it accounts for intra- and inter-generational equity; allows for open participation, if not directly by all affected communities, then at least by their representatives; and is recognised in international agreements for assuring a certain inter-territorial equity.

But sustainability is still commonly deployed to signify an uneasy and frankly irresponsible balance between socioeconomic development and environmental protection. The contradictions inherent in sustainable development emerge at the point at which quantitative economic development overtakes other concerns. In its weakest form, sustainable development becomes 'little more than "sustainable" capitalism' (Pepper 2000, 451). Economic self-interest pushes eco-ethical self-interest into a little corner of sustainability. Herein lies a key vulnerability of anthropocentric eco-ethics. Self-interest that does not perceive the intimate relation between human and nonhuman beings tilts the balance toward the satisfaction of human needs.

The role of culture

Into this struggle for utilitarian public interest comes culture, itself long-straddling pragmatic and ethereal, anthropological and aesthetic definitions and norms, and subject to a relationship to the natural world that is exemplified in struggles over ecological ethics. A complex philosophical heritage underpins artistic ambivalence about transforming the old into the new: anthropocentric and eco-centric worldviews. From an anthropocentric point of view, Bacon avowed four centuries ago that 'commerce between the mind of man and the nature of things ... is more precious than anything on earth' (1620). Two hundred years later, Hegel argued that semiosis is the distinctive quality of humans. It elevates them above other life forms: making meaning is evidence of a beautiful and sublime human quality – putting one's 'will into everything.' An object or place thereby 'becomes mine.' As a consequence, humans, alone among the Earth's inhabitants, have 'the right of absolute proprietorship.' A capacity to restrain ourselves, mastering both 'spontaneity and natural constitution,' distinguishes people from other living things. The inevitable relationship between humanity and nature asserts itself at the core of consciousness as a site of struggle for 'us' to achieve freedom from risk and want. We are unique in our wish and ability to conserve and represent objects, so a strange dialectical process affords us the special right to destroy them. This willpower distinguishes us from other animals because it expresses the desire and capacity to transcend subsistence. Semiotic power legitimizes the destruction of unmarked sites, ones that lack human signage: 'respect for ... unused land cannot be guaranteed.' Nature's 'tedious chronicle' provides 'nothing new under the sun' – valueless without the progress signified by human dominion (Hegel 1954; 242–243, 248–250 and 1988, 50, 154, 61). Hence the anti-indigenous, anti-flora, anti-fauna doctrine of *terra nullius* – among the most powerful of imperial cultural policies – which denied native title to indigenous people due to their ideological and pragmatic lives, which were meant to be harmonised with nature rather than transformative of it.[1]

Conversely, Hume approached these matters from an almost eco-centric persuasion: even if rights are only accorded to those with semiotic abilities, animals deserve them, too, because they 'learn many things from experience' and develop 'knowledge of the nature of fire, water, earth, stones, heights, depths, etc.' Rather than being merely sensate, our fellow creatures infer material truths (1955, 112–113) through what he called 'the reason of animals' (1739).

The duality of nature – that it is simultaneously self-generating and sustaining, yet its survival is contingent on human rhetoric and despoliation – makes it vulnerable, even as its reaction to our interference will strike back sooner or later in mutually-assured destruction: no more nature, no more humanity, no more art. As a consequence, sacred and secular human norms conflict as often as they converge in accounting for changes in the material world and the rights of humanity as its most skillful and willful, productive and destructive inhabitant. As Latour explains:

> From the time the term 'politics' was invented, every type of politics has been defined by its relation to nature, whose every feature, property, and function depends on the polemical will to limit, reform, establish, short-circuit, or enlighten public life. (2004, 1)

This necessitates allocating equal and semi-autonomous significance to natural phenomena, social forces, and cultural meaning in order to understand contemporary life. Just as objects of scientific knowledge come to us in hybrid forms that are coevally affected by social power and textual meaning, so the latter two domains are themselves subject to the natural world (Latour 1993, 5–6). This is why museums focused on nature are encased within imperial domination and industrialisation as well as scientific knowledge, and tightly linked to the Global North's colonising and classifying tendencies over peoples and places (Barrett and McManus 2007). Half of the two hundred million objects housed in British museums fall into this category (Alberti 2008, 73).

Policy implications

Art and custom are now resources for markets and nations, reactions to the crisis of belonging and economic necessity occasioned by capitalist globalisation. They are crucial to advanced and developing economies, and provide the legitimizing ground on which particular groups (e.g. African Americans, lesbians, the hearing-impaired, evangelical Protestants …) claim resources and seek inclusion in national and international narratives (Yúdice 2003).

Cultural industries are getting bigger, with global trade in the culture products increasing from US$559.5 billion in 2010 to US$624 billion in 2011, for example (United Nations 2014). Unsurprisingly, then, questions of the value of cultural production have morphed into questions of economic development, employment, and diversity of access and ownership. A corollary change in terms of cultural policy shifts the emphasis to culture as a fount of economic growth, but one with a far less harmful environmental impact than heavy industry and agriculture. Sustainability in this context is about positioning 'clean' creative and cultural sectors alongside other sectors within the dynamic core of the capitalist economy.

For example, the European Commission defines cultural and creative industries as an economic growth sector, with emphases on education, artists' mobility, regulatory reform, and market access and investment.[2] With the aim to win a place for 'culture-led development' in sustainability debates, UNESCO promotes culture as a fourth pillar of sustainable development, an idea that elevates creative industries to equal partnership with stakeholders working to balance economic growth, social inclusion, and environmental health. Importantly, this has little to do with seeking environmental sustainability within the cultural sector (United Cities and Local Governments 2010; UNESCO 2012; United Nations 2014).

This view of culture as environmentally benign is not limited to cultural policy organizations charged with championing cultural institutions. Surprisingly, it also thrives in political organizations dedicated to environmental well-being. Consider the cultural-policy platforms of major green parties in 2015. In Germany, Canada, New Zealand, and the UK, the Greens' cultural policy focuses on identity, heritage, institutions, funding, ownership participation, and involving artists and other cultural workers in sustainable practices and ideas.[3] The US Green Party lacks a cultural policy, except in relation to mainstream media channels, again with an emphasis on democratic principles, access, ownership, and so on.[4]

While culture is a keyword in Green Party efforts to meet sustainability goals, policy platforms are primarily focused on resisting the dominance of commercial culture and the hyper-consumerism that undermines local participatory culture – a laudable goal, but perversely exclusive of any reference to the real environmental impact of cultural practices. Such a policy discourse reinforces the misleading idea that a movement for ecologically sustainable development has no role to play in the realm of cultural production or artistic practice.

In fact, internal practices of cultural production have social liabilities that directly affect the environment – not in an ideological, expressive, or discursive way, but in the material practices of making, distributing, and consuming culture. These effects derive from materials and energy used to produce movies, performance, and institutional preserves of culture, heritage, and language; the atmospheric effects of digital consumption; and the waste generated by producers and consumers alike. Not even California's Green Party has acknowledged the material ecological problems of making culture, and this with evidence of massive pollution caused by LA-based film and TV production on its doorstep.[5]

Problems for green cultural policy

Green institutional initiatives face many challenges associated with energy consumption and conservation, design and manufacturing processes of information and communication technologies (ICTs), working conditions throughout the global supply chain, and e-waste. The bulk of these problems presumably reside outside the cultural sector, but they are not disconnected, a fact even major Green Parties are ignoring. If cultural policymakers connected upstream and downstream environmental liabilities to the costs of cultural production, they might identify unexpected ways to incorporate environmental accounting into their advocacy efforts, shaping policies that direct non-government, private, and government management protocols to reinforce sustainable practices within the cultural sector itself.

There are already hundreds of accords that aim to protect workers, waterways, plant and animal life, fisheries, archaeological and other cultural-environmental heritage, and atmospheric and ground air quality through the regulation of waste management, trans-border flows of heavy metals, airborne and waterborne pollutants, forests, nuclear energy, and exported hazardous waste. These local, regional, national, and global ecological policies can inform cultural policy where they intersect with matters of climate change, pollution, biodiversity, and habitat. Here are a few examples of environmental issues in which a green cultural policy could play a bigger role.

Making books makes pollution. The production of pulp and paper causes a relatively well-known burden on the environment – deforestation, chemical effluents, emissions, toxic working conditions in printing plants, and so on (National Geographic n. d). Cultural policy could resolve confusion among the patchwork of certification programs claiming to ensure responsible paper use that can sustain forests – there are about fifty such systems in play, with a handful routinely used in the US, for example (Maxwell and Miller 2012, 127).

Movies have a carbon footprint. Like papermaking, filmmaking is energy-intensive and prone to waste and use of materials containing known toxins. As noted above, Hollywood productions are among California's principal polluters (Corbett and Turco 2006). Cultural policy in this area has been captured largely by the industry itself, with studios, producers' organizations, trade organizations, and other private entities involved in greening production practices. These industry actions are meant to substitute for independent policy oversight of this sector (Maxwell and Miller 2012, 83–84), increasing the probability that they never become more than various forms of 'greenwashing,' a public relations strategy to add environmental credibility to industries and thereby stave off regulation. Cultural policy could act as a watchdog to assess the claims of the sector against the actual environmental record of its operations.

Meanwhile, the electronic media provide a complex collection of significant environmental problems – energy consumption and emissions, materials sourcing and toxicity, and electronic waste. There are between ten and fifteen billion high-tech devices needing electricity today, and 15 percent of global residential energy is spent powering domestic digital technology. If energy demand continues to grow at this rate, the residential electricity needed to power electronics will rise to 30 percent of global consumption by 2022, and 45 percent by 2030 (International Energy Agency 2009). When residential use is added to the electricity it takes to make and distribute these goods, the total energy consumed translates into carbon emissions that are about the same as current levels from aviation – and this does not account for the energy to make chemicals and gases that go into the production of semiconductors or the energy used to dispose or recycle the devices. Cultural policy doesn't currently address high-energy profiles of digital cultural production, an area of significant importance to green cultural policy-making.

This is only a glimpse of some of the problems cultural policymakers will face were they to begin to generate positions and research that considers cultural practices in the context of sustainability benchmarks. Each problem arose in a particular historical context of emerging intersections of politics, economics, and technology. Today they are all subsumed in vital ways by market criteria associated with digital capitalism. The most obvious sign of this shift in the cultural sector is the incorporation of non-profit cultural institutions via digitisation of administration and operations. Digital technology now permeates the all forms of culture – in the technology used to make culture, administer and operate cultural institutions, and consume their output (Maxwell 2015).

Digital capitalism and cultural policy

In the US and the UK, the most powerful non-profit arts organizations all invest heavily in moving towards digitisation in various ways. This transformation can be understood as a matter of survival in a world where the public's cultural affections are increasingly focused on commercial electronic screen content. Behind the rhetoric justifying digital schemes lie external pressures, including diminishing benefactor support, rising electronic consumption/participation relative to on-site arts programming, and the breathtaking uptake of mobile devices – tablets, smartphones, notebooks, and laptops. This has contributed the lion's share of global spending on consumer electronics, which reached US$1 trillion for the first time in 2012. As this occurred in the wake of the worst economic crisis since the 1930s, it reinforced the idea that digital investments are immune to recession and offer a lifeline to cultural institutions who have few alternatives to engage with consumers entranced by digital entertainments ('Gartner Says' 2013).

Unsurprisingly, a flurry of excitement about digitisation can be found in the way arts and cultural groups are promoting these technologies as enhancements of on-site exhibition and performance, on-line distribution, promotion, and as catalysts for enlarging stand-alone digital art collections and exhibitions. The more successful cultural institutions are distinguished by their ability to, among other things, 'crowdfund' and sell digital commodities – mobile applications, electronic books, music, recorded performances, games, etc. – as well as physical goods via online retail. And virtually all British arts and cultural organizations report high levels of confidence in digital systems as drivers of growth, innovation, and consumer outreach. That makes for the continued investment and deployment of more and more digital technology, with a vanguard of 'cultural digerati' leading the laggards into the future (Digital R&D Fund for the Arts 2013).

While it is vital for these institutions to increase attendance and participation in an era of increased governmental/neoliberal surveillance, it's also expensive to do so with digital systems, which are not simply installed then safely forgotten. On-line marketing schemes using social media, for example, must be well-designed, maintained, and upgraded. They require ongoing expenditure on hardware and software as well as investment in training existing staff or hiring employees who are adept at operating these systems. As digitisation consumes more and more of cultural institutions' revenue, digital technology introduces the same bias in cultural and arts provision that we've seen in businesses and non-profits like universities. Among other characteristics, this includes a greater share of administration controlled by enterprise resource planning (ERP) systems with locked-in partnerships for database management and performance audits. Only a handful of ERP systems offer services addressed to non-profit operations (mostly education and government) though all are hungry for this business.[6] In most cases, this method foists institutional roles and functions designed for businesses onto staff whose work has traditionally been organised and assessed by non-business criteria. The shift also entails a greater monetization of audience value: size of attendance, internet views, and click-throughs become more important than measuring the social significance of arts organizations as, for example, public goods that sustain cultural infrastructure beyond the fickle nature of market whimsy.

Finally, digitisation encourages arts and culture administrators and artists themselves to endorse educational changes to meet the demand for skilled high-technology workers within 'their' organizations. This exemplifies one of the latest instances of a sixty-year trend of 'corporate educational provision' of workers 'suitably trained' for digital capitalism and all that this brings with it: a back door allowing training of 'human capital' inside public institutions, with 'vocational objectives,' precarity, and the reproduction of system-serving routines (Miller 1993; Schiller 1999, 204–205 and 2016). This education/employment dimension is critical: just as digitisation via online sales, marketing, and audience analytics is perceived as a crucial means of raising revenue, the digitisation of training in the arts and cultural sector – increasingly in university programs of digital humanities and the like – proposes dramatic, untested changes in the way we are asked to teach, interpret, and measure the value of artistic and cultural resources. Digital technology is not a neutral set of tools that benignly build up arts and culture. It comes loaded with ideological baggage and a dismal record of toxic harm to the environment and workers.

Digitisation also raises environmental concerns that existing cultural policies have ignored, in particular its relation to energy consumption, health risks, and e-waste. Museums, for example, tend to be electricity hogs and poor partners in recycling efforts (Museum Association 2008, 4). Digital technologies can reduce energy consumption through light-emitting diodes and 'smart' air-quality and temperature controls, but audience and visitor attraction through ICTs stimulates energy use, waste, and long-term environmental harm.

The performing arts range in size and complexity, but many scenarios require lots of energy and produce lots of waste, neglecting reuse and recycling routines – problems that multiply with touring. Of course, there are green artists keen to change these dirty practices, but sustainability seems easier to foster in small-scale productions (Beer 2012). Attempts to green these activities at national levels has shown some success, but bureaucrats in charge of these programs still tend to enter digital solutions on the plus side as presumptively sustainable practices. Environmental harm that occurs beyond the confines of these organizations' immediate operations is easy to ignore or treat as peripheral to such greening strategies.

And as long as we don't see the smokestacks and pollution that accompany electricity needed for digitisation, high-wattage operations of digital networks, office equipment, and video displays can be sold as clean, environmentally benign technologies ('Managing Energy' 2011). But these systems are plugged into the utility grid, which makes them part of a global problem of climate change mentioned above (International Energy Agency 2009).

Moreover, enormous amounts of data pass daily through massive networks and data centres – the 'cloud' – now scattered across the globe. Data centres' energy demands rise at a steady pace, with business practices that range from serious plans to reduce reliance on coal-fired energy to widespread examples of waste and thoughtless energy management. At current levels, cloud computing eats up energy at a rate somewhere between what Japan and India consume (Greenpeace 2012). The environmental impact of this networked culture depends on the type of energy production used to power the grids – coal-fired power being the biggest menace.

Cultural organizations that increase content provision to mobile devices have joined another unsustainable trend. There are nearly fourteen billion networked mobile devices in use worldwide today. But we're not just talking about people following map directions to the theatre or museum. Wireless connectivity consumes a tremendous amount of electricity – up to 90 percent of the total energy consumed by mobile telecommunication connections (Center for Energy Efficient Telecommunications 2013; Maxwell and Miller 2013).

Rising resistance against dirty corporate sponsorship[7]

Cultural policy can also challenge cultural organizations to divest from sponsorship deals with fossil fuel corporations. Over the past decade, BP has dedicated much of its public relation efforts to glossing its reputation as one of Britain's principal cultural institutions, boasting that it 'has proudly supported arts and culture in the UK for over 35 years'[8] (Chase 2010; Reynolds 2012). In the US, BP paid the Los Angeles County Museum of Art US$25 million in 2007, in return for which the Museum christened a BP Grand Entrance.[9] When one of the its oil rigs exploded in the Gulf of Mexico in 2010, BP quickly withdrew much of its marketing in the US and UK. Still, the company felt no compunction about retaining its offer to name the 'BP Sea Otter Habitat' at the Long Beach's Aquarium of the Pacific, which opened a month after the spill (though the oily sponsors failed to show up at the opening, perhaps in order to avoid acknowledging negative externalities and protests) (Boehm and Sahagun 2010; Reynolds 2012).[10]

BP also participates in more overtly ideological activities, notably through educational programs at Britain's Science Museum, where school students are encouraged to embrace the wonders of energy generation via 'an interactive game where visitors play the energy minister and have to efficiently power a make-believe country by balancing economic, environmental and political concerns before the prime minister fires them' (Viney 2010). The game sets up BP and the Science Museum as reasonable actors capable of a measured and fair-minded engagement and positions the firm as a benign intermediary between present and future, science and childhood, truth and innovation.

Chevron in Colombia endeavours to promote the country's cultural development ['promover el desarrollo cultural de Colombia'], by sponsoring exhibits like the one at the Museo del Gas de Riohacha that explores pre-invasion and colonial settlements and the ongoing cultures of indigenous peoples, such as the Wayúu ('Ficha Técnica' 2013). The reality is that Chevron disrupts the Wayúu's form of life, who have protested.[11]

Like the Wayúu, cultural policy could become more alert to real environmental harms caused by embedded cultural practices of fossil fuel corporations involved in arts and cultural sponsorship. A green cultural policy could also draw on the lessons of activists and artists who have mounted spectacular forms of resistance to corporate greenwashing, rethinking culture as a ground of struggle in both its objects of critique and its self-reflexive tactics.

RisingTide UK's Art Not Oil project takes as its motto: 'For creativity, climate justice & an end to oil industry sponsorship of the arts' (Rising Tide 2012). Since 2004, RisingTide UK has challenged artists to work in sustainable ways as they work against the unsustainability of Shell, BP, and their kind, by undermining their greenwashing efforts in arts sponsorship. Art Not Oil operates on-line galleries designed to criticise and undermine 'the caring image' propagated by corporate polluters (for example, BP's Portrait Award and Shell's exhibit of 'Wildlife Photographer of the Year' at Britain's Natural History Museum). These activists want to see 'Big Oil' go 'the way of Big Tobacco in being unwelcome in any gallery, museum, opera house or theatre.'[12]

This is much more than an issue of consumerism. It is about large institutions and their place within international and national power élites, drawing on minimal, cheap sponsorship to gloss their image and win goodwill from the public while maintaining oligarchical ties. Hence the Tate's Director, Nicholas Serota, avowing during the spill of the year before that 'You don't abandon your friends because they have what we consider to be a temporary difficulty' (quoted in Liberate Tate, Platform, and Art Not Oil 2011, 12).

There are many other examples of artists and performers fed up with greenwashing efforts of fossil fuel corporations: Reclaim Shakespeare Company's critique of the British Museum's complicity with its 'Out Damn Logo' flash mob;[13] 'Good Crude Britannia' and the 'Greenwash Guerrillas;'[14] and Toronto's artist-run Whippersnapper Gallery featuring Brazilian street artists creating gigantic urban sculptures from garbage (Kocialkowska 2012; 'Activistas y artistas' 2010; Bain and McLean 2013, 107). The Liberate Tate group mounted several intense actions using spectacle to highlight the museum's sycophancy to polluters,[15] including the notorious simulacrum of oil dripping over a cringing, abject artist on the floor of the Tate where BP's proud 'Single Form' exhibit, dedicated to the human body, took place ('Human Cost;' 'Repudian artistas' 2011). They followed this a year later with 'Floe Piece,' a street performance in which they lugged fifty-five melting kilos of Arctic ice from Occupy London on the steps of St Paul's Cathedral to the Tate's Turbine Hall (Culture Beyond Oil 2011, 19; Anderson 2012; Lam et al. 2013).[16] After years of pressure, Tate Modern and BP ended their partnership, without admitting a causal relationship to these protests, but it is reasonable to assume that either or both of these institutions decided that damage had occurred to their reputations, singly or collectively ('Cuatro museos' 2011; Khomami 2016).

Conclusion

It is a positive sign that certain segments of the cultural industries have pursued strategies and design innovations in response to the eco-crisis, rather than denying its existence. Meanwhile, green arts activists are raising awareness of the harmful game behind corporate sponsorship that uses cultural partners to divert attention from environmental despoliation resulting from corporate misconduct. Arts activist groups opposed to greenwashing have shown us all a way forward. And there is clearly a link between attempts to counter the economic crisis and the struggle against global warming through publicly-funded programs that shift investment to green practices in the cultural sector, including where companies have moved to renewable sources of energy generation such as solar, wind, and biomass and reduce energy consumption by retrofitting buildings.

However progressive and lasting these initiatives prove to be, the defining political economy of digital capitalism has been very effective in hampering the ability for green thinking to flourish in the cultural arena. As we've seen, a vanguard of cultural organizations in the US and UK are expanding the footprint of digital technologies by promoting them as drivers of growth, innovation, and consumer outreach without regard for their ideological influence or environmental impact. The traditional role of public culture is being reshaped to fit enterprise management systems, while arts administrators and other cultural leaders buy into the idea that this is all clean and environmentally benign – a position that disavows growing evidence of carbon emissions owing to the mobile electronics and high-wattage network operations that underpin digitized arts exhibition, promotion, and audience analytics.

Cultural policy has yet to take a position of leadership on these matters. This is reflected most alarmingly by the platforms of major Green Parties and major cultural institutions. It's time that cultural policy become an environmental policy and not just a side-lined player in the global movement for sustainable development.

It can do this by encouraging state and non-state policy-making that fosters conditions in which green cultural practices can thrive in arts and cultural organizations. This is one goal of IMAGINE 2020, a network of eleven European arts organizations funded by the European Union to reorganize cultural industries to meet the challenges of the ecological crisis, asking how the arts and cultural sector can make 'changes necessary to stabilise the climate and secure a sustainable future' (IMAGINE n. d.). Green cultural policy must also press for environmentally truthful bookkeeping in the cultural sector by factoring in eco-system and atmospheric liabilities associated with all operations, from architecture to corporate sponsorship to digitisation of cultural practices, performance and exhibition. The time has come to reform old business accounting practices that fail to add the environmental costs into the bottom line of artistic and cultural industriousness. To measure the true value of cultural institutions, we must see them as vital environmental participants with a stake in the future of the planet and all its inhabitants.

Notes

1. http://www.migrationheritage.nsw.gov.au/exhibition/objectsthroughtime/bourketerra/.
2. http://ec.europa.eu/culture/policy/cultural-creative-industries/index_en.htm.
3. http://www.gruene-bundestag.de/service-navigation/english/culture_ID_377806.html; http://www.greenparty.ca/en/policy-background-2015/part-l; https://home.greens.org.nz/policysummary/arts-culture-and-heritage-policy-summary; https://policy.greenparty.org.uk/culture,-media-and-sports.html.
4. https://www.greenparty.org/Platform.php.
5. http://www.cagreens.org/platform/arts-and-culture.
6. http://erp-software.findthebest.com/.
7. This section draws in part from Ahluwalia and Miller 2014.
8. http://www.bp.com/en/global/corporate/about-bp/bp-worldwide/bp-united-kingdom/bp-in-the-community/arts-and-culture.html; http://www.bp.com/content/dam/bp/pdf/investors/BP_Annual_Report_and_Form_20F_2012.pdf.
9. http://www.lacma.org/sites/default/files/bpgef.pdf.
10. http://www.aquariumofpacific.org/exhibits/northern_pacific_gallery/otters.
11. http://www.fundaciongasnaturalfenosa.org/es-ES/MuseoGas/Paginas/subhome.aspx http://chevrontoxico.com/take-action/colombia; http://www.youtube.com/watch?v=5RKr2NKdsgQ.
12. http://www.artnotoil.org.uk/about.
13. http://www.britishmuseum.org/whats_on/past_exhibitions/2012/shakespeare_staging_the_world.aspx.
14. http://greenwashguerrillas.wordpress.com.
15. http://liberatetate.wordpress.com/liberating-tate/about/).
16. http://platformlondon.org/2014/01/24/shell-no-longer-sponsoring-southbank-classic-series-a-timeline/.

Disclosure statement

No potential conflict of interest was reported by the authors.

References

"Activistas y artistas critican la relacion de centros culturales ingleses con la petrolera BP [Activists and Artists Criticize the Relationship of English Cultural Centers with British Petroleum]." *Terc3ra*, 2010, January 7. Accessed August 9, 2015. http://www.tercerainformacion.es/spip.php?article16502

Ahluwalia, P., and T. Miller. 2014. "Greenwashing Social Identity." *Social Identities: Journal for the Study of Race, Nation and Culture* 20 (1): 1–4. doi:10.1080/13504630.2013.878983.

Alberti, Samuel J. M. M. 2008. "Constructing Nature behind Glass." *Museum and Society* 6 (2): 73–97.

Anderson, S. 2012. "Art Collective Liberate Tate Uses Arctic Ice to Protest at Gallery's BP Sponsorship." *Independent*, January 16. Accessed August 9, 2015. http://www.independent.co.uk/arts-entertainment/art/news/art-collective-liberate-tate-uses-arctic-ice-to-protest-at-gallerys-bp-sponsorship-6290448.html

Bacon, F. 1620. *The Great Instauration*. http://www.constitution.org/bacon/instauration.ht.

Bain, A., and H. McLean. 2013. "The Artistic Precariat." *Cambridge Journal of Regions Economy and Society* 6 (1): 93–111.

Barrett, J., and P. McManus. 2007. "Civilising Nature: Museums and the Environment." In *Water Wind Art and Debate*, edited by G. Birch, 319–344. Sydney: University of Sydney Press.

Beer, T. 2012. "An Introduction to Ecological Design for the Performing Arts." In *Proceedings of the Cultural Ecology Symposium*, Accessed January 23, 2013. https://www.academia.edu/4974188/An_Introduction_to_Ecological_Design_for_the_Performing_Arts

Boehm, M. and L. Sahagun. 2010. "BP Oil Spill Poses PR Dilemma for Nonprofits." *Los Angeles Times*, May 19. Accessed January 23, 2012. http://articles.latimes.com/2010/may/19/local/la-me-bp-donations-20100519

Center for Energy Efficient Telecommunications. 2013. *The Power of Wireless Cloud: An Analysis of the Energy Consumption of Wireless Cloud*. Accessed January 23, 2014. http://www.ceet.unimelb.edu.au/pdfs/ceet_white_paper_wireless_cloud.pdf

Chase, S. 2010. "Art Not Oil: Shedding Light and Shadow on the Oil Industry (and Beyond) Since 2004." *Art Not Oil*, Accessed January 23, 2012. http://www.artnotoil.org.uk/

Commoner, B. 1971. *The Closing Circle*. New York: Knopf.

Corbett, C. J., and R. P. Turco. 2006. *Sustainability in the Motion Picture Industry. Report*. Prepared for the Integrated Waste Management Board of the State of California, November. Accessed January 23, 2012. http://www.personal.anderson.ucla.edu/charles.corbett/papers/mpis_report.pdf

"Cuatro museos británicos renuevan patrocinio con BP con polémica de fondo [Four British Museums Renew BP Sponsorship with Controversy in the Background]." *Prensa Libre*, 2011, December 19. Accessed August 9, 2015. http://www.prensalibre.com/internacional/Museos-britanicos-renuevan-patrocinio-BP_0_611939054.html

Curry, P. 2006. *Ecological Ethics: An Introduction*. Cambridge, MA: Polity.

Digital R&D Fund for the Arts (Arts Council England, Nesta and the Arts and Humanities Research Council). 2013. *Digital Culture: How Arts and Cultural Organisations in England Use Technology*. Accessed March 30, 2016. http://native.artsdigitalrnd.org.uk/wp-content/uploads/2013/11/DigitalCulture_FullReport.pdf

"Gartner Says Worldwide IT Spending on pace to Reach $3.7 Trillion in 2013." *Gartner*, 2013, July 2. Accessed August 9, 2015. http://www.gartner.com/newsroom/id/2537815

Greenpeace International. 2012. *How Green is Your Cloud?* April. Accessed March 30, 2016. http://www.greenpeace.org/international/Global/international/publications/climate/2012/iCoal/HowCleanisYourCloud.pdf

"Ficha Técnica de Colombia [Technical Data on Colombia]." *Chevron*, 2013, April. Accessed August 9, 2015. http://www.chevron.com/documents/pdf/colombiafactsheetspanish.pdf

Hegel, G. W. F. 1954. *The Philosophy of Hegel*. Edited by C. J. Friedrich. Translated by C. J. Friedrich, P. W. Friedrich, W. H. Johnston, L. G. Struthers, B. Bosanquet, W. M. Bryant, and J. B. Baillie. New York: Modern Library.

Hegel, G. W. F. 1988. *Lectures on the Philosophy of World History. Introduction: Reason in History*. Translated by H. B. Nisbet. Cambridge: Cambridge University Press.

Hume, D. 1739. *A Treatise of Human Nature*. http://michaeljohnsonphilosophy.com/wp-content/uploads/2012/01/5010_Hume_Treatise_Human_Nature.pdf.

Hume, D. 1955. *An Inquiry Concerning Human Understanding with a Supplement: An Abstract of a Treatise of Human Nature*. Edited by C. W. Hendel. Indianapolis, IN: Bobbs-Merrill.

IMAGINE 2020. n. d. *Art and Climate Change Network*. Accessed March 30, 2016. http://www.imagine2020.eu/

Intergovernmental Panel on Climate Change. 2007. *Climate Change 2007: Synthesis Report Summary for Policymakers*. Geneva: World Meteorological Organization.

International Energy Agency. 2009. *Gadgets and Gigawatts: Policies for Energy Efficient Electronics – Executive Summary*. Paris: Organization for Economic Cooperation and Development.

Khomami, N. 2016. "BP to End Tate Sponsorship after 26 Years." *Guardian*, March 11. Accessed March 30, 2016. http://www.theguardian.com/artanddesign/2016/mar/11/bp-to-end-tate-sponsorship-climate-protests

Kocialkowska, K. 2012. "Flashmob Protest Sets Sights on British Museum." *New Statesman*, November 16. Accessed March 30, 2016. http://www.newstatesman.com/culture/art-and-design/2012/11/flashmob-protest-sets-sights-british-museum

Lam, S., G. Ngcobo, J. Persekian, N. Thompson, A. S. Witzke, and Liberate Tate. 2013. "Art, Ecology and Institutions: A Conversation with Artists and Curators." *Third Text* 27 (1): 141–150.

Latour, B. 1993. *We Have Never Been Modern*. Translated by C. Porter. Cambridge, MA: Harvard University Press.

Latour, B. 2004. *Politics of Nature: How to Bring the Sciences into Democracy*. Translated by C. Porter. Cambridge, MA: Harvard University Press.

Lewis, J., and T. Miller, eds. 2002. *Critical Cultural Policy Studies*. Boston, MA: Blackwell.

Liberate Tate, Platform, and Art Not Oil. 2011. *Culture Beyond Oil*. Accessed March 30, 2016. http://platformlondon.org/2011/11/27/read-online-now-not-if-but-when-culture-beyond-oil/

"Managing Energy Costs in Museums." 2011. *Energy Right*. Accessed August 9, 2015. http://www.energyright.com/business/pdf/Museums_ESCD.pdf

Maxwell, R. 1995. *The Spectacle of Democracy*. Minneapolis: University of Minnesota Press.

Maxwell, R. 2015. "Social Liabilities of Digitising Cultural Institutions: Environment, Labor, Waste." In *The Routledge Companion to the Cultural Industries*, edited by J. O'Connor and K. Oakley, 392–401. London: Routledge.

Maxwell, R., and T. Miller. 2012. *Greening the Media*. New York: Oxford University Press.

Maxwell, R., and T. Miller. 2013. "The Material Cellphone." In *The Oxford Handbook of the Archaeology of the Contemporary World*, edited by P. Graves-Brown, R. Harrison, and A. Piccini, 699–712. Oxford: Oxford University Press.

Miller, T. 1993. *The Well-tempered Self: Citizenship, Culture, and the Postmodern Subject*. Baltimore, MD: The Johns Hopkins University Press.

Miller, T. 2016. "Cybertarian Flexibility – When Prosumers Join the Cognitariat, All That is Scholarship Melts into Air." In *Precarious Creativity: Global Media, Local Labor*, edited by M. Curtin and K. Sanson, 19–32. Berkeley: University of California Press.

Miller, T., and G. Yúdice. 2002. *Cultural Policy*. London: Sage.

Museum Association. 2008. *Sustainability and Museums – Your Chance to Make a Difference*. Accessed March 30, 2016. http://www.museumsassociation.org/campaigns/sustainability/sustainability-report

National Geographic. n. d. *Paper Buying Guide*. Accessed August 9, 2015. http://environment.nationalgeographic.com/environment/green-guide/buying-guide/paper/environmental-impact/

"Repudian artistas la asociación de la galería Tate con la British Petroleum [Artists Repudiate BP's Sponsorship of Tate]." *La Jornada*, 2011, April 21. Accessed August 9, 2015. http://www.jornada.unam.mx/2011/04/21/cultura/a03n1cul

Pepper, D. 2000. "Environmentalism." In *Understanding Contemporary Society: Theories of the Present*, edited by G. Browning, A. Halci, and F. Webster, 445–462. London: Sage.

Pollin, R. 2015. "Think We Can't Stabilize the Climate While Fostering Growth? Think Again." *The Nation*, October 27. Accessed August 9, 2015. http://www.thenation.com/article/think-we-cant-stabilize-the-climate-while-fostering-growth-think-again/

Reynolds, J. 2012. "BP Seeks 'More Positive' Sentiment with Return to Advertising." *Marketing Magazine*, November 20. Accessed August 9, 2015. http://www.marketingmagazine.co.uk/article/1160524/bp-seeks-more-positive-sentiment-return-advertising

Rising Tide. 2012. "Action: Greenwash. Shell-out Sponsorship." *Marketing Magazine*, September 21. Accessed August 9, 2015. http://risingtide.org.uk/action/greenwash

Schauer, T. 2003. *The Sustainable Information Society: Vision and Risks*. Vienna: European Support Centre of the Club of Rome.

Schiller, D. 1999. *Digital Capitalism – Networking the Global Market System*. Cambridge, MA: The MIT Press.

UNESCO. 2012. *Culture: A Driver and an Enabler of Sustainable Development*. Paris. Accessed August 9, 2015. http://www.un.org/millenniumgoals/pdf/Think%20Pieces/2_culture.pdf

United Cities and Local Governments. 2010. *Culture: Fourth Pillar of Sustainable Development*. Barcelona: UCLG. Accessed August 9, 2015. http://www.agenda21culture.net/index.php/docman/-1/393-zzculture4pillarsden/file

United Nations. 2014. *Resolution Adopted by the General Assembly on 20 December 2013 (a/RES/68/223). Culture and Sustainable Development*. February 12.

Viney, Leslie. 2010. "Fuelling the Future." *Aral*. Accessed August 9, 2015. http://www.aral.de/assets/bp_internet/globalbp/STAGING/global_assets/downloads/B/BPM_05one_Energy_text.pdf

Yúdice, G. 2003. *The Expediency of Culture: Uses of Culture in the Global Era*. Duke University Press.

Cultural sustainability as a strategy for the survival of museums and libraries

Kirsten Loach, Jennifer Rowley and Jillian Griffiths

Cultural sustainability has become a growing priority within sustainable development agendas, and is now often depicted as a fourth pillar, equal to social, economic, and environmental concerns. Museums and libraries play a unique role within cultural sustainability by preserving their communities' heritage. However, sustainability policy and research within these sectors still tends to focus on the social, economic, and environmental pillars. This article provides a critique of sustainability policy and research for museums and libraries. It argues that more explicit coverage of cultural sustainability is required to not only improve the contributions of museums and libraries to cultural sustainability, but also to provide an increased understanding and appreciation of the value of these institutions necessary for their continued survival.

Introduction

Libraries, particularly through their special collections, and museums maintain important cultural artefacts that represent a significant part of the heritage of the communities that they serve. Indeed, not only their collections, but also the museums and libraries themselves, including their history and buildings, are a cultural asset that can enrich local communities and, alongside other heritage attractions contribute to tourism associated with a city or region.

One of the primary aims of museums and libraries is to hold these cultural assets in trust for their communities, yet a series of challenges in recent years have put the long-term survival of these institutions at risk, with implications for the sustainability of the cultural assets within their care. Cuts to public funding and reducing revenues for charitable organisations (ACE 2011), together with difficulties in maintaining relevance within increasingly competitive leisure and information markets (Kazi 2012), mean that both museums and libraries face an ongoing battle to justify their existence and secure their futures.

Finding themselves lacking in support for their cultural mission, organisations have been encouraged to adopt more sustainable business models based upon the triple bottom line approach, which evaluates their work according to their contribution to the wider social, economic, and environmental sustainable development goals of society (Jankowska and Marcum 2010, Stylianou-Lambert *et al.* 2014). Yet whilst such measures can often help to ensure the general sustainability of their organisations, it can also lead to the neglect of their original mission, with the pressure to meet targets and demonstrate value in these three areas leading to the 'acquisition, preservation, and research of the collections' becoming 'considered subordinate' to these other 'aims' (Anderson 2009, 6).

However, there is increasing recognition that culture is of equal importance as social, economic, and environmental concerns in a sustainable society. Indeed, the inclusion of a concern for culture within sustainable development agendas was a central focus of the United Nations' post 2015 sustainability goals (IFACCA 2013). With the preservation of cultural heritage and the promotion of cultural vitality having been identified as key to enabling cultural sustainability (Soini and Birkeland 2014), this would seem to be a prime opportunity for museums and libraries to demonstrate the true value of their work. Yet to date there has been limited acknowledgment of the notion of cultural sustainability as an equal concern within sustainability policies for museums and libraries, and as a result, their work to sustain culture continues to be considered as subsidiary to demonstrating their contributions to social, economic, and environmental concerns.

Accordingly, this article aims to highlight the disparity that currently exists between museum and library practices that have cultural sustainability at their core, and policy that values the work of these institutions in sustaining culture according to its ancillary benefits rather than its intrinsic value. It suggests that if one of the functions of policy is to align practice with wider agendas in society, then policies for museums and libraries should be revised in order to reflect the growing consensus that cultural sustainability should be considered as a definitive outcome in its own right. This would then provide further justification for the future support of museums and libraries, by helping to articulate the value of their unique role in sustaining culture beyond its instrumental role in social, economic and environmental issues. Specifically, this article:

(1) Profiles the museum and library sectors in the UK.
(2) Reviews the use of the triple bottom line in sustainability policy and research within the museum and library sectors.
(3) Explores the growing consensus surrounding culture as the 'fourth pillar' of sustainability.
(4) Considers the implications of the lack of recognition of culture as an equal pillar within sustainability policy and research in the museum and library sectors.
(5) Proposes directions for future research and development.

Profile of the museum and library sector in the UK

The Museums Association estimates that there are around 2500 museums in the UK. These range from national museums run by central government, whose collections are 'considered to be of national importance'; to local authority run museums that hold collections which tend to 'reflect local history and heritage'. In addition to these, many university museums maintain collections relating 'to specific areas of academic interest', and a diverse range of independent museums 'owned by registered charities and other independent bodies or trusts', also hold materials that vary considerably in their area of interest, focusing on anything from tanks to pencils (Museums Association 2015).

The UK also has an estimated 4145 public libraries (Public Libraries News 2015). Working to 'provide free services that empower people with access to resources', these libraries are generally run by local authorities (GOV.UK 2013), and, as with museums, exist alongside a variety of other kinds of library. Akin to national museums, national libraries contain 'a high concentration of the nation's treasures', often working to collect together 'the literary production of the nation' (IFLA 1997). Academic libraries exist to support the work of students and researchers by providing access to relevant resources (CILIP 2014), whilst special libraries, that are often privately owned and sometimes form part of a larger business or organisation, hold collections that tend to be of a more specialist interest specific to the requirements of the institution that they support (Merriam-Webster 2015).

This list is by no means exhaustive. There are numerous other types of library and museum, and the ways in which they are classified can also often be far more complex than suggested, owing to systems of governance that can sometimes cross between public, private and academic sectors. Nevertheless, the central mission of all of these organisations revolves around the maintenance of collections for the benefit of users. Museums aim to honour 'the legacy of collections, information and knowledge contributed by people in the past' in order to pass it on 'to future generations' (Museums Association 2008, 4); whilst the main purpose of libraries is said to revolve around the 'selection, organization, preservation, and dissemination of information' (ALA 2015). This again involves the management of collections, whether in physical or digital form.

Regardless of any differences in specific missions or aims in maintaining these collections, a diverse range of cultural assets reside within the care of many of these institutions. Taking the museums and libraries of Manchester as an example, the focus of collections can vary from archaeology, anthropology and natural history at the university owned Manchester Museum (Manchester Museum 2015), to the history of the working classes at the Working Class Movement Library, which is an independent registered charity (WCML 2010). The history of theatre in the city resides within the special collections at the central public library (Manchester City Council 2015), whilst it is possible to explore the history of science and engineering within the collections of the Museum of Science and Industry, which is part of the nationwide Science Museum Group (MOSI 2015).

These museum and library collections are often housed within historic buildings that can be considered cultural assets in their own right. Continuing with the example of Manchester, the neo-gothic Manchester Museum was designed by the renowned Victorian architect Alfred Waterhouse (Manchester Museum 2015), and the neoclassical circular Central Library was designed by Vincent Harris and built in the 1930s (Pidd 2014). Such buildings are iconic landmarks within the city, and have strong links to the community in which they are based. For example, the Portico Library was built in 1806 as Manchester was in the grip of its 'boomtown' phase, and its members included many closely involved in the industrial revolution (Portico Library 2015).

Museums and libraries clearly make significant contributions to the cultural landscape, and maintain a vast array of cultural heritage for their communities. The role that these organisations play is however far more complex than simply preserving cultural heritage for posterity. Indeed, the museum sector, in particular, has long recognised that organisations have a greater responsibility to society than simply preserving and interpreting cultural artefacts, and should play an active role in improving society by working to address contemporary issues and using their expertise to make a positive difference to their communities (Janes and Conaty 2006).

This perspective is now a fundamental part of museum theory and practice. The Museums Association's 'Museums 2020' initiative for the future development of the sector provides further clarification of how museums are expected to benefit society, ranging from 'improving people's lives, building communities, strengthening society and protecting the environment' (Museums Association 2012, 3). Meanwhile, libraries are expected to have a similar wide-ranging role in inspiring and supporting communities, through having an impact on health and wellbeing, providing social and educational benefits, and making contributions at an economic level (ACE 2014a, Fujiwara et al. 2015).

Having a more active role in society in this way is essential for achieving the long-term sustainability of museums and libraries, especially when the public funding of cultural organisations at the cost of other vital services is being questioned (ACE 2011). Engaging with contemporary concerns provides a sense of relevance to the work that organisations undertake in preserving heritage that has clear and immediate benefit for communities, thus counteracting the notion that such work is simply an 'add-on', or 'nice to have' addition to society (ACE 2011, 3).

The triple bottom line in museums and libraries

As the Museums Association's 'Museums 2020' initiative suggests, it is not however enough for there to be a 'generalised sense that a museum provides public benefit by merely existing' (Museums Association 2012, 4). In order to prove their value and continue to be supported, it is essential that museums as well as libraries develop 'defined and explicit' explanations of how their activities benefit wider society (4).

As a concern that permeates all levels of society, sustainable development provides a comprehensive approach by which organisations can demonstrate such value. Having originated from a concern

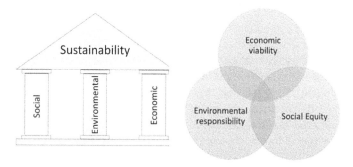

Figure 1. Popular depictions of the three pillars of sustainability, with the Venn diagram emphasising the interdependence of the three components.

over the rapid depletion of ecological resources, the sustainable development ethos recognises that we must move away from 'exclusively economic' ideas about development to a more holistic approach (Hawkes 2001, 9). If society is to develop in a way that 'meets the needs of the present without compromising the ability of future generations to meet their own needs' (WCED 1987, 16), then economic growth must be balanced against not only a concern for the protection of the natural environment, but also a concern for the social wellbeing of humanity. These three interdependent aspects of human existence are considered to be of equal importance in enabling society to continue to function, and are commonly referred to as the three pillars of sustainability, as if any one of the pillars is found to be weak, then the whole system becomes unsustainable (Figure 1).

Organisations are now increasingly expected to demonstrate their contributions to sustainability according to these three pillars. This has led to what is known as the triple bottom line approach being adopted across many sectors, which evaluates an organisation according to its wider social, economic, and environmental impact. As organisations that have a fundamental obligation to have socially responsible relationships with their communities, it is not surprising that the applicability of such measures were quickly recognised in both the museum and library sectors. There is now a wealth of policy and research to guide both museums and libraries in becoming more sustainable organisations, and institutions are increasingly expected to align their practices and missions with wider sustainable development agendas.

Museums are expected to 'achieve greater social outcomes and impact' (Museums Association 2013, 3), 'enrich[ing] the lives of individuals, contribut[ing] to strong and resilient communities, and help[ing] create a fair and just society' (2), whilst libraries are expected to 'clarify' and 'design impact measures' of their social objectives' (Shared Intelligence 2013). Numerous reports also strive to demonstrate the contributions of organisations to the economy. For example, the 2015 'Economic impact of Museums in England' report estimates that the nation's museums 'generate an average of £3 income for every £1 of public sector funding invested in the sector' (Kendall 2015). Similarly, the 2014 'Evidence review of the economic contribution of libraries' works to provide insight of the 'contribution public libraries can make at an economic level' (ACE 2014b). Attention has also been paid to environmental concerns, with 'SMART' targets having been developed for museums to help enable them to become greener institutions (Madan 2011, 82), and groups having been set up to consider how libraries can become more environmentally sustainable (IFLA 2014).

These initiatives clearly reflect sustainable development concerns, and an increasing acceptance of the triple bottom line approach to assessing the value of organisations across society. There are many beneficial effects of adopting this approach for museums and libraries. It enables them to demonstrate their continued relevance to society, and provides them with alternative ways to measure the value of their services, which are often difficult to demonstrate solely in terms of economic profit (ACE 2014b). Many actions that contribute to wider sustainability goals can also have a positive effect on the sustainability of organisations themselves. For example, efforts to reduce energy consumption according to environmental goals can enable financial savings to be made, and outreach projects working towards wider social wellbeing can act as a valuable marketing exercise, promoting wider awareness and helping to develop a positive image of an organisation and its work. At policy level, it also provides policymakers with targets that have long-term relevance and that are applicable to every community, enabling the development of policies that are relevant to institutions across an entire sector.

Despite these many benefits, concerns over the use of the triple bottom line within museums and libraries have been raised. Whilst the adoption of this approach may help to ensure the general future of an institution, it does not allow for adequate recognition of the unique role of museums and libraries in sustaining cultural heritage for their communities. As Campolmi (2013, 239) suggests, 'Preserving but also creating culture makes museums [and by inference, many libraries] core mission different from that of any other media, cultural institutions, commercial businesses and industrial firms'. By evaluating the work of museums and libraries according to the triple bottom line, the unique value of their work in 'preserving and creating culture' is lost, being considered only according to its contribution to wider sustainability goals, rather than according to any intrinsic cultural value that it may hold.

This approach to evaluating culture through its wider impact rather than its intrinsic value is by no means new. Employing instrumental arguments to demonstrate 'culture's contribution to other kinds of good' has been common practice since the 1980s, and has partly arisen owing to the difficulties that exist in understanding and demonstrating the value of culture itself (Holden 2004, 15). Whilst this approach is clearly beneficial in helping cultural institutions to develop socially responsible relationships with their communities, there has been growing concern that this practice of evaluating cultural activity according to its instrumental value can have negative repercussions for the cultural sector. Indeed, as Holden suggests, it has meant that

> The cultural aims and practices of organisations have been subverted. Energies have been directed into chasing funding and collecting evidence rather than achieving cultural purposes. In the search for outcomes and ancillary benefits, the essence of culture has been lost. (2004, 20)

Being based upon demonstrating wider impact on social, economic, and environmental concerns, sustainability policies for museums and libraries can be seen to reinforce this approach to evaluating cultural activity through its instrumental value. It is therefore arguable that the increased focus upon meeting the targets of funders and demonstrating value according to these policy agendas can have such negative repercussions as those suggested by Holden. Indeed, as Anderson (2009, 6) suggests, working towards such policy agendas can even lead to the 'acquisition, preservation, and research' of collections becoming 'considered subordinate' to these other 'aims', with the continuity and development of collections suffering as a result.

The fourth pillar: cultural sustainability

Recent changes within the sustainable development field however have the potential to develop a wider appreciation and understanding of the unique role that museums and libraries play in sustaining cultural heritage. Cultural sustainability, originally considered by many as a component of social sustainability, is now often regarded as a distinct component of equal importance to other sustainability concerns. Indeed, many sustainable development models now depict culture as the 'fourth pillar', situated alongside social, economic, and environmental concerns (Hawkes 2001, i; Figure 2).

Defining exactly what we mean by 'culture' has long been a difficult task. Definitions of the term have changed greatly over the centuries, and vary considerably according to the discipline from which it is approached (Barthel-Bouchier 2013). Culture can of course refer to 'intellectual and creative products', such as those which museums and libraries work to conserve and produce (CIDA 2000, 1). However, it can also refer to 'the beliefs and practices' of a society, being part of its 'fabric' and shaping the way in which 'things are done and our understanding of why this should be so' (1).

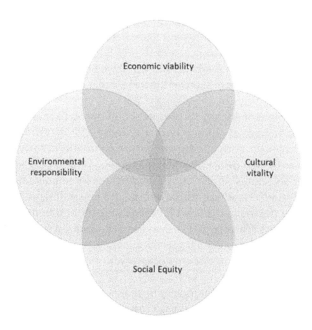

Figure 2. A depiction of the four pillars of sustainability, showing the maintenance of cultural vitality as being of equal importance to environmental, social, and economic concerns.

This second definition would seem to support the thesis that culture is essential for a sustainable society to be possible. Social cohesion depends upon the shared 'patterns of thought and behaviour, values, and beliefs'(Barthel-Bouchier 2013, 11) that culture encompasses. It is also through culture that we learn about 'economic, social, and environmental issues', and develop our ideas about how society should 'address' them (Duxbury and Gillette 2007, 10). From this perspective, whilst culture may have struggled to achieve validation alongside other sustainability goals, it can in fact be considered fundamental to the entire sustainability movement. Culture is not only integral to the existence of a society or social group in the first place, but is also what provides us with the means of 'comprehending' and 'implementing' the changes in our ideas about living that are required to enable a more sustainable society to be possible (Hawkes 2001, 25).

There is still much work required to fully understand and develop the notion of cultural sustainability. Indeed, owing to the 'iterative and reciprocal relationship, in which culture constructs society but society also shapes culture', there are still many difficulties that exist in trying to separate cultural and social sustainability concerns (Dessein *et al.*2015, 25). Nevertheless, certain concerns have been identified that can be considered key to enabling cultural sustainability. Indeed, Soini and Birkeland's (2014, 221) analysis of the scientific discourse surrounding cultural sustainability suggests that whilst it may still be 'at an early stage in its conceptual evolution', the need for the protection of cultural heritage and the strengthening of cultural vitality have emerged as two key 'story lines' within the literature surrounding the term. These concerns, it is proposed, can most clearly be seen to form the 'fourth, cultural pillar of sustainability parallel to ecological, social, and economic sustainability' (220).

As such, the protection of cultural heritage assets, which provide a core means by which cultural values and meanings are transferred, is now considered by UNESCO (2013) to be crucial for cultural sustainability to be possible. These assets include both tangible forms of cultural heritage, such as buildings, monuments, books, and works of art; and intangible cultural heritage, such as folklore, traditions, and languages. Of course, the management of such cultural assets is far more complex than simply ensuring their preservation, as they cannot exist in isolation from the wider cultural needs of society. This more dynamic relationship between cultural heritage and society has many similarities to the relationship between ecological resources and society. Both can be described as forming a 'stock' of 'capital' which is 'inherited from our forebears and which we pass on to future generations' (Throsby 1997, 15), but which must equally be utilised for the benefit of the current population.

To this end, Throsby identifies five key sustainability principles originally devised to aid in the sustainable management of ecological resources, but owing to their similarities, can equally be applied to the management of cultural heritage. These include ensuring equity in terms of access to cultural resources for both current and future generations; fostering cultural diversity, and applying the precautionary principle when managing cultural heritage to prevent irreversible damage or loss. In addition, it is also considered necessary to maintain an awareness of the interconnectedness of the cultural, economic, social, and environmental systems, and the consequent effects that any decisions made when managing cultural heritage may have on these other sustainability concerns (Throsby 2011). If, as has been suggested, the protection of cultural assets is as central to cultural sustainability as the protection of ecological resources is to environmental sustainability, then it would seem necessary for similar principles to be applied to the management of cultural heritage.

Interestingly, this is not the only comparison to be drawn between the cultural and environmental sustainability spheres. In a similar way to how organisms are linked together with their environment as part of an ecosystem, in the last decade the idea that 'cultural activities' are 'linked together' in 'dynamic ways' has also been recognised (Holden 2015,3). The AHRC's report entitled 'The ecology of culture' proposes that in order to understand 'the complex interdependencies that shape the demand for and production of arts and cultural offerings' (2), rather than considering culture as an economy, it is far more useful to take an 'ecological approach' (2). The report suggests that rather than following the traditional linear and economically focused approach to evaluating cultural production, it is far more profitable to consider the cultural sector in terms of its dynamic nature, concentrating on the

'relationships and patterns within the overall system, showing how careers develop, ideas transfer, money flows, and product and content move, to and fro, around and between' the various organisations and individuals involved with the cultural sector. (Holden 2015, 2)

Just as those working in the field of ecology have realised that environmental problems must be addressed according to an awareness of the 'wholeness and interconnectedness' of ecological systems, so it is now becoming clear that cultural 'producers, advocates, and policymakers' must also take a similar stance to 'strengthen the arts and cultural sphere' (Holden 2015, 6). The AHRC's report makes a number of preliminary suggestions of approaches that could be taken in order to achieve this, based on considering the roles that different stakeholders play in sustaining culture, the complex networks that exist between them, and how best to increase the durability and productivity of these cultural systems. In practice, developing such perspectives of the cultural sector can aid those involved in its future development. For example, mapping local cultural ecologies, which involves 'Combining descriptions of activity, infrastructure, history, and demographics … with data about cultural participation and its objective and subjective effects' (24), can help to determine the main strengths and weaknesses of the sector within a specific locality, and thus aid local authorities in deciding 'where their investment is best deployed' (32).

Just as an acute awareness of complex ecosystems and the careful management of ecological resources underpins environmental sustainability, so there would seem to be an increasing recognition that a similar approach is required for our cultural systems in order for cultural sustainability to be possible. If culture is as fundamental to enabling a sustainable society as has been suggested, then more strategic methods of encouraging cultural vitality and managing our cultural heritage, as key components of the fourth pillar, would certainly seem necessary.

Integration of cultural sustainability in sustainability policy and research for museums and libraries

The idea that culture should be considered as a distinct pillar within sustainable development agendas is now gaining widespread acceptance. Indeed, the need for greater consideration of cultural sustainability was a primary focus in the United Nation's post 2015 sustainability goals (IFACCA 2013). Along with the growing consensus surrounding the idea that the protection of cultural heritage is crucial for cultural sustainability to be possible (UNESCO 2013), this would seem to be a prime opportunity to demonstrate the value of the work of museums and libraries in sustaining culture beyond its impact on social, economic, and environmental concerns. Yet despite this, the focus of sustainability research within museums has tended to remain upon their relationship 'with primarily environmental and secondarily economic and social sustainability' (Stylianou-Lambert *et al.* 2014, 569).

This would also appear to be the case within library research, with the majority of studies focusing on 'greening' initiatives (Jankowska and Marcum 2010, 162). Even research or initiatives focusing specifically on the maintenance of either physical or digital collections within libraries again tend to focus on the environmental, economic and social aspects of the sustainability of these collections (Hamilton 2004, Jankowska and Marcum 2010, Chowdhury 2014). Little reference is made to cultural sustainability either as a way to guide the development of more sustainable practices or to provide explanation for why this work is necessary, despite the fact that such projects are often dealing directly with the preservation of cultural artefacts.

A similar story is told within cultural policy, with the Museums Association's (2008) document 'Sustainability and museums: your chance to make a difference' again focusing on 'Economic, environmental and social' concerns (5). Aspects of what could be considered cultural sustainability are included in their 'Principles for sustainable museums', such as the need to 'Acknowledge the legacy contributed by previous generations and pass on a better legacy of collections, information and knowledge to the next generation' (Museums Association 2016). However, the methods of measuring sustainability in their 'Sustainability Checklist' remain rooted in attributing objectives and targets to 'the three main aspects of sustainable development', which are considered to be 'social, economic, and environmental' concerns (2016).

It is arguable that cultural sustainability concerns are innate within the practices of museums and libraries, and as a result do not need further coverage in sustainability policy. Indeed, as the Museum Association's 'Museums Change Lives' report suggests, initiatives working towards 'improving lives, creating better places and helping to advance society' are built on 'the traditional role of preserving collections and connecting audiences with them'(2013, 3). However, such an approach continues to value the role that organisations play in sustaining culture according to wider 'social outcomes and impact' (3), rather than according to its own merit.

Sustaining culture may be central to the work of museums and libraries, yet cultural sustainability is rarely considered as a definitive outcome within sustainability research and policy within the sector. The role that museums and libraries play within sustainable development continues to be valued according to its social, economic, and environmental impact, perpetuating the notion that culture can only be valued according to its ancillary benefits. This denies organisations the opportunity to be valued according to their unique contributions to sustainable development that explicit recognition of cultural sustainability as an equal pillar would allow.

Encouraging steps have however been made within recent museum research. Stylianou-Lambert *et al.*(2014) provide a theoretical model by which the sustainable development of museums can be assessed according to all four areas of sustainability, with a particular focus on identifying gaps in the 'parameters of cultural sustainability'(566). These parameters are 'constructed on the basis of the broad discussions of culture as a fourth pillar of sustainable development … the recommendations of museum associations and the most recent debates about multiculturalism, inclusion and community participation'(569–570). The aim of this model is to provide a list of the key responsibilities of museums within the cultural sustainability sphere, and these are broken down into seven separate areas, which are described as 'Heritage preservation', 'Cultural skills and knowledge', 'Memory/identity', 'New audiences/inclusion', 'Cultural diversity/intercultural dialogue', 'Creativity/innovation', and 'Artistic vitality' (570).

Stylianou-Lambert et al. conducted their research across the museums sector in Cyprus, and the model was developed in order to aid cultural policy-makers in identifying 'weaknesses or gaps' in particular areas of cultural sustainability within different museum environments (Stylianou-Lambert et al. 2014, 572). For example, the research found state museums to 'place their emphasis on heritage preservation, the passing on of specialized cultural skills and knowledge, as well as the construction of public memory and a sense of national identity'. However, they were considered less active in 'the development of new audiences, the representation of cultural diversity, as well as creativity, innovation, and artistic vitality', which would suggest that policy would need to be amended in order to encourage development within these areas (582).

This study marks a significant move away from the use of the triple bottom line approach, to include cultural sustainability as an equal concern within sustainable development models for museums. Further replications of this study are however required in other countries as well as in other cultural heritage organisations such as libraries. In addition, a range of linked studies might support the development of a better understanding as to how cultural sustainability might be delivered in different contexts. This would seem vital to generate greater understanding of the different pressures affecting the sustainability of cultural heritage within the diverse institutional contexts explored earlier in this article.

Furthermore, the focus of the model devised by Stylianou-Lambert et al. is upon developing 'broader (external) cultural policies' (Stylianou-Lambert et al. 2014, 569), rather than on internal practices within museums and how these may need to be adapted in order for organisations to demonstrate their contributions to wider cultural sustainability agendas. Without detailed consideration of cultural sustainability at practice level, and the development of 'milestones, benchmarks or measurement facilities' in order to 'assist institutions in assessing their progress towards sustainability', many organisations find 'the practical application of holistic sustainability principles to their operations challenging' (Adams 2010, 26–29). In consequence, whilst such policies may aim to help institutions demonstrate their value to wider society, the translation of policy into practice remains problematic, and as has previously been the case with the triple bottom line, may lead to organisations failing to include it as 'a core part of their work and planning' (Museums Association 2009, 5).

Adams (2010) attempts to address this issue, and draws on existing publications and governmental guidelines within the sustainable development field in order to develop a set of indicators for use within museums that incorporates all four pillars. The benefit of this model is that it provides museums with clear actions in order to work towards sustainability. For example, in terms of increasing environmental sustainability, it is suggested that organisations review their total water use and non-renewable energy use over twelve months, as well as the ratio of waste recycled to waste sent to land fill over the same period (46). The overall sustainability goals are also specific to the organisations themselves, with, for example, the economic goal being defined as 'To have a balanced and diverse budget' (46). In comparison to the policy focused model of Stylianou-Lambert et al. (2014, 570), which includes 'Cultural tourism' and 'Economic revitalization' of the local community as the key parameters of museums' role within economic sustainability, the development of such specific goals and indicators as provided by Adams can help towards making sustainability more relevant and manageable to practitioners at an organisational level.

However, whilst Adams' (2010) model includes cultural sustainability as an equal concern alongside the triple bottom line, it does not adequately address the complex nature of culture, or fully explore the role that museums play. The main cultural sustainability goal for museums is defined as being 'to hold the collection in perpetuity and maintain its quality'. The suggested core indicators for doing so focus on conservation measures, such as the 'Proportion of collection surveyed for conservation in the last 12 months', or the increasing or decreasing percentage of items within the collection that rate highly in terms of condition (46). It is clear, however, that cultural sustainability and the role that museums as well as libraries play within it is far more complex than the preservation of cultural artefacts. As explored earlier in this article, museums and libraries are organisations that often have complicated links to the cultural history of their local communities; maintaining historic buildings, hosting a diverse range of cultural events, offering a wide variety of opportunities for research, and providing cultural inspiration to academics, artists, writers and the general public alike. If the full extent of the cultural value of organisations is to be harnessed for the purpose of expressing contributions to cultural sustainability, then models and indicators need to be developed that more fully reflect the diverse and complex nature of this role.

Proposals for future research and development

For museums and libraries to receive adequate recognition of their unique value in sustaining culture, it is imperative that the concept of cultural sustainability is more fully introduced and developed within cultural policy contexts, and is considered as central rather than subsidiary to other sustainability concerns. However, further research is first required so that the value of the role that museums and libraries play in sustaining culture can be articulated in greater depth than the criteria currently provided by broader sustainable development agendas, and with greater breadth beyond preservation and conservation practices. Such research could enable the contributions of museums and libraries to cultural sustainability to be more adequately expressed within sustainability policies, thus enabling wider appreciation of the value of these organisations to society. This would seem especially necessary within the library sector, where the role of organisations in sustaining culture is often not as immediately discernible as it is in museums, and has consequently remained comparatively underexplored.

To achieve a deeper understanding of the role that museums and libraries play within cultural sustainability, it will be necessary to revise sustainability models. Models so far have concentrated on reflecting external sustainability concerns, which consider environmental, social, economic, and cultural concerns to be equally weighted. However, as the main strengths of these organisations lie in sustaining culture, it could perhaps be more productive to consider their role in sustainability first and foremost according to their role in cultural sustainability. This would not only ensure that their full value in sustaining culture is recognised and harnessed for the purposes of cultural sustainability, but would also help to make sustainability seem more relevant to museum and library professionals, who sometimes struggle to understand the applicability of sustainable development concepts to their organisations (Museums Association 2009).

Rather than seeing all four dimensions of sustainability as equal pillars within the museum or library environment, it may in fact be beneficial to utilise sustainability models to consider how social, economic, and environmental structures within these organisations work to support their cultural contributions (Figure 3). In terms of social structures, it could be helpful to investigate the role of governing bodies, staff, the community, and other external bodies that play a supportive role through associations, partnerships, and collaborations in sustaining the cultural value of individual organisations. Economic

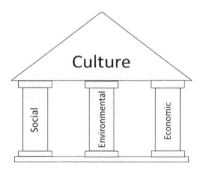

Figure 3. Re-imagining the four pillars: social, economic, and environmental structures supporting museums and libraries in sustaining culture.

considerations would include an investigation of funding and income streams, ways of reducing costs, and the development of business strategies in order to make the cultural contributions of organisations more economically sustainable. Lastly, environmental concerns would focus on the physical conditions and processes required for the conservation of collections, archives, and buildings, and providing the environment necessary for the physical survival of cultural heritage assets within organisations.

Such a model would still need to be informed by external sustainability concerns, as organisations would still bear a responsibility towards wider society, but it would enable sustainable development concerns to be better aligned with the strength of museums and libraries in sustaining culture. This alternative perspective could also help to highlight any conflicts that may exist between organisations' cultural missions and wider sustainability goals. For example, environmental considerations would need to incorporate both a concern for the conservation needs of collections as well as for wider responsibilities to the natural environment, which owing to collection conservation practices not always being eco-friendly, can often be opposed to each other. Trying to find ways to resolve these issues could help to make the application of sustainability measures more practicable within museum and library environments, and again help to increase the uptake of sustainability within the core strategies of organisations.

Conclusion

This article has explored the use of sustainable development concepts within cultural policy to provide justification of the value of museums and libraries to society. It argues that whilst cultural sustainability has become an increasing concern in wider sustainable development agendas, it has not yet been given adequate coverage within sustainability policy and research in museums and libraries. As a result, the work of these institutions in sustaining culture continues to be valued according to its instrumental role in social, economic, and environmental sustainability, rather than according to its intrinsic cultural value.

Museums and libraries have an inherent investment in sustaining and promoting culture, and the growing concern for cultural sustainability provides a compelling perspective from which they can re-establish an understanding of how crucial their work is to society. Formulating sustainability policies for museums and libraries that include cultural sustainability as an equal concern alongside their commitments to social, economic, and environmental impact would help to develop understanding of this role and appreciation of the unique value of these institutions to society, thus helping to secure their future.

Disclosure statement

No potential conflict of interest was reported by the authors.

Funding

This work was supported by the Arts and Humanities Research Council [grant number 8H/LO12197/1].

References

ACE (Arts Council England), 2011. *Culture, Knowledge and Understanding: Great Museums and Libraries for Everyone*. London: Arts Council England. Available from: http://www.artscouncil.org.uk/media/uploads/pdf/culture_knowledge_and_understanding.pdf

ACE (Arts Council England), 2014a. *Evidence Review of the Economic Contribution of Libraries*. Manchester, NH: Arts Council England. Available from: http://www.artscouncil.org.uk/media/uploads/pdf/Evidence_review_economic_contribution_libraries.pdf

ACE (Arts Council England), 2014b. Now published: Evidence Review of the Economic Contribution of Libraries. *Arts Council England*, 4 June. http://www.artscouncil.org.uk/news/arts-council-news/now-published-evidence-review-economic-contributio/

Adams, E., 2010. *Towards Sustainability Indicators for Museums in Australia*. BSc diss., University of Adelaide.

ALA (American Library Association), 2015. *Code of Ethics of the American Library Association*. American Library Association.http://www.ala.org/advocacy/proethics/codeofethics/codeethics [Accessed 23 April 2015]

Anderson, M.L., 2009. Museum values. *In*: S. Holo and M. Alvarez, eds. *Beyond the Turnstile: Making the Case for Museums and Sustainable Values*. Lanham: Altamira Press, 5–7.

Barthel-Bouchier, D., 2013. *Cultural Heritage and the Challenge of Sustainability*. Walnut Creek: Left Coast Press.

Campolmi, I., 2013. Sustainability in Modern Art Museums. Management Challenges and Cultural Policies. *Il Capitale Culturale: Studies on the Value of Cultural Heritage*, 8 (2013), 235–250. Available from: https://riviste.unimc.it/index.php/cap-cult/article/viewFile/563/517

Chowdhury, G., 2014. Sustainability of Digital Libraries: a Conceptual Model and a Research Framework. *International Journal on Digital Libraries*, 14 (3–4), 181–195. doi:10.1007/s00799-014-0116-0.

CIDA (Canadian International Development Agency), 2000. *Culture*. Quebec: Canadian International Development Agency. Available from: http://www.oecd.org/social/gender-development/1896320.pdf

CILIP (Chartered Institute of Library and Information Professionals), 2014. *Academic Librarian*. Chartered Institute of Library and Information Professionals. Available from: http://www.cilip.org.uk/cilip/jobs-careers/types-job/librarian-roles/academic-librarian

Dessein, J., Soini, K., Fairclough, G., and Horlings, L., eds., 2015. *Culture in, for and as Sustainable Development: Conclusions from the COST Action IS1007 Investigating Cultural Sustainability*. Jyväskylä: University of Jyväskylä.

Duxbury, N. and Gillette, E., 2007. *Culture as a key Dimension of Sustainability: Exploring Concepts, Themes, and Models*. Creative City Network of Canada. Available from: http://tosca.vtlseurope.com:8098/arxius/pdf/E130054.pdf

Fujiwara, D., Lawton, R., and Mourato, S., 2015. *The Health and Wellbeing Benefits of Public Libraries: Full Report*. Manchester, NH: Arts Council England. Available from: http://www.artscouncil.org.uk/media/uploads/Health_and_wellbeing_benefits_of_public_libraries_full_report.pdf

GOV.UK, 2013. *Policy: Library Services*. GOV.UK. Available from: https://www.gov.uk/government/policies/library-services

Hamilton, V., 2004. Sustainability for Digital Libraries. *Library Review*, 53 (8), 392–395. doi:10.1108/00242530410556210.

Hawkes, J., 2001. *The Fourth Pillar of Sustainability: Culture's Essential Role in Public Planning*. Common Ground Publishing. Available from: http://www.culturaldevelopment.net.au/community/Downloads/HawkesJon%282001%29TheFourthPillarOfSustainability.pdf

Holden, J., 2004. *Capturing Cultural Value: how Culture has Become a Tool of Government Policy*. London: Demos. Available from: http://www.demos.co.uk/files/CapturingCulturalValue.pdf

Holden, J., 2015. *The Ecology of Culture: a Report Commissioned by the Arts and Humanities Research Council's Cultural Value Project*. Wiltshire: Arts and Humanities Research Council. Available from: http://www.ahrc.ac.uk/News-and-Events/News/Documents/AHRC%20Ecology%20of%20Culture%20(A).pdf

IFACCA (International Federation of Arts Councils and Culture Agencies), 2013. *Culture as a Goal in the post-2015 Development Agenda*. International Federation of Arts Councils and Culture Agencies. Available from: http://www.ifacca.org/publications/2013/10/24/culture-goal-post-2015-development-agenda/

IFLA (International Federation of Library Associations), 1997. *Section of National Libraries: Guidelines for Legislation for National Library Services*. International Federation of Library Associations. Available from: http://archive.ifla.org/VII/s1/gnl/gnl-i1.htm

IFLA (International Federation of Library Associations), 2014. *About the Environmental Sustainability and Libraries Special Interest Group*. International Federation of Library Associations. Available from: http://www.ifla.org/about-environmental-sustainability-and-libraries

Janes, R.R. and Conaty, G.T., 2006. *Looking Reality in the Eye: Museums and Social Responsibility*. Calgary: University of Calgary Press.

Jankowska, M.A. and Marcum, J.W., 2010. Sustainability Challenge for Academic Libraries: Planning for the Future. *College & Research Libraries*, 71 (2), 160–170. doi:10.5860/0710160.

Kazi, N., 2012. The Identity Crisis of Libraries in the Attention Economy. *Library Philosophy and Practice (e-journal)*, 1 January. Available from: http://digitalcommons.unl.edu/libphilprac/684?utm_source=digitalcommons.unl.edu%2Flibphilprac%2F684&utm_medium=PDF&utm_campaign=PDFCoverPages

Kendall, G., 2015. England's Museums Generate £3 for every £1 of Public Funding. *Museums Association*, 9 March. Available from: http://www.museumsassociation.org/museums-journal/news/09032015-englands-museums-generate-3-for-every-1-public-funding

Madan, R., 2011. *Sustainable Museums: Strategies for the 21st Century*. Edinburgh: MuseumsEtc.

Manchester City Council, 2015. *Libraries: Theatre Collection*. Manchester City Council. Available from: http://www.manchester.gov.uk/info/447/rare_books_and_collections/334/theatre_collection [Accessed 23 April 2015].

Manchester Museum, 2015. *The History of the Manchester Museum*. Manchester Museum. Available from: http://www.museum.manchester.ac.uk/aboutus/history/ [Accessed 23 April 2015].

Merriam-Webster, 2015. *Special Library*. Merriam-Webster. Available from: http://www.merriam-webster.com/dictionary/special%20library [Accessed 23 April 2015].

MOSI (Museum of Science and Industry), 2015. *SMG: a Family of Museums*. Museum of Science and Industry. Available from: http://www.mosi.org.uk/about-us/smg-a-family-of-museums.aspx [Accessed 23 April 2015].

Museums Association, 2008. *Sustainability and Museums: your Chance to Make a Difference*. London: Museums Association. Available from: http://www.museumsassociation.org/download?id=16398

Museums Association, 2009. *Sustainability and Museums: Report on Consultation*. London: Museums Association. Available from: http://www.museumsassociation.org/download?id=17944

Museums Association, 2012. *Museums 2020 Discussion Paper*. London: Museums Association. Available from: www.museumsassociation.org/download?id=806530

Museums Association, 2013. *Museums Change Lives: the MA's Vision for the Impact of Museums*. London: Museums Association. Available from: www.museumsassociation.org/download?id=1001738

Museums Association, 2015. *Frequently Asked Questions*. Museums Association. Available from: http://www.museumsassociation.org/about/frequently-asked-questions [Accessed 23 April 2015].

Museums Association, 2016. *Principles for Sustainable Museums*. Museums Association. Available from: http://www.museumsassociation.org/campaigns/sustainability/principles-for-sustainable-museums [Accessed 11 March 2016].

Pidd, H., 2014. Manchester Central Library Reopens after £50m Revamp. *The Guardian*, 21 March. Available from: http://www.theguardian.com/uk-news/2014/mar/21/manchester-central-library-reopens-50 m-pound-revamp

Portico Library, 2015. *The collection*. Portico Library. Available from: http://www.theportico.org.uk/library

Public Libraries News, 2015. *What's Happening in Your Library?* Public Libraries News. Available from: http://www.publiclibrariesnews.com/ [Accessed 23 April 2015].

Shared Intelligence, 2013. *Demonstrating Increased Social Impact is the Biggest Challenge Libraries Will Face*. Shared Intelligence. Available from: http://www.sharedintelligence.net/projects/demonstrating-increased-social-impact-is-the-biggest-challenge-libraries-will-face/

Soini, K. and Birkeland, I., 2014. Exploring the Scientific Discourse on Cultural Sustainability. *Geoforum*, 51 (2014), 213–223. Available from: http://www.academia.edu/5720777/Exploring_the_scientific_discourse_on_cultural_sustainability

Stylianou-Lambert, T., Boukas, N., and Christodoulou-Yerali, M., 2014. Museums and Cultural Sustainability: Stakeholders, Forces, and Cultural Policies. *International Journal of Cultural Policy*, 20 (5), 566–587. doi:10.1080/10286632.2013.874420.

Throsby, D., 1997. Sustainability and Culture Some Theoretical Issues. *International Journal of Cultural Policy*, 4 (1), 7–19. doi:10.1080/10286639709358060.

Throsby, D., 2011. *The Economics of Cultural Policy*. Cambridge: Cambridge University Press.

UNESCO (United Nations Educational, Scientific and Cultural Organisation), 2013. *Introducing Cultural Heritage into the Sustainable Development Agenda*. United Nations Educational, Scientific and Cultural Organisation. Available from: http://www.unesco.org/new/fileadmin/MULTIMEDIA/HQ/CLT/images/HeritageENG.pdf

WCED (World Commission on Environment and Development), 1987. *Our Common Future*. World Commission on Environment and Development. Available from: http://www.un-documents.net/our-common-future.pdf [Accessed 23 April 2015].

WCML (Working Class Movement Library), 2010. *Introduction to Our Collection*. Working Class Movement Library. Available from: http://www.wcml.org.uk/wcml/en/contents/ [Accessed 23 April 2015].

Caretakers of the Earth: integrating Canadian Aboriginal perspectives on culture and sustainability into local plans

M. Sharon Jeannotte

ABSTRACT

While still contested in most jurisdictions, a consensus on the four-pillar approach to sustainable development is slowly emerging. This perspective attempts to integrate the environmental, social, economic and cultural elements of a community into local sustainability planning processes and has been widely adopted in Canada as the basis of Integrated Community Sustainability Plans. However, Aboriginal perspectives have generally been marginalised in such efforts, largely because Aboriginal peoples take a more holistic approach to both sustainability and culture than Western-educated planners and decision makers. This article examines current approaches and methodologies adopted by Aboriginal and non-Aboriginal communities in Canada to integrate culture in sustainability planning and presents several case studies that examine the application of medicine wheel and other Aboriginal integrative worldviews to community sustainability planning. It discusses whether Aboriginal perspectives on culture can provide an alternative narrative that will advance our understanding of culture's role in community sustainability and counteract the monocultural perspectives that are the legacy of colonialism throughout the world.

Introduction

'Culture' and 'sustainability' are two of the most complex policy areas in society today. Many academics, institutional stakeholders and practitioners are arguing for a fresh approach to development theory that takes into account the role culture plays in creating a sustainable, just and fair society (Zukin 1996, World Commission on Culture and Development 1996; Schech and Haggis 2000; Cowan, Dembour, and Wilson 2001; Nederveen Pieterse 2010). Clammer (2012), in commenting on this shift in development theory, has suggested:

> The problem is the core values of our culture and the difficulty of changing them even when rationality points to the need, and indeed the necessity, for urgent and radical change. What is needed ... is a 'new story' – a new conception of the earth, its history, our place as one species among many in that story, and our vision of what we want our collective (human and non-human) future to be like. This is fundamentally not a question of politics, but of culture, the site of our core values, habitual practices, modes of expression and creativity and models of selfhood. It is not, then, just a matter of changing culture in more humane and ecologically just directions: culture is the *means* by which those changes take place. (158)

An alternative 'story' does in fact exist, but it is not new and predates current views of nature, culture and development by many thousands of years. For the past 200 years, starting with the Enlightenment and intensifying during the Industrial Revolution, Western philosophy has espoused 'ethical, political and aesthetic arguments that are constructed upon a view of culture as offering an essential correc-tive to "nature'" (Soper 1995, 28–29). This perspective views the two as opposites rather than as part of an existential continuum. In the global capitalist system, this worldview has culminated in what author and environmental activist Klein (2014) has called a mentality of 'extractivism', which sees it as humanity's right to 'bend complex natural systems to our will' and 'to extract ever more without facing consequences' (25). Aboriginal or Indigenous cultures[1], in contrast, are characterised as 'regenerative', which Klein (quoting Missisauga Nishnaabeg writer Leeanne Simpson) describes as 'a way of living designed to generate life, not just human life but the life of all living things' (443).

Aboriginal cultures in Canada are embedded in place and cannot be separated from the natural order that surrounds them. As Culhane (1998) has stated, 'The fusion of Indigenous cultures with their land is so complete that the only way to take the land is to destroy the Indigenous culture' (49). Many contemporary Aboriginal scholars have described how rupturing this relationship with the land and with traditional communities, a result of Canadian government policies, has contributed to both indi-vidual trauma and community dysfunction (Clarkson, Morrissette, and Régallet 1992; Broad, Boyer, and Chataway 2006; Episkenew 2009). It is for this reason that Aboriginal peoples view culture and cultural policies as being at the heart of both recovering and rebuilding their communities. Aboriginal peoples also suggest that their commitment to the Earth and to the future seven generations can serve as an example to the rest of society. As Clarkson, Morrissette, and Régallet (1992) state, 'Indigenous people have kept alive the knowledge and the relationships with the land that have become opaque to western people. As a result, they are the key to the future survival not only for Indigenous societies, but for humanity' (74).

Recent European research on the conceptual underpinnings of culture's role in sustainability has suggested three possible models, which roughly parallel the approaches taken in the three case studies in this article. The first role, characterised as 'culture *in* sustainable development' corresponds to the four-pillar approach and views culture as 'linked but autonomous, alongside separate ecological, social, and economic considerations and imperatives of sustainability' (Dessein et al. 2015, 28). Instead of viewing culture as in opposition to nature and sustainable development, it presents it as being equally supportive as other key factors. The second role is 'culture *for* sustainable development', which moves culture into 'a framing, contextualising and mediating mode that can balance all three of the pillars and guide sustainable development' (28). It is somewhat akin to the new 'narrative frames' or discourses that Redclift (2006) and others have suggested are needed to develop new metaphors for and stories about sustainability. In this model, the context (including in this case, the colonial context) is central to the sustainability narrative. The third role – 'culture *as* sustainable development' – 'sees culture as the necessary overall foundation and structure for achieving the aims of sustainable development' (Dessein et al. 2015, 29). In this conceptualization, culture takes on a transformative role and 'involves practicing a new understanding of the human place in the world, and recognising that humans are an inseparable part of the more-than-human world' (31). As this article argues, culture as a foundation for sustainability is, perhaps, not so much a *new* understanding as much as it is an old one, embodied in the concept of the medicine wheel and other traditional Indigenous teachings from around the world While these teachings take many forms in different cultures, this article will focus on examples common to Canada's Aboriginal peoples.

This article first describes how Aboriginal culture has been treated within Canada's colonial history over the past 500 years. This often traumatic story serves as the backdrop and bridge to an overview of medicine wheel and other integrative Aboriginal worldviews and their application to the sustaina-bility of communities. Following a review of current approaches adopted by Aboriginal and non-Ab-original communities in Canada to integrate culture in sustainability planning, three case studies are presented, illustrating the application of traditional teachings to Aboriginal community development and discussing the general applicability of these concepts to contemporary debates about culture's role in sustainability, with a focus on local community planning. Then, linking the case studies to the conceptual frames described above, it considers the following questions: Can Aboriginal perspectives on culture provide an alternative narrative that will help planners better understand culture's role in community sustainability? Can these perspectives be more broadly applied internationally to incorporate marginalised voices into cultural policy discourse, to support cultural diversity and to promote a more holistic approach to sustainability?

Colonialism and Canada's cultural policies

Established in 2008 to reveal the truth about the history of Canada's residential schools for Aboriginal peoples and to guide the process of healing within Aboriginal families and between Aboriginal peoples and other Canadians, the Truth and Reconciliation Commission of Canada (TRCC) held national and community-level events, gathered documents and statements about residential schools and their legacy, and developed a set of recommendations. Its final report, published in 2015, concluded that the central element of the Canadian government's policy with regard to Aboriginal residential schools was cultural genocide, which it defined as 'the destruction of those structures and practices that allow the group to continue as a group' (TRCC 2015, 1). The forcible relocation of Aboriginal children to residential schools was intended, in the words of the Truth and Reconciliation Commission, 'to eliminate Aboriginal governments; ignore Aboriginal rights; terminate the Treaties; and through a process of assimilation, cause Aboriginal peoples to cease to exist as distinct legal, social, cultural, religious, and racial entities in Canada' (TRCC 2015, 1).

In Canada, residential schools were a major element of colonialism, the central mechanism used by European empires to consolidate economic, political and spiritual control of conquered territories. Canadian colonialism was initially imperial in nature, driven by the extractive logic of resource exploitation as embodied in the fur trade. Aboriginal peoples played essential and central roles in the harvesting, transportation and distribution networks of the fur market (Innis 1999; Dickason and MacNab 2009). However, it was settler colonialism that underpinned Canadian Aboriginal policy in the twentieth and twenty first centuries. Paquette, Beauregard, and Gunter (2015) have argued that settler colonialism – focused on acquisition of land rather than resource extraction – required the permanent displacement of the Indigenous population, rather than its exploitation.

As Canadian settlers sought to detach themselves from the imperial powers of Great Britain and France and establish a distinct identity, settler nationalism succeeded settler colonialism as the driving force behind cultural policy as well as Aboriginal policy. Landmark Canadian cultural policy documents, such as the report of the Royal Commission on National Development in the Arts, Letters and Sciences (1951), were instrumental in fostering a cultural policy focused on the creation of a pan-Canadian identity, one which was 'infused with settler nationalism – a nationalism that embraces expression of English and French as conditions and foundations of "national unity"' (Paquette, Beauregard, and Gunter 2015, 6). Canada's policies of bilingualism, biculturalism and, later, multiculturalism, have never been fully able to address the 'complexity generated by Indigenous populations as a challenge to the Canadian-European narrative of cultural identity' (8).

Exclusion from the national narrative is another artifact of colonial legacies – what Santos (2004) has described as the production of non-existence. Five logics underpin this non-existence: the monoculture of knowledge, the monoculture of linear time, the monoculture of classification into hierarchies, the monoculture of the universal and the global, and the monoculture of capitalistic productivity. Aboriginal peoples continue to struggle against these monocultures, which have characterised them as ignorant (lacking knowledge), residual ('backward' in terms of linear time or progress), inferior (in the racial hierarchy), local (or lacking global and universal credibility) and non-productive (lazy, inefficient and lacking in the skills necessary to fit within capitalist modernity) (Santos 2004, 239).

Aboriginal scholar Episkenew (2009) contends that exclusion from the 'authorised story of the creation of the Canadian nation-state' has contributed to the postcolonial trauma of Aboriginal peoples. She argues that 'Implicit in our exclusion is the understanding that we are not noteworthy enough to remember, not significant enough to perceive, and not desirable enough to have a place in the future of the Canadian collective' (71). She adds that the inclusion of Aboriginal narratives in the national narrative is necessary, not only to heal individual wounds suffered by individuals, but also to inspire 'social regeneration by providing eyewitness testimony to historical injustices' (75). A few Aboriginal scholars have attempted to address this exclusion by documenting the contributions of Aboriginal peoples to Canada's identity and culture (Newhouse, Voyageur, and Beavon 2005; Valaskakis 2005; King 2012), but it is a project very much in early stages.

In Aboriginal cultures, stories and narratives are central to their worldview with regard to sustainability and balance. Elder Reg Crowshoe, in his testimony before the Truth and Reconciliation Commission, emphasised that 'when we talk about stories, we talk about defining our environment and how we look at authorities that come from the land' (TRCC 2015, 18). He explained that reconciliation between Aboriginal and non-Aboriginal Canadians would have to include reconciliation with the natural world or, as the Commission observed, 'humans must journey through life in conversation and negotiation with all creation' (18).

Role of culture in Aboriginal and Western sustainability conceptualisations

While there are many ways in which Aboriginal societies express their cultural worldviews, one compelling example is the medicine wheel, a cultural symbol that can be used to convey a variety of teachings or meanings in a holistic and balanced way. The medicine wheel is a circle divided into parts (usually four) that counterbalance each other. The four segments most often represent the four cardinal directions, the four seasons and the four stages of life, but they can also denote 'the many aspects of creation, such as the races of people, plants, the natural elements, aspects of being or character, animals and other living beings' (Four Directions Teachings 2012). The quadrants are equal and joined by a sequence that proceeds in a clockwise direction, with the centre representing the balanced nature of the universe or Creation. The wheel is therefore a symbol of wholeness and inter-connectedness and is used as a sacred geometry to illustrate the cycles of nature at both macro and micro levels (Four Directions Teachings 2012). It reflects a worldview based on principles of harmony and balance, the basis of Aboriginal ways of knowing, going beyond epistemology or traditional indigenous knowledge (which has been incorporated into some sustainable development projects (Sillitoe 1998) (See Figure 1).

The medicine wheel was often an integral part of Aboriginal cultural landscapes. Throughout North America, but especially western Canada, medicine wheel circles were constructed of stone, antlers and other natural materials to mark special 'locations of power' within the landscape encountered by the nomadic peoples who lived there. At these locations, the power of the land was particularly evident – for example, at the crests of hills or near bodies of water. The medicine wheel also includes a vertical power axis that connected this world with the cosmos above and below. In traditional Plains life, this circle-axis motif was reflected in everyday life through the use of stone circles to hold tipis in place (tipi rings), the central poles of the tipis, circular shields made of buffalo skin, ceremonies centred on the sun dance, placement of sites on hilltops, the veneration of certain trees or mountains and medicine

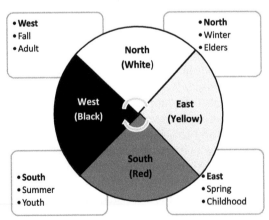

Figure 1. Depiction of a traditional medicine wheel. Source: Illustration by author, based upon the version used by the Anishnabe Peoples. Other variations may be used by other Aboriginal Peoples. (See Pitawanakwat 2006).

lodges where healing and other rituals were performed (Wilson 2005). As Wilson puts it, 'people tended to view themselves as 'written by' the landscape, and not the reverse' (6).

Contemporary Aboriginal peoples in Canada continue to view this connection to the land as fundamental to their identity and to their wellbeing. In a treatise on indigenous peoples and sustainable development, Clarkson, Morrissette, and Régallet (1992) describe this relationship in the following terms:

> Westerners tend to equate culture with language or other outward manifestations such as dress, music, dance and art. However, our culture is more than this. It is a way of life. People cannot maintain their culture unless they can continue to reproduce themselves physically. Our cultures, and we venture to say all Indigenous cultures, are based upon a spiritual and material dependence on the land. To the degree that this relationship is severed, Indigenous culture will disappear. (66)

A sacred responsibility is derived from this relationship, one in which Aboriginal peoples are caretakers of the earth, treating 'plants, animals, minerals, human beings and all life as if they were a part of ourselves' with a responsibility to ensure survival for the seventh generation (Clarkson, Morrissette, and Régallet 1992, 12). The medicine wheel in many contemporary Aboriginal societies continues to serve as a metaphor for this concept of balance among the political, social, economic and spiritual aspects of life (Clarkson, Morrissette, and Régallet 1992, 23).

Each Aboriginal nation has interpreted the relationship with sustainability in its own way. For example, E. Richard Atleo, hereditary chief of the Nuu-chah-nulth people of Vancouver Island, describes the Nuu-chah-nulth people's theory of *tsawalk* or reality as based on four principles: (1) recognition, (2) consent, (3) continuity and (4) respect. Recognition is considered an important methodology for dealing with complexity and applies to all life forms. Consent is 'defined by a range of behaviour that is mutually agreeable and reciprocal within a society' and reflects 'a consensus that reality is characterised by purposeful diversity' (Atleo 2011, 93). Continuity is based on respect and requires that 'life forms must learn to co-manage their common reality' through 'protocols' to govern predation (122). Sacred respect posits that 'all life forms have value and all are to be allowed to live sustainably because of this value' (117). These protocols often take the form of myths that serve as guides to understanding the nature of reality. The belief system and cultural practices embodied in these myths have been 'developed to maintain and to enhance life's major purpose, namely, the development of harmonious relationships between and among all life forms' (54). Contemporary Nuu-chah-nulth communities continue to be guided by these principles as conveyed through traditional songs, dances, regalia and stories that have been passed orally from generation to generation.

The Inuit of northern Canada use the term *Qaujimajatuqangit* to describe 'all aspects of traditional Inuit culture, including values, world-view, language, social organization, knowledge, life skills, perceptions, and expectations' (quoted in Wenzel 2004, 240). *Qaujimajatuqangit* is a unified system of beliefs founded on four laws or *malagait*: (1) working for the common good, (2) respecting all living things, (3) maintaining harmony and balance and (4) continually planning and preparing for the future (Tagalik 2009, 1). The Government of Nunavut, the Inuit territory created in northern Canada in 1999, educates non-Inuit administrators, scientists and other personnel on the role of this concept in Inuit life to ensure that the breadth of Inuit culture is 'considered in all areas of policy development' (Wenzel 2004, 241) and provides over C$1.3 million annually toward strengthening Inuit societal values and traditional knowledge as embodied in *Qaujimajatuqangit* (Government of Nunavut 2015, F-8).

More generally, while medicine wheel and other Aboriginal holistic teachings have been used as a conceptual base for policy and practice in a variety of disciplines, such as psychology (Thomason 2010; France and Rodriguez n.d), social work (Hart 1999), organisational theory (Chapman, McCaskill, and Newhouse 1991) and medicine (Currie et al. 2013), they have not been widely applied in the context of local sustainability policies in Canada.[2] With the adoption of the four-pillar model of sustainability as the basis of Integrated Community Sustainability Plans (ICSPs) in Canada, Aboriginal perspectives were marginalised in these efforts. Yet many Aboriginal communities in Canada have made traditional teachings central to sustainable development planning and have attempted to reconcile them with the four-pillar model through a variety of 'bottom up' approaches. The tensions inherent in this process provide an opportunity to study the relationship between these two narratives and to critically examine how integrative Aboriginal conceptions of culture have been applied in the context of community sustainability planning.

Culture in ICSPs

In 2006, the Canadian federal government's External Advisory Committee on Cities and Communities put forward a vision and approach to long-term sustainable development for cities and communities based on a four-pillar model of sustainability that included environmental responsibility, cultural vitality, social equity and economic viability. As an incentive to encourage this type of planning, the federal government agreed to transfer a portion of its Gas Tax revenues to the provincial governments. In return, the provinces were required to transfer these monies to the municipalities, conditional upon the municipalities producing ICSPs based on the four-pillar framework.[3] In a position paper on ICSPs, the federal government stated:

> In Canada, sustainability is founded on development as a qualitative concept, incorporating notions of improvement and progress, which includes cultural and social, as well as economic and environmental dimensions. It has been recognised that as Canadian communities become increasingly diverse, culture plays an important role in building social cohesion, a sense of community and a shared value set that is rooted in local diversity. Cultural investments can reinforce place-based community development objectives related to employment and innovation, neighbourhood revitalization and environmental sustainability. (Government of Canada 2005, 12)

In a section devoted to cultural sustainability, the government reinforced this message, adding that 'past approaches to cultural policy have tended to focus on supporting the elements of the cultural production cycle: creation, production and dissemination. This perspective could be broadened to examine the role of culture in the long-term development, vibrancy and cohesion of communities' (15).

These general directions from the federal government provided the framework for the development of the ICSPs, with the provinces and territories producing more detailed guides to help municipalities develop ICSPs. Of the 17 ICSP guides produced by provinces, territories, private and non-profit organizations to help municipalities draft these plans (which in 2005 were quite new), only nine ventured to provide a definition of 'culture' or 'cultural sustainability'. Among a broad range of interpretations, only those from the northern territories of Nunavut and Yukon focused on anthropological definitions emphasizing community identity and values. The Canadian provinces tended to emphasise expressive definitions of culture, such as heritage infrastructure and arts and culture activities and resources. Only Québec's guide to sustainability used a definition that combined the two, incorporating both anthropological aspects (language, beliefs and ways of living together) and the ways that society expresses itself through the arts and letters (Duxbury and Jeannotte 2012).[4]

While some communities achieved a balanced approach to local sustainability in their plans, this tended to be the exception rather than the rule. With regard to the general use of an integrated framework, Duxbury and Jeannotte (2012) concluded:

> While the explicit adoption of a four-pillar model of sustainability has been a major step toward an integrated approach, its contribution to a more holistic understanding of the place of culture in sustainable development is less clear. This research suggests that while the inclusion of culture within city planning is gradually advancing, *integration* of cultural considerations within a holistic sustainability planning paradigm has not yet been achieved. (13)

One possible reason for this shortfall, they suggest, may be that the narrative frame used in conventional sustainability planning does not discuss 'resiliency and change, nor the need for a systems approach that links past, present and future' (13). They also found that concrete actions were often disconnected from holistic definitions of sustainability and that culture-related items within economic and social sustainability contexts tended to be 'minor' suggestions that were usually delayed in subsequent action plans.

Wheels and pillars – Reconciling approaches to culture within ICSPs

At the outset, it should be noted that all First Nations communities in Canada (but not Inuit or Métis ones) are subject to *separate* community planning approaches, mandated or supported by the Department of

Indigenous Affairs and Northern Development.[5] While it is beyond the scope of this article to describe the many types of community plans that have been developed *apart* from ICSPs, research on these other types of planning processes by Wesley-Esquimaux and Calliou (2010) has identified seven key factors in successful indigenous community development, the first of which is identity and culture. They concluded that 'we need to find processes to bring culture back in' and that one of the ways that this can be done is by adopting a 'wise practices' approach, which they see as being closer to indigenous approaches than the best practices hierarchical, 'one-size-fits-all' model. They define 'wise practices' as 'locally-appropriate actions, tools, principles, or decisions that contribute significantly to the development of sustainable and equitable social conditions' (19). Wise practices rebuild balanced communities by tapping into 'implicit and explicit communal wisdom, a sense of cultural identity, an appreciation for time and deep practice, a respect for togetherness and reciprocity, and deeply-seeded reverence for traditional teachings' (21). They endorse a variation of the medicine wheel approach as the basis of successful community sustainability planning, which has been confirmed in empirical studies of planning processes in First Nations communities (Indian Affairs and Northern Development 2004, 2006; Smart Planning for Communities n.d.).

About 40 Canadian communities with large Aboriginal populations drafted ICSPs, most within the three northern territories. Within the Northwest Territories, eight Aboriginal communities developed ICSPs; within the Yukon Territory, 19 did so; and within Nunavut, three were identified.[6] While some of them attempted to incorporate the medicine wheel/traditional culture worldview into the planning process, the results were mixed. This section examines three ICSP case studies to illustrate how the communities treated culture within their sustainability plans. The case studies were chosen to include one from each territory, to illustrate three distinct approaches to including culture in local sustainability planning and to provide insight into how Aboriginal ontologies fit within post-colonial discourse on the role of culture in community sustainability.

Nunavut – City of Iqaluit – Iqaluit Sustainable Community Plan

Nunavut, a large territory in Canada's far north, is the traditional home of the Inuit people. Its capital, Iqaluit (population 6699 in 2011), is located on Frobisher Bay on the southeastern corner of Baffin Island, and is the largest community in the territory (population 31,906). Iqaluit's population profile is 59% Inuit and 41% Qallunaat (non-Inuit) (Statistics Canada 2011a).

The area was occupied first by the Dorset and then by the Thule Inuit cultures from approximately 500 BC. The first colonial contact occurred when Sir Martin Frobisher, arrived in 1576 while searching for the Northwest Passage to Asia. Whalers, missionaries and traders followed, introducing diseases such as measles and influenza that devastated the local population. By the 1930s, game had been over-hunted and fur prices collapsed, bringing much hardship to the local population. In the 1940s, the U.S. Army constructed a military base in the area, and the Canadian government later built a radar station that attracted many non-Inuit workers. In the 1960s, the Canadian government established permanent administrative services in Frobisher Bay (the former name of Iqaluit), which attracted still more southerners, including teachers, doctors and government workers. Faced with these cultural pressures, in 1976, the Inuit Tapirisat of Canada (the national organization of Inuit peoples) began to press for their own sovereign Nunavut territory,[7] and in 1993, the Nunavut Land Claims Agreement was signed by the Government of Canada and the Government of the Northwest Territories, which led to the creation of Nunavut in 1999 with Iqaluit as its capital (*Iqaluit ...* 2014).

The City of Iqaluit began work on an ICSP in 2006, taking approximately eight years to produce its first Sustainable Community Plan.[8] The final *Iqaluit Sustainable Community Plan* takes a long-term, 50-year perspective, makes no reference to the four-pillar approach to sustainability, and instead bases its sustainability narrative on Inuit *Qaujimajatuqangit*. It states that 'Inuit *Qaujimajatuqangit* helps us to better understand and adapt to today's changes and challenges. It recognises that everything is related to everything else, in such a way that nothing can stand alone. This is actually the pulse of our sustainability' (4).

Inuit *Qaujimajatuqangit* also guided the process by which the plan was developed, such that 'opportunities for respectful dialogue, discussion, questioning, and listening revolved around these concepts' (4). The aim of the consultations was 'to present a deep understanding of our historical, cultural and political contexts' which was considered 'essential when our entire community must work together on universal problems like sustainability' (4). The process began with a year of conversations and interviews with city councillors and community members, which eventually led to the hiring of a sustainability coordinator. After funding was secured in 2010, the Sustainable Iqaluit initiative was launched in 2011 and, over the next two years, consultations were undertaken with residents to garner their views on sustainability in the community.

Community participation was highly interactive. For example, a community Storytelling Activity involved 65 people and a four-day Community Exhibit attracted over 300 people, who 'discussed, drew, wrote, played, shared old photographs and stories, watched locally produced videos, drank tea, ate bannock and cookies, signed up for Working Groups, and took information home with them' (*Iqaluit* 2014, 12) About 70 people participated in eight Working Groups on specific topics and another 25 people attended a long-term Inuit residents meeting.

At these gatherings, participants asserted that the community was based on *relationships* anchored in the culture. One stated that 'Cultural connections to the land are hugely important to the quality of life of Iqalummuit and contribute positively to the health, education, family, community, culture and spirit of the community' (Sustainable Iqaluit 2012, 5). Another stated that 'Inuit are the land – the land is an extension of ourselves' (5). In addition to educating non-Inuit residents on *Qaujimajatuqangit* and strengthening the status of Inuktitut (the Inuit language), the participants wanted to 'balance living concurrently in two (or more) very different cultures' (11). Expressive elements of culture identified as being important included Inuit celebrations and festivals, an Inuit museum, and 'more Inuit artistic presentations, fairs, performances, art markets, film screenings; more public art, wall murals, sculptures/carvings; more Inuit art, books, prints, shows, TV and Inuit Broadcasting Corporation programming; more Inuit fashion, videogames, cartoons, animated films, illustrated books; more dancing, music concerts, theatre' (11).

The *Iqaluit Sustainable Community Plan* reflected these sentiments in its final report. It is organised by three relationships: *relationship to our environment, relationship to social and family wellbeing,* and *relationship to a productive society*. It is only at this point that the report indicates that 'These relationships correspond to the three 'pillars' of sustainability (environment, socio-cultural, economic) that are typically used in sustainable community plans in the South' (*Iqaluit* 2014, 14). In the 'Action Plan' section of the report, cultural considerations are part of each of the three relationships. For example, in the 'Relationship to social and family wellbeing' section, the municipal goal of promoting a more 'recognizably Inuit cultural community' includes an action to 'support more Inuit art and cultural representations in public spaces' (25) and a series of actions to be carried out by community organizations to support Inuit artists and cultural expression (26). Cultural actions are also part of the 'Relationship to a productive society' section, with community groups being asked to provide learning and volunteer opportunities in the arts to create more awareness of the city's history and culture (46, 49). It is difficult to determine whether these proposed actions will be fulfilled, but the *Iqaluit Sustainable Community Plan* demonstrates a determination to build a sustainable community on a solid foundation by asserting its unique cultural voice, taking into account the changing circumstances and population profile of the City. The Plan recognises the 'pillars' used in southern Canadian sustainability plans, but is solidly grounded in the Inuit *Qaujimajatuqangit* worldview.

Northwest Territories – Hamlet of Ulukhaktok – Integrated Community Sustainability Plan

The Northwest Territories (NWT) is a vast northern region of Canada with a sparse, widely distributed population of 41,462, according to the 2011 Census (Statistics Canada 2011a). The Inuvialuit are one of three Inuit groups in Canada located outside the Nunavut territory, and have lived in this area for thousands of years, following the wildlife that inhabits both the land and the sea. There are six Inuvialuit communities in the western Arctic, each of which is culturally grounded in a particular hunting region (Slavik 2010, 4). The Hamlet of Ulukhaktok[9]. is situated on the west coast of Victoria Island in the Inuvialuit Settlement Section of the NWT. It is home to just over 400 Inuvialuit people, the majority of whom speak Kangiryuarmintun, a dialect of two other Inuit languages and English. The hamlet was incorporated in 1984 and is challenged by its remote location, which makes the cost of living very high.

European contact began in the late eighteenth century, centred on the fur trade, and hunting and fishing continue to be integral to the way of life of the residents of the hamlet. Animals commonly hunted are caribou, musk ox, polar bear, wolves and Arctic fox. Printmaking and arts and crafts are the other major source of income and the community has a commercial outlet – the Ulukhaktok Arts Centre – that sells these products online (http://ulukhaktok.com). A unique feature of the community is the world's most northern golf course, which hosts a celebrity golf tournament every summer (Hamlet of Ulukhaktok 2010, 3, 8).

Each community in the NWT was required to complete an ICSP by March 31, 2010 that included a community strategy, a capital investment plan, a community energy plan and a human resource plan. In January 2009, the Department of Municipal and Community Affairs hosted a workshop where administrative officers and elected officials from several small communities in the region, including Ulukhaktok, were provided with an overview of the ICSP process and were introduced to the NWT ICSP 'tool', a software program that provided a template for completing an ICSP (Municipal and Community Affairs 2009). Despite this training, the Hamlet of Ulukhaktok decided to hire a firm of architects and engineers to help complete the plan.

The Ulukhaktok ICSP, covering the period 2010–2014, does not mention the four-pillar approach to sustainability, although it refers to the NWT government's financial assistance to local governments under the Gas Tax Agreement for municipal infrastructure to 'maintain or enhance economic, social and cultural opportunities and wellbeing, while protecting and improving the quality of the environment' (6). Very little information is provided in the ICSP about the process followed to develop the plan, except that there was 'an information-gathering phase, focus group sessions with staff and members of Town Council, meetings with the SAO [Senior Administrative Officer], an Open House for the public and a presentation to the Hamlet Council' (3). A key message from the community was that 'the Hamlet wants to be culturally vibrant with everyone working together to have a healthy place to live' (3). Wellness, values and traditional knowledge were identified as important to the community, as were country (traditional) food and protection for the language. Concerns were also expressed about traditional harvesting, improving infrastructure and fostering economic growth (8).

In the ICSP, a series of sustainability goals were spelled out, including two related to culture

Goal D: Improve communication and cultural awareness including traditional values, skills, family and wellness

Goal E: Foster and strive for a strong arts and crafts community (10–11).

However, there is no information as to how strategies such as increasing the number cultural and arts events in the community would be carried out.

One cannot help but feel that a great deal was left out of the ICSP due to the restrictive nature of the process.[10] The hamlet administration clearly lacked the capacity to engage in this type of bureaucratic process, as evidenced by the decision to hire a consulting firm to assist in the plan's development. Yet, with access to Gas Tax revenues at stake, it was imperative that a sustainability plan be prepared and submitted by the deadline. It appears that a process was undertaken, but despite hints that the over-whelmingly Inuvialuit population wished to maintain and build upon its traditional way of life, the ICSP provides only a cursory overview of the challenges faced by the community and of the measures that it might take to deal with them in a sustainable way. There is no reference to the traditional worldview of the Inuvialuit, centred on the relationship with the creatures inhabiting the land and the sea, which, if included, would certainly have had an impact on the achievement of goals related to environment and culture. With a bureaucratic emphasis on the plan, rather than on the context for sustainability, it is difficult to see how Ulukhaktok will address significant issues affecting its traditional way of life, such as climate change, which is only mentioned briefly in the context of its energy plan.

Yukon Territory – The City of Dawson and Tr'ondëk Hwëch'in Community Integrated Community Sustainability Plan

The City of Dawson, or Dawson City as it is commonly known, has a population of just over 1300 people (Statistics Canada 2011a) and is situated in the central part of the Yukon (population 33,897), the geographically smallest of Canada's three northern territories. According to the 2011 National Household Survey, 420 people or about 32% of the City's residents identified themselves as having Aboriginal origins (Statistics Canada 2011b). The community is located on the site of a traditional Tr'ondëk Hwëch'in fishing camp and sprang into being as a result of the 1896 Klondike Gold Rush, which brought thousands of miners and settlers into Tr'ondëk Hwëch'in territory. By 1898, Dawson City had become known as the 'Paris of the North' with an estimated population of 40,000.

The Tr'ondëk Hwëch'in First Nation has lived in the area for thousands of years, existing on the abundant salmon in the Yukon River, as well as the caribou and other big game that inhabited the region. First contact with Europeans dates back to the late 1700s, when fur traders established trading posts in the area, but colonial impact was minimal until the 1896 Gold Rush, which displaced the Tr'ondëk Hwëch'in to a nearby village. In an effort to protect their culture, the Tr'ondëk Hwëch'in entrusted their traditional sacred objects, songs and dances to neighbouring First Nations in Alaska. They did not return to Dawson City until the 1950s, long after the mining boom had collapsed and the City's population had plummeted to less than 1000. In 1998, the Tr'ondëk Hwëch'in signed Final and Self-Government Agreements with the federal government that granted them lands and authorities. They now work closely with the City of Dawson on social, economic and cultural development initiatives.

In the 1960s, when the National Historic Sites and Monuments Board designated 17 buildings in the community as being nationally significant, Dawson City began to attract tourists. Although placer mining is still carried out in the area, tourism has become an important economic asset due to the historic townscape, Gold Rush attractions, a vibrant arts and culture scene and the Tr'ondëk Hwëch'in heritage. The Dawson City Arts Society and its partners, including the Tr'ondëk Hwëch'in, created the Klondike Institute of Arts and Culture and the Yukon School of Visual Arts in the late 1990s. The Tr'ondëk Hwëch'in also opened the Dänojä Zho Cultural Centre in 1998 to showcase their heritage and culture (City of Dawson 2007a).

The Tr'ondëk Hwëch'in and the City of Dawson worked together to produce their ICSP, entitled *After the Gold Rush – The Integrated Community Sustainability Plan*. It is a long-term, 20-year comprehensive plan, developed after extensive consultation with the community. Instead of the four-pillar approach, the two entities based their vision on six sustainability dimensions – culture, economy, built environment, governance, society and natural environment – visualised as a series of intersecting circles that show the links between them (see Figure 2). The circular and interlinked relationship among the dimensions bears a strong similarity to the medicine wheel and is reinforced by the accompanying text which states that 'Sustainability is about understanding the connections between and achieving balance among the dimensions of our community' (16).

A community vision ('Honouring the past, Sharing the present, Embracing the Future'), a statement of community values and a set of 10 sustainability principles were developed after a series of community consultations that included community questionnaires, newsletters, four public meetings, a school writing contest, a municipal open house, discussions at the Community Support Centre and meetings with numerous organizations and groups (City of Dawson 2007b). These consultations helped to define what 'sustainability' meant to residents based on the answers to three questions: What is important to you about the community today? When you think about the community's future, what changes would you most like to see? What could be done to make this happen? Residents stated that they valued the historic character and heritage of the community, the natural environment, inclusiveness, a vibrant arts and cultural scene, a strong First Nation community, a healthy community and a sustainable society. In the final section of the ICSP, Dawson City's sustainability priorities were categorised under the six sustainability dimensions and linked to one or more of the values derived from the consultations.[11]

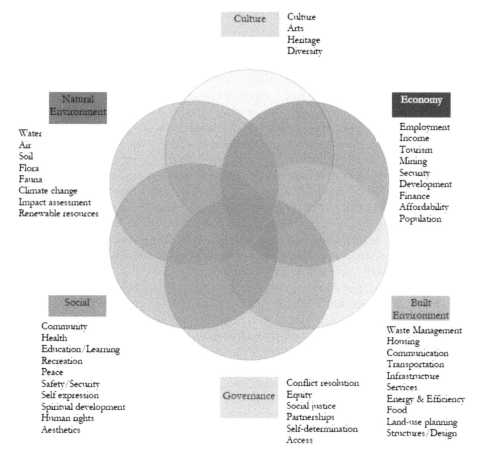

Culture
Culture
Arts
Heritage
Diversity

Natural Environment
Water
Air
Soil
Flora
Fauna
Climate change
Impact assessment
Renewable resources

Economy
Employment
Income
Tourism
Mining
Security
Development
Finance
Affordability
Population

Social
Community
Health
Education/Learning
Recreation
Peace
Safety/Security
Self expression
Spiritual development
Human rights
Aesthetics

Governance
Conflict resolution
Equity
Social justice
Partnerships
Self-determination
Access

Built Environment
Waste Management
Housing
Communication
Transportation
Infrastructure
Services
Energy & Efficiency
Food
Land-use planning
Structures/Design

Figure 2. After the gold rush sustainability dimensions. Source: After the Gold Rush –The Tr'ondëk Hwëch'in and City of Dawson Integrated Community Sustainability Plan, 2007.

The plan was adopted by both the Tr'ondëk Hwëch'in Chief and Council and the City of Dawson Mayor and Council and will be incorporated into other local policies and plans.

The ICSP represents an attempt to blend the cultural approaches of the two communities into one document. At the top of the list of challenges, as in most northern communities, is climate change, and the ICSP states that 'Tr'ondëk Hwëch'in has a vast knowledge of the region and sustainable stewardship. Adopting traditional values throughout community life can enhance long-term community health and environmental protection' (10). At the same time, it recognises that 'The community's strong heritage provides huge cultural and economic development opportunities' (11). As the ICSP also observes, 'History has given the community a unique perspective and an ability to embrace challenges' (11). The many political, social and economic upheavals it has witnessed since the two cultures came together have fostered a combined approach to sustainability, based on a blending of cultural worldviews.

Concluding thoughts

The ICSP process in Canada was an ambitious attempt at multi-level governance to identify pathways to sustainability, enlisting not only the federal, provincial, municipal and First Nation governments but also stakeholders and citizens through participatory means. The genius of the policy initiative was its recognition that definitions of sustainability are place-based and specific, and therefore must flow from below. Its greatest weakness may have been its somewhat ingenuous expectation that local governments would have the tools, knowledge and desire to engage seriously in such a process. Nevertheless, as Duxbury and Jeannotte (2012) have observed, 'Cultural change occurs when we think and speak differently' (13). The examples they studied suggested that many communities were beginning to 'speak differently' about sustainability using a narrative that incorporates culture into the discourse. Their study also found, however, that the four-pillar model sometimes worked against an integrated approach to sustainability and confined culture in a separate box when examining its role in community sustainability.

In the three case studies presented in this article, it is clear that the City of Iqaluit has adopted 'culture *as* sustainable development' as the conceptual frame for its ICSP, reflecting perhaps the demographic dominance of the Inuit in that community. The Hamlet of Ulukhaktok, on the other hand, although it is an Aboriginal community, appears to have been forced by circumstances to adopt a more Western frame for its ICSP, although even the four-pillar approach or 'culture *in* sustainable development' is not highly evident in the final results. Dawson City's ICSP represents an interesting attempt to blend Western and Aboriginal concepts in a type of 'culture *for* sustainable development' approach that uses a narrative about the community to bridge the traditional cultural orientation of the Tr'ondëk Hwëch'in people with the more 'pillar-like' approach of Dawson City's majority non-Aboriginal population. All the plans used the bureaucratic frame of ICSP planning methodologies in order to access Gas Tax revenues, but the two communities that made a serious attempt to integrate Aboriginal worldviews into their ICSPs were arguably more successful in 'telling the story of culture' in their communities and using culture as a base for their sustainability planning.

The case studies, although few in number and limited to Canada's North, provide potential lessons for other jurisdictions that are attempting to advance sustainability *and* to adopt more inclusive cultural policies. Can the notion of 'culture *as* sustainable development' be applied or adapted more widely in urban and rural communities outside of Canada's North? Perhaps the answer is 'yes' – the integrative worldviews centred on concepts of interconnectedness and balance, which are embodied in Aboriginal symbolic concepts such as the medicine wheel, have much to contribute to contemporary debates about sustainability and provide a counter-model to the extractivist mentality that has been the dominant worldview over the past two centuries.

In a Canadian context, the integration of Aboriginal worldviews and knowledge into local sustainability planning constitutes one step in the reconciliation process that the Truth and Reconciliation Commission recommended. In a broader context, this integration could begin to address the monocultural logics that have marginalised Aboriginal/Indigenous cultures in both sustainability planning and cultural policies and contributed to their relative absence in both spheres.

In many parts of the world, countries are faced with growing cultural diversity and intensifying pressures to address all aspects of sustainability – environmental, economic, social and cultural. Places that were once home to embedded monocultures are now experiencing rapid cultural change. Narratives that were told in relative isolation must now be expanded to include the global as well as the local and the future as well as the past. Voices that were traditionally excluded now have to be heard. More than ever, cultural policies that recognise and embrace diversity, inclusiveness and balance are central not only to local sustainability planning but also to the broader stories that nations and societies tell about themselves and their place in the world.

There are, as Santos points out, alternatives to monocultures. These alternatives include new ecologies of knowledge, temporalities, recognition, scale and productivity that confront colonial mentalities, broaden the diversity of social practices and productive behaviour, and constitute alternatives to hegemonic global capitalism. To the extent that these begin to find a place in the lexicon of cultural policy, they will represent a symbolic enlargement of the cultural sphere beyond its current institutional boundaries and provide a possible template for change at the sub-national, national and international levels.

Notes

1. The term 'Indigenous' is increasingly being used in both domestic and international contexts to describe peoples who were called 'native', 'Indian' or 'First Nations' and who were living in Canada when Europeans arrived. I have used the term 'Aboriginal' throughout this article because Canada's Constitution recognises *three* Aboriginal peoples – First Nations, Inuit and Métis (mixed race Aboriginal peoples) and is therefore the more inclusive term.
2. One exception is a study of the quality of life of Aboriginal peoples in the Greater Vancouver Region conducted by Cardinal 2005.
3. Canada is a federal state comprising ten provinces and three territories. Jurisdictional relationships are complex: provinces have responsibility for municipalities, but the federal (national) government has the power to intervene in 'urban' issues such as public transportation, housing and infrastructure.
4. Québec did not require its municipalities to produce ICSPs, instead adopting Agenda 21 for Culture as its guide to sustainability planning.
5. The federal government has clear fiduciary responsibility only for First Nations communities, comprising 634 recognised governments or bands located throughout Canada.
6. However, a Nunavut website provides links to 24 Integrated Community Infrastructure Sustainability Plans that focus only on *infrastructure* that might potentially be financed using Gas Tax revenues (http://www.buildingnunavut.com/en/communityprofiles/communityprofiles.asp).
7. At the time, Nunavut was part of the Northwest Territories.
8. This was in contrast to many southern Canadian communities, which tended to produce plans in a matter of a few months.
9. The name means 'the place where ulu parts are found' (the ulu being an Inuit woman's knife used in for a variety of purposes, including skinning animals).
10. Much of the plan consists mainly of grids outlining strategies under each goal, but columns in the grids for budgets and time frames for each strategy were not filled in.
11. For example, preservation and retention of the historic townscape was slotted under the 'built environment' dimension, but also linked to the values related to historic character and heritage, a strong First Nation and a sustainable society (City of Dawson 2007a, Appendix I: Community Objectives).

Disclosure statement

No potential conflict of interest was reported by the author.

References

Atleo, E. R. 2011. *Principles of Tsawalk – An Indigenous Approach to Global Crisis*. Vancouver: UBC Press.
Broad, G., S. Boyer, and C. Chataway. 2006. "We Are Still the Aniishnaabe Nation: Embracing Culture and Identity in Batchewana First Nation." *Canadian Journal of Communication* 31 (1): 35–58.
Cardinal, N. 2005. *An Urban Aboriginal Life – The 2005 Indicators Report on the Quality of Life of Aboriginal People in the Greater Vancouver Region*. Vancouver: Centre for Native Policy and Research.
Chapman, I., D. McCaskill, and D. Newhouse. 1991. "Management in Contemporary Aboriginal Organizations." *The Canadian Journal of Native Studies* 11: 333–349.
City of Dawson. 2007a. *After the Gold Rush – The Integrated Community Sustainability Plan. Volume I: The City of Dawson and Tr'ondëk Hwëch'in Community Vision*. Dawson City: Dawson.
City of Dawson. 2007b. *After the Gold Rush – The Integrated Community Sustainability Plan. Volume III: Appendices and Background Documents*. Dawson City: Dawson.
Clammer, J. 2012. *Culture, Development and Social Theory – Towards an Integrated Social Development*. New York: Zed Books.
Clarkson, L., V. Morrissette, and G. Régallet. 1992. *Our Responsibility to the Seventh Generation – Indigenous Peoples and Sustainable Development*. Winnipeg: International Institute for Sustainable Development.
Cowan, J. K., M.-B. Dembour, and R. A. Wilson, eds. 2001. *Culture and Rights: Anthropological Perspectives*. Cambridge: Cambridge University Press.

Culhane, D. 1998. *The Pleasure of the Crown: Anthropology, Law and First Nations*. Vancouver: Talonbooks.

Currie, C., T. C. Wild, D. P. Schopflocher, L. Laing, and P. Veugelers. 2013. "Illicit and Prescription Drug Problems among Urban Aboriginal Adults in Canada: The Role of Traditional Culture in Protection and Resilience." *Social Science and Medicine* 88: 1–9.

Dessein, J., K. Soini, G. Fairclough, and L. Horlings, eds. 2015. *Culture in, for and as Sustainable Development: Conclusions from the COST Action IS1007 Investigating Cultural Sustainability*. Jyväskylä: University of Jyväskylä.

Dickason, O., and D. MacNab. 2009. *Canada's First Nations: A History of Founding Peoples from Earliest times*. 4th ed. Don Mills, ON: Oxford University Press.

Duxbury, N., and M. S. Jeannotte. 2012. "Including Culture in Sustainability: An Assessment of Canada's Integrated Community Sustainability Plans." *International Journal of Urban Sustainable Development* 4 (1): 1–19.

Episkenew, J. 2009. *Taking Back Our Spirits: Indigenous Literature, Public Policy, and Healing*. Winnipeg: University of Manitoba Press.

Four Directions Teachings. 2012. *Introduction and Overview*. Accessed April 15, 2013. http://www.fourdirectionsteachings.com/Teacher_Resource_Kit.html

France, H., and C. Rodriguez. n.d. *Within Indigenous Context: Transpersonal, Circle Work and the Medicine Wheel*. Accessed October 26, 2015. http://www.web.uvic.ca/~hfrancer/indigenoushealing.pdf

Government of Canada. 2005. "Integrated Community Sustainability Planning – A Background Paper." Discussion Paper for Planning for Sustainable Canadian Communities Roundtable, organized by the Prime Minister's External Advisory Committee on Cities and Communities, Ottawa, September 21–23. Government of Canada.

Government of Nunavut. 2015. *Main Estimates 2015–16*. Accessed September 11, 2015. http://www.gov.nu.ca/sites/default/files/main_estimates_2015-2016_-_english_-_for_web.pdf

Hamlet of Ulukhaktok. 2010. *Integrated Community Sustainability Plan*. Yellowknife: FSC Architects & Engineers (now part of Stantec).

Hart, M. A. 1999. "Seeking Mino-Pimatasiwin (the Good Life): an Aboriginal Approach to Social Work Practice." *Native Social Work Journal* 2 (1): 91–112.

Indian Affairs and Northern Development. 2004. *First Nations Stories: Building Sustainable Communities in British Columbia*. Ottawa: Department of Indian Affairs and Northern Development.

Indian Affairs and Northern Development. 2006, August. *CCP Handbook: Comprehensive Community Planning for First Nations in British Columbia*. Ottawa: Department of Indian Affairs and Northern Development.

Innis, H. A. 1999. *The Fur Trade in Canada: An Introduction to Canadian Economic History*. 12th ed. Toronto: University of Toronto Press.

Iqaluit sustainable community plan – part one – overview. 2014. Iqaluit: Municipal Corporation of the City of Iqaluit.

King, T. 2012. *The Inconvenient Indian: A Curious Account of Native People in North America*. Toronto: Anchor Canada.

Klein, N. 2014. *This Changes Everything – Capitalism vs. the Climate*. New York: Simon & Schuster.

Municipal and Community Affairs. 2009. *Workshop Summary Report*. Yellowknife: Government of the Northwest Territories. Accessed October 29, 2015. http://www.maca.gov.nt.ca//wp-content/uploads/2011/09/MACA_SCG_Inuvik-Workshop-Summary-Report_2009.pdf

Nederveen Pieterse, J. 2010. *Development Theory: Deconstructions/Reconstructions*. 2nd ed. London: Sage.

Newhouse, D. R., C. J. Voyageur, and D. Beavon. 2005. *Hidden in Plain Sight: Contributions of Aboriginal Peoples to Canadian Identity and Culture*. Toronto: University of Toronto Press.

Paquette, J., D. Beauregard, and C. Gunter. 2015. "Settler Colonialism and Cultural Policy: The Colonial Foundations and Refoundations of Canadian Cultural Policy." *International Journal of Cultural Policy*. doi:10.1080/10286632.2015.1043294.

Pitawanakwat, L. 2006. *Ojibwe/Powawatomi (Anishnabe) Teaching*. Accessed April 15, 2013. http://www.fourdirectionsteachings.com/transcripts/ojibwe.pdf

Redclift, M. R. 2006. "Sustainable Development (1987–2005) – An Oxymoron Comes of Age." *Horizontes Antropológicos* 12 (25): 65–84.

Santos, B. de Sousa. 2004. The World Social Forum: Toward a Counter-Hegemonic Globalisation (Part I). In *The World Social Forum: Challenging Empires*, edited by J. Sen, A. Anand, A. Escobar and P. Waterman, New Delhi: Viveka Foundation. Accessed July 5, 2016. http://www.choike.org/nuevo_eng/informes/1557.html

Schech, S., and J. Haggis. 2000. *Culture and Development: A Critical Introduction*. Oxford and Malden, MA: Blackwell.

Sillitoe, P. 1998. "The Development of Indigenous Knowledge." *Current Anthropology* 39 (2): 223–252.

Slavik, D. 2010. *Inuvialuit Knowledge of Nanuq: Community and Traditional Knowledge of Polar Bears in the Inuvialuit Settlement Region*. Whitehorse, Yukon: Wildlife Management Advisory Councils for the North Slope and Northwest Territories and the Inuvialuit Game Council.

Smart Planning for Communities, n.d. *Uncovering the Wisdom of Community: The Aq'am Community's Inclusive Planning Process*. Vancouver: SPC Stories from the Field.

Soper, K. 1995. *What is Nature? Culture, Politics and the Non-human*. Oxford: Blackwell.

Statistics Canada. 2011a. *Census*. Accessed July 5, 2016. http://www12.statcan.gc.ca/census-recensement/index-eng.cfm

Statistics Canada. 2011b. *National Household Survey*. Accessed July 5, 2016. http://www12.statcan.gc.ca/nhs-enm/index-eng.cfm

Sustainable Iqaluit. 2012. *What We Heard – A Summary of past Voices.* Iqaluit. Accessed July 13, 2016. https://sustainableiqaluit1.files.wordpress.com/2012/05/what-we-heard-final-eng-web.pdf

Tagalik, S. 2009. *Inuit Qaujimajatuqngit: The Role of Indigenous Knowledge in Supporting Wellness in Inuit Communities in Nunavut.* Prince George, BC: National Collaborating Centre for Aboriginal Health.

Thomason, T.C. 2010. *The Medicine Wheel as a Symbol of Native American Psychology.* Accessed April 15, 2013. http://www.cgjungpage.org/learn/articles/culture-and-psyche/908-the-medicine-wheel-as-a-symbol-of-native-american-psychology

TRCC (Truth and Reconciliation Commission of Canada). 2015. *Honouring the Truth, Reconciling for the Future: Summary of the Final Report of the Truth and Reconciliation Commission of Canada.* Winnipeg: Truth and Reconciliation Commission of Canada.

Valaskakis, G. G. 2005. *Indian Country: Essays on Contemporary Native Culture.* Waterloo, ON: Wilfrid Laurier University Press.

Wenzel, G. W. 2004. "From TEK to IQ: Inuit Qaujimajatuqangit and Inuit Cultural Ecology." *Arctic Anthropology* 41 (2): 238–250.

Wesley-Esquimaux, C., and B. Calliou. 2010. *Best Practices in Aboriginal Community Development: A Literature Review and Wise Practices Approach.* Banff, AB: The Banff Centre.

Wilson, M. C. 2005. "The 'Placing' of Identity in Nomadic Societies: Aboriginal Landscapes of the Northwestern Plains of North America." *Material Culture Review/Revue De La Culture Matérielle*, 62 (Fall), 7–19. Accessed July 5, 2016. https://journals.lib.unb.ca/index.php/MCR/article/view/18057/19365

World Commission on Culture and Development. 1996. *Our Creative Diversity.* Paris: UNESCO.

Zukin, S. 1996. "Cultural Strategies of Economic Development and the Hegemony of Vision." In *The Urbanization of Injustice*, edited by A. Merrifield and A. Swyngedouw, 223–243. London: Lawrence & Wishart.

Cultural policies for sustainable development: four strategic paths

Nancy Duxbury ⓘ, Anita Kangas ⓘ and Christiaan De Beukelaer ⓘ

ABSTRACT

In the Sustainable Development Goals adopted by the United Nations in 2015, the role of culture is limited. We argue that culture's absence is rooted in the *longue durée* of interplay among theoretical and policy debates on culture in sustainable development and on cultural policy since the mid-twentieth century. In response to variations in concepts and frameworks used in advocacy, policy, and academia, we propose four roles cultural policy can play towards sustainable development: first, to safeguard and sustain cultural practices and rights; second, to 'green' the operations and impacts of cultural organizations and industries; third, to raise awareness and catalyse actions about sustainability and climate change; and fourth, to foster 'ecological citizenship'. The challenge for cultural policy is to help forge and guide actions along these co-existing and overlapping strategic paths towards sustainable development.

Introduction

On 25 September 2015, the Sustainable Development Goals (SDGs) were adopted by the 193 Member States of the United Nations and took effect on 1 January 2016. These goals follow the earlier Millennium Development Goals (MDGs) as a normative and technical framework for concerted government action towards global development. The adjustment from 'development' to 'sustainable development' is significant, as it signals both a shift in objectives (towards sustainability) and a shift in scope (from 'developing' countries to all countries). This act has put sustainability at the centre of global political debate, policy, and programmes for years to come.

In this context, sustainability is not simply defined as one easy-to-reach goal, but as a complex set of visions for the future of humanity. It is worth citing the explanation provided on the SDG website at some length:

> We envisage a world free of poverty, hunger, disease and want, where all life can thrive. We envisage a world free of fear and violence. A world with universal literacy. A world with equitable and universal access to quality education at all levels, to health care and social protection, where physical, mental and social well-being are assured …

> We envisage a world of universal respect for human rights and human dignity, the rule of law, justice, equality and non-discrimination; of respect for race, ethnicity and cultural diversity; and of equal opportunity permitting the full realisation of human potential and contributing to shared prosperity …

> We envisage a world in which every country enjoys sustained, inclusive and sustainable economic growth and decent work for all. A world in which consumption and production patterns and use of all natural resources – from air to land, from rivers, lakes and aquifers to oceans and seas – are sustainable. One in which democracy,

good governance and the rule of law as well as an enabling environment at national and international levels, are essential for sustainable development, including sustained and inclusive economic growth, social development, environmental protection and the eradication of poverty and hunger … (UN 2015, n.p.)

This extensive set of visions (slightly reduced here) encompasses a very broad conceptualisation of 'sustainability' that intertwines environmental health, vibrancy, and biodiversity with social justice, equity, and inclusivity; individual opportunity, well-being, and capability development; and a sense of global citizenship based on human rights and dignity, democracy, and good governance (cf. Sen 2010). The vision is operationalized through 17 goals,[1] which are elaborated through 169 specific targets to be achieved over the next 15 years and indicators that track the achievement of the targets. Critics have already questioned the effectiveness of such a wide-ranging agreement with its comprehensiveness of topic areas. Langford (2016), for example, points to its breadth as potentially providing 'a convenient cover for problematic compromises and a conservative capture of the monitoring process' and notes that its effectiveness as a political resource and implementation success depends on the organizations and agencies that drove its expansiveness to push for targets that are salient, demanding, and operationalisable.

In the debates preceding the adoption of the SDGs, particularly in the context of the Open Working Group of the General Assembly on Sustainable Development Goals (OWG) that was established in January 2013 to engage in an extensive public consultation process, interest groups of different kinds actively lobbied for the inclusion of 'their' activities and goals in the list of objectives. Culture-focused initiatives were largely aimed at obtaining an explicit mention and integration of culture in the post-2015 development agenda, with a particular focus on introducing a cultural goal. UNESCO's dominant narratives in this context were of culture (and the cultural sector more specifically) as an 'enabler' and a 'driver' of sustainability (see, e.g. Hosagrahar 2012). The Group of Friends of Culture and Development, comprising 29 countries from all regions, also advocated for fully integrating culture in the post-2015 development agenda. Moreover, an unprecedented coalition of international NGOs led a global campaign to establish a goal focused on culture in the post-2015 development agenda (IFACCA, United Cites and Local Governments – Committee on Culture, International Federation of Coalitions for Cultural Diversity, and Cultural Action Europe 2013).[2] In these initiatives, culture was defined as 'both a vector to foster other sustainable development goals and a development end in itself' (IFACCA, United Cites and Local Governments – Committee on Culture, International Federation of Coalitions for Cultural Diversity, and Cultural Action Europe 2013, 7).

In the final SDG (and Targets) approved by the UN's General Assembly, the actual place and role of culture in the goals is limited. The document mentions culture (linked with terms such as civilization, diversity, inter-cultural, heritage, and tourism) in four areas – education, economic growth, consumption and production patterns, and sustainable cities – but fails to identify culture as a stand-alone goal. As both David Throsby and Y. Raj Isar note (in this special issue), the final goals do not refer to the case for integrating culture into sustainable development planning and decision-making, and in spite of several years of advocacy and research demonstrating the impacts of culture-led development projects (e.g. MDG Achievement Fund 2013), it remains unclear in the SDG documents precisely how culture can contribute to attaining these objectives. Furthermore, the failure to consider culture as an important pillar of sustainable development in the SDGs overlooks the contributions that indigenous peoples can make regarding how to ground sustainable development and understand 'the foundation of culture as key to sustaining and balancing development with nature and people' (Watene and Yap 2015, 53; Throsby and Petetskaya 2016; Jeannotte, in this issue).

In this context, this article aims to clarify how cultural policy/ies can contribute to sustainable development trajectories. To historically contextualise this question, it presents the key outlines of the often parallel but occasionally intersecting trajectories of 'culture and sustainable development' and 'cultural policy' discourses. It grapples with the plurality of conceptual approaches that have resulted and concludes by exploring four roles for cultural policy in an attempt to make our era that of sustainability.

Chronological and conceptual trajectories

Culture and sustainable development

While environmental discourse grew slowly from the 1950s in the context of worsening socio-economic and ecological conditions (Quental, Lourenço, and Nunes da Silva 2011), the integrating concept of 'sustainable development' first appeared in the international policy arena in 1980 when the International Union for the Conservation of Nature and Natural Resources published the *World Conservation Strategy*, proclaiming 'the overall aim of achieving sustainable development through the conservation of living resources' (iv). In the strategy, 'development' was defined as 'the modification of the biosphere and the application of human, financial, living and non-living resources to satisfy human needs and improve the quality of human life' (1). The section 'Towards Sustainable Development' identified the main agents of habitat destruction as poverty, population pressure, social inequity, and the terms of trade.

During the 1980s (often viewed as a time of stagnation in sustainable development policy and a 'lost decade' in global development), 'a debt crisis, mounting unemployment, adjustment to these new economic realities, budgetary cuts across the board, and the threat of a new arms race' resulted, in many countries, in 'embracing efficiency, rather than equity and solidarity, as guiding principles, and in a weakening of the spirit of international cooperation' (Pronk 2015, 368). As a critical response to the economic logic of development thinking, the human development approach emerged in the late 1980s. This approach was an attempt to provide a framework to conceptualise and measure development as the opportunities people have to build a life 'they value and they have reason to value' (Sen 1999, 291). The process of enlarging people's choices has two sides: the formation of human capabilities and the use people make of their acquired capabilities (e.g. for leisure, productive purposes, or being active in cultural, social and political affairs) (UNDP 1990). The policy imperative of the human development reports is to make the non-economic count as well.

Critical academic research emphasised a growth of interest in culture and a turn away from economy. New conceptualizations, such as 'signifying practices' (Williams 1958), cultural capital and social distinction (Bourdieu 1984), human development, capability and freedom (Sen 1987, 1999), central human capabilities and human rights (Nussbaum 1995, 2006), cultural capacity and the capacity to aspire (Appadurai 2004), and cultural values and cultural capital (Throsby 1999), allowed for several interpretations of the role of culture in (economic) development and the articulation of a world in which development can either fail or succeed. Underlying these works was the idea that development should not be considered as a finality (generally expressed in a monetary value derived from work), but the extent to which people are able to participate in political, social, and economic life (Sen 1999). This liberal and methodologically individualist political philosophy focuses on individuals in societies, rather than countries' average economic wealth (expressed in GDP per capita).

The normative framework was operationalized for policy and analysis by Mahbub ul Haq, who led the development of the Human Development Index (HDI) for the United Nations Development Programme (UNDP). This index included health and education alongside income (GDP/capita) to give governments an incentive to invest in public services that would increase the education and health of their citizens. By strengthening all three levels of performance, countries would gain a higher HDI score and rise in the ranking of countries. The UN MDGs, the first global set of measurable development objectives, were built directly on these principles of human development. The role of culture, however, remained limited in both the literature on human development (see Rao and Walton 2004; De Beukelaer 2015) and the MDGs (Baltà Portolés 2013, Throsby in this issue).

In 1987, the World Commission for the Environment and Development published the report, *Our Common Future*. The UN Working Group had been inspired by the earlier report to the Club of Rome, *The Limits to Growth* (Meadows et al. 1972). Under the direction of Gro Harlem Brundtland (whose name would be used to informally refer to both the commission and the report), the World Commission defined 'sustainable development' as: 'development that meets the needs of the present without compromising the ability of future generations to meet their own needs'. It contained within it two key concepts: that of 'needs' ('in particular the essential needs of the world's poor, to which overriding priority should be given') and that of 'limitations imposed by the state of technology and social organisation on the environment's ability to meet present and future needs' (WCED 1987, 42, 43). The Brundtland Commission introduced a new principle into global development discourse, 'sustainability', considered 'an essential precondition to be met in order to safeguard a common future' (Pronk 2015, 368). The Commission pointed out that 'sustainable development must not endanger the natural systems that support life on Earth: the atmosphere, the waters, the soils, and the living beings' (55). From its perspective, there was no single focus (or object) of sustainability but, instead, all the economic, social, and environmental systems must be simultaneously sustainable. Satisfying any one of these sustainability pillars without also satisfying the others was deemed insufficient because they are interdependent, and all needed to be addressed urgently.

Meanwhile, UNESCO had organized the World Conference on Cultural Policies in Mexico City in 1982 and put forward with great conviction the idea that 'Culture constitutes a fundamental part of the life of each individual and of each community ... and development ... whose ultimate aim should be focused on man ... must therefore have a cultural dimension' (UNESCO 1982, 78, 79). The World Decade for Cultural Development (1988–1997) was first raised at the Mexico Conference, and later approved and proclaimed by the United Nations General Assembly. Promoting genuine diversity across business, education, and the state, the Decade had two principal objectives: greater emphasis on the cultural dimension in the development process, and the stimulation of creative skills and cultural life in general.

In the Decade's final report, *Our Creative Diversity* (1996), the World Commission on Culture and Development brought into focus the particular roles of culture within this conceptually evolving constellation. The report linked cultural policy and sustainable development and connected culture to a range of economic, political, and societal issues. Paralleling the process that had led from the Brundtland Report to the Rio Summit (1992) and beyond, the World Commission on Culture and Development was an important model for a new discussion about culture and development. *Our Creative Diversity* defined the concepts of 'culture', 'cultural development', and 'culturally sustainable development'. Culture was seen as having both an instrumental role in promoting economic progress and a constituent role as a desirable end itself, the characteristic of civilization that gives meaning to existence. However, a country does not contain only one culture, and the Commission pointed to accepting diversity in individual choices and group practices. In defining 'culturally sustainable development', it noted that as 'we shift our attention from [a] purely instrumental view of culture to awarding it a constructive, constitutive and creative role, we have to see development in terms that include cultural growth' (25). Although not published in the report, the Commission also discussed 'cultural sustainability', linked to 'cultural valuations and cultural activities' (Throsby 1997, 10).

In this context, the idea of 'cultural development' was introduced as a way of balancing cultural and economic policy objectives (UNESCO 1998, 14–19). It included aims to facilitate cultural diversity and give local communities opportunities for cultural expression, and to encourage cross-sectoral partnerships as tools for supporting sustainable cultural activity. The conditions for 'culturally sustainable development' called for public policy that would simultaneously encompass community demands for nonmaterial well-being, inter-generational equity (that is, the distribution and preservation of resources for future generations), and the interdependence of economic and cultural variables (Throsby 1997, 33).

The release of *Our Creative Diversity* was quickly followed up by the Intergovernmental Conference on Cultural Policies for Development, held in Stockholm in 1998, and the resulting *Action Plan on Cultural Policies for Development* (UNESCO 1998). Rooted in human development thinking, the report advocated that to achieve 'the social and cultural fulfilment of the individual' (Principle 2), cultural policy should be one of the main components of 'endogenous and sustainable development policy', positioned within an integrated approach. It also recommended that any policy for development must be 'profoundly sensitive to culture itself' and take into account cultural factors.

In the early 2000s, the idea to translate some of these challenges into binding legal documents gathered momentum. This eventually culminated in the 2005 UNESCO *Convention on the Protection and Promotion of the Diversity of Cultural Expressions* (henceforth 'the Convention'), building on the earlier

2003 UNESCO *Convention for the Safeguarding of Intangible Cultural Heritage* and the 2001 UNESCO *Universal Declaration on Cultural Diversity*.

The *raisons d'être* of *Our Creative Diversity* (1996) and the 2005 Convention differ significantly. The former focused on culture (primarily as a 'way of life') in relation to development processes, as it put forward the role of culture in considering the future we want, thereby putting culture at the core of attempts to rethink the global ethics (and pragmatics) of development. The latter, on the contrary, focuses on culture (as 'cultural expressions') as a trade issue,[3] largely due to the fact that trade was the principal area for U.S. opposition to the Convention. It serves as a legal document to protect the right of countries to support cultural production, which would otherwise be considered as unfair state support under WTO free trade agreements. While the Convention pays lip service to 'sustainability', this term remains disconnected from its strong normative dimensions as conceived in the Brundtland report (De Beukelaer and Freitas 2015). The first *Global Report* on the Convention (UNESCO 2015) provides a stronger engagement with sustainability than the Convention itself, but remains overall more focused on 'sustainable systems of governance for culture' than the integration of 'culture in sustainable development frameworks' (Throsby 2015).

Evolutionary currents of cultural policy

Within such international political-conceptual currents, national cultural policy regimes reflect the histories of nation building, the making of the modern state, institutional arrangements, and the modes of government specific to each country. They also reflect the patterns of the national art and cultural fields, their internal hierarchies, and the contents of art and culture that were included or excluded in the policy regime (Miller and Yúdice 2002; Kangas 2004; Milz 2007; Dubois 2015). It is difficult to generalise about the evolution of cultural policies before the Second World War; however, the postwar period signified a clear change in the formation of cultural policy and in the ways it was implemented. Formalised cultural policy efforts emerged internationally and in the 1940–1950s, many countries established small administrative organisations for culture (e.g. Arts Councils, Ministries of Education and/ or Culture). During this time, the concept of culture was restricted, with the scope of cultural policy tightly linked to value appraisal of what deserved to be conceived as culture and what did not in cultural policy-making practices (Volkerling 1996; Gray 2007).

From the 1960s, UNESCO has played a strong role in strengthening national cultural policies. In 1967, UNESCO organized a roundtable meeting in Monaco, which highlighted that each country has a different general concept of the action that public authorities should take in the cultural field, and of its justification and aims, and it was not UNESCO's role to define the cultural policy of states. At the same time, there was a recognised need for exchange of information and experience between countries. An examination of the idea of cultural policy during this meeting resulted in two hegemonic keystones emerging: First, a thesis: 'Economic and social development should go hand in hand with cultural development' (UNESCO 1969, 10), which emphasised the importance of integrating cultural policy in general planning. Second, as far as possible, 'all barriers (geographical, financial, and social) to accessing culture should be removed', which reinforced that the arts and cultural activities should be a part of the services of the welfare state and should be available to everyone. This approach was grounded on the view that the arts were potentially of benefit to everyone, regardless of age, sex, race, or class.[4]

In the 1970s, strong discussions about 'new cultural policy' brought forth a new vocabulary featuring the concepts of 'democratization of culture' and 'cultural democracy'. Both concepts aimed to promote cultural participation, widen access to cultural life, and ensure an active share in it. While 'democratization of culture' aims to ensure the widest possible dissemination of works of art and of the mind which cultivated people consider being of capital importance, 'cultural democracy' emphasises the ambition to promote the greatest possible diversity of forms of cultural expression, encouraging active participation in community cultural life and in policy decisions that affect the quality of cultural life (Mennell 1979; Bennett 1996; Evrard 1997; Kangas 2003, 2004). This decade also featured the strengthening of institutionalisation and professionalism in the cultural fields (UNESCO 1981).

During the 1970s, cultural policy became a growing part of governments' welfare policy. The benefits and relevance of culture to society as a whole became a priority within this purview, with a general emphasis on cultural participation. This social role of culture was considered both in terms of social class levels and in the context of geographical distribution. Local and regional authorities began to take on new tasks, aiming to provide their populations with a coherent range of cultural facilities and services, and local cultural offices were established in many cities. Through these developments, the definition of culture broadened, still encompassing professional arts development but also beginning to lean towards a more anthropological definition incorporating cultural identity and diversity, while cultural policy was increasingly linked to education, social, and urban policy. The need for a cultural dimension in projects of social integration, particularly in disadvantaged urban areas, began to be recognised and the role of socio-cultural animators was emphasised (Council of Europe 1978). At the international level, UNESCO-organized intergovernmental continental conferences focused on the roles of cultural professionals, the cultural dimension of development, and the struggle against social exclusion.[5]

While the 1970s was a period of ideological realignment, the 1980s was a time for practical structuring and effectuation. The economic stagnation of the early 1980s, combined with a growing neoliberal political zeitgeist, meant that national governments reconsidered their tasks in various fields, including culture. The cultural sector still focused on high artistic quality and professionalism but, at the same time, funding contexts became more market-oriented and budget cuts had to be made. Governments encouraged institutions to acquire extra earnings in order to reduce their dependence on public subsidies. The changed economic conditions played a part in criticism of public administration and public cultural services in the context of the market economy (Kangas 2004). A new term, 'instrumental cultural policy', gained in popularity as cultural productions and investments were increasingly used as instruments to attain goals in areas other than the cultural sector (e.g. regional and urban development) (Vestheim 1994; McGuigan 2004). At the same time, the main targets of cultural policy were still the promotion of artistic creativity and making it easier for people to access art activities, making the participants more 'civilized', and defining art by means of the 'art world' and 'culturally competent' audiences.

Propelled by a neoliberal tide, the UN World Decade for Cultural Development (1988 to 1997) was grounded in a multi-ethnic definition and appreciation of culture (discussed previously), as well as the formation of cultural policy with an eye to the impacts of globalization on the state and the market. A new policy discourse of 'creative industries' and a policy practice, known as the 'creative industries model' in the U.K. and Australia,[6] became successful exports to other parts of the world, linking together a seemingly heterogeneous set of sub-sectors as the 'creative industries'. Highly capital-intensive sectors (e.g. film, radio, and television), the arts, and heritage were associated with both economic and social welfare discourses. Cultural policy also became strongly linked with global information society policy, and the implications of technological change and convergence (Rabinovich 2007). The significance of creativity as a driver of economic growth in cities, regions, and advanced capitalist economies increased with the rise of 'creative city' aspirations internationally, fuelled by works such as Landry (2000) and Scott (2000). In the transition of consensus towards neoliberal policies, market forces became more generally accepted and in international organisations such as UNESCO, cultural and creative industries appeared as a strategic concept in intergovernmental conferences and recommendations.[7] Debates among policymakers, consultants, and academics influenced a re-emerging cultural industries agenda at the United Nations. In the first instance, the 'cultural industries' became central to the 2005 UNESCO Convention (see above). Later, UNCTAD built on the 'creative industries' in the articulation of their *Creative Economy Reports* (2008, 2010, forthcoming), and the Special Edition of the report published by UNESCO (2013). Collectively, these documents have propelled the 'cultural' and 'creative' industries into cultural policy and development policy debates around the world (De Beukelaer and O'Connor 2016).

In sum, cultural policy discourses do not exist in isolation from the major debates (ideologies) of the day and at the same time there is also continuity across the periods (Sokka and Kangas 2007). Over time, new ways of considering the borders of the cultural field have challenged the definition of cultural policy.

Within the cultural policy field, explicitly instrumental policies aiming to use culture to overcome societal challenges have been developed in attempts to strengthen the case for public expenditure on culture. Through these trajectories, cultural policy expanded in two main areas. First, the capacity of arts and culture has been used to regenerate cities and peripheral areas, even if the intended 'Bilbao effect' proved difficult to attain elsewhere (Plaza and Haarich 2009). Cultural industries, creative arts and heritage have been used to attract investment into cities and regions (linked to competitiveness), even if this essentially led to a zero sum game among those who actively compete (and created only 'losers' among the cities that did not take part in this competition). In these situations, local governments benefit from successfully realised cultural projects: the image of the region, suburb, or district alters, wealthy consumers and taxpayers may move there, and the value of the land and the estates and services increases. At the same time, one of the effects of regeneration policies may be gentrification: the area becomes more expensive to live in, and lower social classes are forced to move away (Peck 2005). Local, regional, and national policy schemes have differed on how they have set their respect priorities in these matters (Vicario and Martínez Monje 2003; Kangas 2004; Wilks-Heeg and North 2004). Second, cultural activities have been used to improve social inclusion, provide social welfare, and foster social cohesion (Jeannotte 2000; Duxbury 2002; NESF 2007, Støvring 2012), even if the sector remains deeply reliant on free and speculative labour (Gollmitzer and Murray 2009; Ross 2010; Randle 2015) and, as research in the U.K. shows, succeeding in the arts and culture requires ample social and economic capital (O'Brien 2014). As Belfiore (2002) has stated, 'Many attempts have been made to demonstrate that culture is a peculiarly successful means of promoting social cohesion, inclusion or regeneration, but they miss the point if they regard culture as one means to social regeneration among various possible others' (104; see also Belfiore and Bennett 2008).

Discrepancies of concepts, frameworks, and dimensions of sustainability and culture

As outlined in the previous section, the historically weak position of *culture* in major sustainable development policy documents has inspired numerous initiatives to conceptualise and articulate a 'place' for culture in sustainability or sustainable development, which has resulted in a wide array of perspectives and definitions. As Isar (in this special issue) highlights, the concepts and frameworks that have evolved to situate culture in sustainability contexts have demonstrated substantial flexibility and a widening plurality of approaches over time. While flexibility can enable meaningful modifications and adaptations of conceptual constructs and frameworks to specific contexts (whether political, cultural, economic, or geographic), this 'elasticity' is now becoming a liability to the design and advancement of policy.

Scholarly analyses tend to divide the concept of sustainable development into multiple dimensions: environmental, economic, social, cultural, and sometimes others (e.g. Seghezzo 2009; Hasna 2012; Peterson 2016). This conceptual practice of compartmentalisation has been widely criticized (e.g. Gibson 2006; Connelly 2007; Griggs et al. 2013; Boyer et al. 2016; Coutinho de Arruda and Lino de Almeida Lavorato 2016) with the main difficulty building on the paradox that all these elements are equally part of the sustainability conundrum, yet political discourse typically does not allow for the layered complexity that is needed to inclusively tackle these issues.

In general, the dimensions of sustainability are considered to overlap and bear equal importance, with arguments demonstrating how the dimensions cannot be completely separated and how 'real' sustainability can be achieved only when all dimensions are combined or intersected (Elliott 2006; Connelly 2007). However, the tendency to define different dimensions of sustainable development reinforces administrative and policy separation in practice. Furthermore, the dimensions can also be seen as contradictory, proposing a need to make value judgments between different dimensions. One of them may be considered to be primary, followed by others. Within this contentious and shifting framework, the social and cultural dimensions of sustainability, sometimes reported as a socio-cultural dimension, are tightly interconnected but feature distinct subjects and priorities.[8]

The varied use of the term *culture* in both academic and policy discourses adds further ambiguity to the overall debate. The mainstream field of sustainability has considered culture mainly in terms of societal values, general perceptions, and consumption practices (e.g. Assadourian, Starke, and Mastny 2010; Caradonna 2014; Robertson 2014). In this context, debates on the interrelationships among

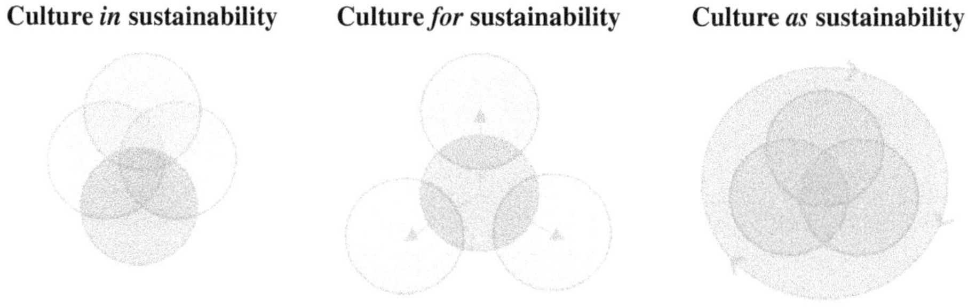

Culture *in* sustainability   **Culture *for* sustainability**   **Culture *as* sustainability**

Figure 1. Three approaches for exploring culture-sustainability relations.
Notes: These diagrams represent three approaches to culture (represented in darker shading) in sustainable development (the three other circles represent the social, economic, and environmental dimensions): 'Culture added as a fourth pillar (left diagram), culture mediating between the three pillars (central diagram) and culture as the foundation for sustainable development. The arrows indicate the ever-changing dynamics of culture and sustainable development (right diagram)' (Dessein et al. 2015, 29).

nature and culture have traditionally had a primarily rural and long-term inflection (e.g. Pilgrim and Pretty 2013). Consideration of the place of culture in urban sustainable development has inspired the emergence of works with attention to the role of community arts, everyday creativity, and artists in cities aiming to contribute to the goal of a sustainable future (e.g. Hristova, Dragićević Šešić, and Duxbury 2015; Blanc and Benish 2016). Acknowledging different perspectives on the topic, thus making cultural policy actors more conscious of co-existing narratives about culture and sustainable development and the assumptions that underlie them, enables greater attention to be focused on negotiating and reconciling (if necessary) the prevailing tensions and contradictions (Torggler et al. 2015).

Dessein et al. (2015) have introduced three approaches that outline the ways in which culture is predominantly positioned vis-à-vis sustainability and its general role in each situation (see Figure 1, in which the more darkly shaded circles represent culture). They have been elaborated as 'culture *in* sustainability', 'culture *for* sustainability', and 'culture *as* sustainability' and provide one framework from which to organize diverse discourses and examine prevailing conceptual issues. The first representation, 'culture *in* sustainability', considers culture as having an independent or autonomous role in sustainability: culture becomes the fourth dimension of sustainability. The approach views cultural sustainability as parallel to ecological, social, and economic sustainability, with all comprising interconnected dimensions of sustainability. The second representation, 'culture *for* sustainability', stresses culture having a mediating role to achieve economic, social, and ecological sustainability. The third representation, 'culture *as* sustainability', considers culture not only as an instrument but a necessary foundation for meeting the overall aims of sustainability. In this approach, culture encloses all other dimensions of sustainability and becomes an overarching concern or paradigm of sustainability.

The representations highlight one of the main issues encountered in aligning these discourses, the 'multi-interpretability' of the key terms *culture* and *sustainability/sustainable development* (Soini and Birkeland 2014, 213). The figures serve as an analytical tool to assist in organising, comparing, and aligning different discourses, and provide a framework from which to explore and assess each general approach in more detail (e.g. Soini and Dessein 2016). However, they do not aim to reconcile the competing paradigms toward an integrated model, and their applicability to the international cultural policy context is yet to be explored.

Cultural policy for sustainable development

In terms of policy, we focus now on the domain of cultural policy and how it is located relative to sustainability. A core issue in this endeavour is that cultural policy requires close attention *within* the realm of activity under its mandate, yet sustainability is a multisectoral, complex bundle of issues and policies that inevitably cross boundaries between sectors and policy fields. As is common in cultural

Table 1. Four strategic lines of cultural policy for sustainable development.

Primary objectives	Roles of cultural policy	Culture concept	Sustainability concept
To safeguard and sustain cultural practices and rights	Regulator and Protector	Cultural practices and rights of groups	Sustaining diverse cultural practices and environments into the future
To 'green' the operations and impacts of cultural organizations and industries	Translator and Politicking	The production and dissemination of cultural expressions through events, products, services, etc. as well as modes and habits of cultural consumption	Environmental sustainability, possibly also linked to social, cultural, and economic sustainability (includes reducing economic costs by focusing on resource efficiency)
To raise awareness and catalyse action about sustainability and climate change through arts and culture	Animator and Catalyst	Artistic and creative expressions – as works of art in themselves and explicitly (or sometimes) implicitly instrumentalised	Environmental sustainability dominant, possibly linked also to social, cultural, and economic sustainability
To foster global ecological citizenship to help identify and tackle sustainability as a global issue	Educator and Promoter	Identity and creative expression	Integrated social, economic, cultural, and environmental dimensions

Source: The authors.

policy, culture is primarily defined as creative or artistic expression and heritage. The connection of this definition to a more anthropological notion of culture as a way of life is also in play, recognising that the unresolved tension between these two notions tends to impede a systematic engagement with culture for sustainable development.

While some organisations and commentators argue that cultural and creative industries have an intrinsic capacity to contribute to sustainable development, such claims go largely unchecked. We argue that these industries, along with other cultural, creative, and artistic activities, do not intrinsically nor automatically contribute to sustainable development, but may do so under certain circumstances and conditions.

How can cultural policies contribute to sustainable development trajectories? The challenge for cultural policy is to embody very different roles in relation to sustainable development. Synthesizing the key dimensions of contemporary discussions about culture and sustainability addressed by the articles in this special issue, four key objectives in regard to cultural policy emerge: (1) to safeguard and sustain cultural practices and rights; (2) to 'green' the operations and impacts of cultural organizations and industries; (3) to raise awareness and catalyse actions about sustainability and climate change; and (4) to foster 'ecological citizenship'. Building from this, in Table 1 we dissect these four strategic lines to identify their primary objectives, the roles cultural policy plays, and the key concepts of culture and sustainability that are prevalent within each approach.

(1) Cultural policy to safeguard and sustain cultural practices and rights

This approach puts an emphasis on the cultural policy values of continuity and diversity. It does so by focusing on concerns with the continuity of cultures over time and the value inherent in global cultural diversity (e.g. contexts such as 'cultural crises', intercultural relations, and cultural rights). The discussion extends from the important tools UNESCO has developed to help attain this, such as the *Universal Declaration on Cultural Diversity* (UNESCO 2001), the *Convention for the Safeguarding of Intangible Cultural Heritage* (UNESCO 2003), and the *Convention on the Protection and Promotion of the Diversity of Cultural Expressions* (UNESCO 2005). This strategic line focuses primarily on the need to sustain cultural practices and cultural rights as ends in themselves.

This perspective focuses on the active agency and knowledges embedded in diverse cultural practices that should be safeguarded and sustained within a broader sustainable future. Within this strand, cultural policy plays two primary roles: Regulator and Protector. Within these roles, it advocates for the right for groups and individuals to engage in cultural life and earn a living from creating culture (as enshrined in the Universal Declaration of Human Rights). Examples of this approach can be seen in policies towards Sámi people in Finland, Sweden, Norway, and Russia, which reflect different relations and discrepancies in how cultural policies view (or not) relations between sustainability and collective cultural rights. Linked to the International Labour Organisation Convention concerning Indigenous and Tribal Peoples in Independent Countries (C169, 1989), although only Norway has ratified the Convention, national policy approaches have differed between the countries (see, e.g. Johansson 2016). Some political and legal gains have been made in recent decades, and international negotiations to develop a Nordic Saami Convention among Norway, Sweden, and Finland have been underway since 2011 (Bankes and Koivurova 2013), but progress continues to be precarious (Roy Trudel, Heinämäki, and Kastner 2016). Interlinked with issues of land and water rights, political decision-making, and self-determination, concerns with the survival of languages and the maintenance of cultural traditions and ways of life underline the importance of the transmission and ongoing vitality of Sámi knowledge and practices. In this context, the importance of education and research to the Sámi is highlighted in the establishment and operations of Sámi University of Applied Sciences, Norway. The university cooperates with the Sámi community, particularly focusing on young people, to preserve and promote the Sámi language, traditions, occupations, skills, and knowledge, and to support 'the Sámi society's progress towards equality with the majority society.' Within this perspective, Sámi research has an important role: 'Each Indigenous society needs to build its own scientific capacity, educate its experts and evolve on level with the majority society and language cultures' (Sámi University of Applied Sciences website, http://samas.no/en, 'Our Vision' and 'Research' sections).

Can this approach contribute to expanded notions of sustainability (as the 2005 Convention suggests), even though this is not an essential feature? The challenge is to reconcile and bridge the culture-focussed rationales with broader sustainability concerns and imperatives (see Throsby; and Baltà Portolés and Dragićević Šešić in this issue).

(2)   Cultural policy to 'green' the operations and impacts of cultural organizations and industries

In this strategic line, cultural policy includes an explicit environmental dimension and acts as a vehicle to translate environmental regulation, planning, and restrictions to the organisational models of the cultural sector, and potentially to advance them. It examines how cultural actors (and cultural policy more generally) should integrate principles of sustainability within their work to transform the pragmatic, strategic, and operational practices of the cultural sector in order to encompass greater environmental responsibility. This strand is based in historic precedents in environmental legislation with broad cross-sector applicability, but adapted and tailored to the nature of the cultural sector's operations and its prevailing environmental issues. A primary area in which this approach is found is in the development of cultural facilities within the framework of 'green' building design. For example, the cultural policy of the City of Lyon has taken environmental impacts into account in the development of its opera house, while the Cultural Facilities Plan of Catalonia, Spain (PECCAT) included a set of ten indicators to monitor the environmental sustainability of the cultural facilities developed within the plan (Martínez i Illa and Rius i Ulldemolins 2011). More broadly, the environmental impacts of the operations of cultural organizations and firms in the cultural industries are also being examined. An example of an organisation working on these issues and lobbying for this kind of change in cultural policy is Julie's Bicycle, a U.K.-based charity that aims to connect organisations and individuals in the creative industries to expertise, capacity building, and leadership to reduce their environmental impacts. Here, the sustainability of cultural life itself is taken for granted, but the *environmental* sustainability and impacts of the operations of cultural organizations and the macro systems of the cultural sector are called into question (see Loach, Rowley, and Griffiths; and Maxwell and Miller in this issue).

Within this (underdeveloped) strand, cultural policy plays two primary roles: Translator and Politicking. However, despite incremental advances and a diversity of initiatives – and some mention in policy rhetoric – an integration of environmental dimensions within cultural policy and programme frameworks is still rare (see Moore and Tickell 2014).

(3) Cultural policy to support the cultural sector to raise awareness and catalyse action about sustainability and climate change

This strand emphasises the role for artistic expression in the process towards widespread cultural change and 'way of life' transformation to modes of thinking and manners more complementary to sustainable living (i.e. given climate change and other pressing environmental issues as well as cultural and social crises in the world, issues of inequity, etc.). It is primarily focused on the messaging and meaning-making function of culture, and especially on the messages created by actors in the cultural sector (artists, arts organizations, heritage institutions, etc.). Environmental sustainability is the dominant concern, in many cases interlinked with social, cultural, and economic sustainability issues. Within this strand, cultural policy plays two roles: Animator and Catalyst.

Policy within this approach is reflected in the development of support programs directed specifically to support artistic projects relating to themes of sustainability, although these are often found at a subnational or local level. For example, over the past decade the City of Vancouver, through the Vancouver Board of Parks and Recreation, has supported a series of environmental art projects with a strong public engagement dimension[9] with the importance of this approach acknowledged in the Park Board's environmental education and stewardship action plan, *Rewilding Vancouver: From Sustaining to Flourishing* (2014). At an international level, a network of ten arts organizations within Europe, Imagine 2020, is supported by Creative Europe to fund artistic commissions, foster research and development, and promote sharing of resources, ideas, knowledge and debate of various topics under the umbrella of art and ecology (http://www.imagine2020.eu/about/). Another example of cultural sector action within this strategic line is ArtCOP, the 'artivist' (a conjunction of art and activist) collective that organised artistic interventions in the fringes of the Conference of Parties (COP) in 2015, the global meeting where states negotiated international environmental regulation. While not directly involved in the formal policymaking processes, such activist initiatives produce artistic interventions that can influence the politics and policies of major cultural institutions and the wider general public – from local to international scales (see Maxwell and Miller in this issue).

(4) Cultural policy to foster global 'ecological citizenship'

Nick Stevenson (2003) argues that 'ecological citizenship places its faith in the recovery of public space and human responsibility in order to attend to the environmental crisis. Neither market nor state institutions are likely to offer adequate responses to these issues without an enhanced role for the citizen' (94). In this context, cultural policy, as a tool for creating 'imagined communities' (Anderson 1983), can be one way to foster global citizenship to help identify and tackle sustainability as a global issue. But unlike Anderson's preoccupation with the nation as the locus and focus of such imagined communities, we stress the need to foster a cosmopolitan community, that is, a global community that embraces global awareness about a global challenge, beyond merely national or regional interests and priorities. This objective contrasts quite strongly with the underlying objective of much cultural policy to create and reinforce national identities, where citizens are encouraged to think in terms of their national affiliation rather than as part of humanity as a whole. Ecological citizenship thus presupposes 'cosmopolitan' citizenship – as climate change is an issue that requires concerted action from humanity as a whole (see Isar and Jeannotte in this issue).

This particular role of policy remains most elusive, as it challenges the place and role of cultural policy. Public policy is, by definition, defined and articulated within the framework of a state that has the political legitimacy to enforce it. As there is no such framework at a global level, a truly global policy framework is difficult (and perhaps impossible) to imagine. At the same time, cultural policy – as an instrument in identity politics – has built on, and accentuated, difference. Shifting from a sense of community (i.e. national) belonging to a sense of global belonging (an *imagined humanity* as opposed to *community*) would fundamentally alter the basis of identity politics – at least for those issues that are actually shared by humanity. As our natural environment is arguably the realm that is most cogently contextualising our sense of global belonging and survival today, it can form the bedrock for this renewed sense of belonging, shared human responsibility, and citizenship, with international cultural policy embracing this foundation and cultivating its development. To date – and to the best of our knowledge – this principle has not found its place in actual policy strategies.

In this strand, the focus is on culture both as identity and as creative expression. Sustainability is conceived with integrated social, economic, cultural, and environmental dimensions. Cultural policy can play two primary roles: Educator and Promoter. While creative expression has captured the need to increase awareness of and act upon global sustainability issues, cultural policy largely remains tied up with methodological nationalism. Going beyond efforts to raise awareness and catalyse action, which are encompassed in the previous role, this fourth role aims to construct the worldview that contexualizes and propels these actions, with a focus on (in)forming our collective sense of belonging and responsibility.

Conclusion

Since the mid-twentieth century, repeated international efforts to integrate culture in sustainable development frameworks have reflected the challenging need to balance the integral importance of culture itself with prevailing policy streams, rationales, and broader societal and environmental issues. The result of these efforts is a long-term legacy of policy statements, principles, and other efforts to reinforce the importance of culture in sustainable development, a legacy that is marked by both an expanding array of actors involved in these discourses over time and, intertwined with this, a diversification of concepts, arguments, and approaches. Cultural policy, which as a field embraces a diversity of values, approaches, roles, and rationalizations, has intersected with these discourses from time to time, influenced by the major debates and ideologies of the day. However, in general, the main trajectories of cultural policy have been positioned 'separately' from these debates.

Today, the challenge for cultural policy is to embody very different roles in relation to sustainable development. These different roles often co-exist and overlap. But it is important to clarify *how* they differ and *why*. Most of the differences are down to semantics: *culture* and *sustainability* simply mean different things in these contexts.

In the Brundtland report, sustainable development was characterised by key normative principles: 'Actions are deemed in keeping with sustainable development principles as far as they promote inter- and intra-generational equity, common but differentiated responsibilities, participation and gender equity, and are assessed to be within the planet's ecological means' (Beland Lindahl et al. 2015, 8). Importantly, the Commission notes, if sustainable development is to be meaningful, it 'must involve a consequent engagement with environmental limits' (8, citing Meadowcroft 2013). In situations of local sustainable development negotiations and discourse, these principles can serve as benchmarks in assessing the merits (or otherwise) of alternate 'sustainable' pathways. We argue that they are also useful guidelines in re-visiting cultural policy from a sustainability perspective and context.

Leaping forward almost three decades – within an ever more pressing and critical global environmental context – the SDGs approved in late 2016 maintain these core principles but elaborate a much more comprehensive and complex set of visions to guide collective development efforts. The complexity presents a challenging situation. At a time when environmental crises are dominant, the comprehensive vision appears to dilute this focus. The SDG set of visions is richly aspirational but, as mentioned earlier, their effectiveness as a political resource and implementation success depends on the organizations and agencies that drove its expansiveness to push for targets that are salient, demanding, and operationalisable. Furthermore, the limited references to culture within this expanded frame, despite unprecedented international efforts, indicates that significant challenges remain to effectively intersect with the mechanics of international policy development in this context. With these concerns as backdrop, to advance cultural policy in ways aligned with this envisioned global model of sustainable development, the possible paths and roles for culture must be further clarified, demonstrated, and (in this context) made measurable.

As a contribution towards these goals, this article aims to address and unravel some of the conceptual opacity and inflated claims about the role culture can play in sustainable development. In this process, four possible roles emerge for cultural policy: to safeguard and sustain cultural practices and rights; to 'green' the operations and impacts of cultural organizations and industries; to raise awareness and catalyse action about sustainability and climate change through arts and culture; and to foster global ecological citizenship to help identify and tackle sustainability as a global issue (see Table 1). Examining cultural policy from the context of sustainable development strengthens the argument for cultural policy beyond national borders, which appears increasingly important. This should be developed as a distinctively global exercise by leading actors in international cultural policy and in the 'culture and sustainable development' policy debates. Such an undertaking could involve, for example, the United Nations and UNESCO, the European Union, the European Cultural Foundation, African Union, the Asia-Europe Foundation, Organisation of Ibero-american States for Education, Science and Culture, Association of Southeast Asian Nations, and the different foundations that support 'arts and culture' internationally, but always within national borders. Thus, underlying these four strategic lines, there is an cross-cutting dimension that needs to be integrated into a new sustainability-oriented cultural policy which consists of the conceptual orientations and principles that qualitatively change the way in which goals and strategies are formulated, policies and programs are operated, and decisions are made.

Notes

1. The 17 SDG goals are: (1) End poverty in all its forms everywhere; (2) End hunger, achieve food security and improved nutrition and promote sustainable agriculture; (3) Ensure healthy lives and promote well-being for all at all ages; (4) Ensure inclusive and equitable quality education and promote lifelong learning opportunities for all; (5) Achieve gender equality and empower all women and girls; (6) Ensure availability and sustainable management of water and sanitation for all; (7) Ensure access to affordable, reliable, sustainable and modern energy for all; (8) Promote sustained, inclusive and sustainable economic growth, full and productive employment and decent work for all; (9) Build resilient infrastructure, promote inclusive and sustainable industrialisation and foster innovation; (10) Reduce inequality within and among countries; (11) Make cities and human settlements inclusive, safe, resilient and sustainable; (12) Ensure sustainable consumption and production patterns; (13) Take urgent action to combat climate change and its impacts; (14) Conserve and sustainably use the oceans, seas and marine resources for sustainable development; (15) Protect, restore and promote sustainable use of terrestrial ecosystems, sustainably manage forests, combat desertification, and halt and reverse land degradation and halt biodiversity loss; (16) Promote peaceful and inclusive societies for sustainable development, provide access to justice for all and build effective, accountable and inclusive institutions at all levels; and (17) Strengthen the means of implementation and revitalise the global partnership for sustainable development.
2. See Vlassis (2015) on the history of these negotiations.
3. Due to increased globalisation, cultural expressions such as films, books, music recordings, and so on traveled more easily and rapidly than ever before, yet while some countries had developed strong local markets and significant domestic production, others struggled to produce content in the globalised cultural industries. As well, countries with significant local production, such as France, perceived a threat from the influx of (primarily Anglophone) content that could diminish the cultural character of the country.
4. At the same time, through a separate UN process, The International Covenant on Economic, Social and Cultural Rights (ICESCR) was adopted by the UN General Assembly in 1966 (https://www1.umn.edu/humanrts/edumat/IHRIP/circle/modules/module3.htm).
5. These conferences included: Intergovernmental Conference on Institutional, Administrative and Financial Aspects of Cultural Policies, Venice, 1970; Intergovernmental Conference on Cultural Policies in Europe, Helsinki, 1972; Intergovernmental Conference on Cultural Policies in Asia, Yogyakarta, Indonesia, 1973; Intergovernmental Conference on Cultural Policies in Africa, Accra, Ghana, 1975; and Intergovernmental Conference on Cultural Policies in Latin America and Caribbean, Bogotá, 1978.
6. See the decision in 1997 by the newly elected British Labour government headed by Tony Blair to establish a Creative Industries Task Force as a central activity of its new Department of Culture, Media and Sport (see Flew 2012) and the publication of *Creative Nation* in Australia in 1994 (Government of Australia 1994).
7. Mexico City World Conference on Cultural Policies (MONDIACULT), 1982.
8. For detailed discussions of social sustainability, see Boström (2012).
9. The environmental art projects supported have addressed a range of environmental topics of importance to city residents, with broader conceptual and pragmatic resonance in society, such as: how to ethically coexist and collectively define shared urban spaces with urban animals; how contemporary city gardens and plants can be used to support and extend multi-cultural traditions in an urban environment; and how green waste can be creatively repurposed. For details, see: http://vancouver.ca/parks-recreation-culture/environmental-art.aspx.

Disclosure statement

No potential conflict of interest was reported by the authors.

ORCID

Nancy Duxbury ⓘ http://orcid.org/0000-0002-5611-466X
Anita Kangas ⓘ http://orcid.org/0000-0002-7962-8225
Christiaan De Beukelaer ⓘ http://orcid.org/0000-0002-9045-9979

References

Anderson, B. 1983. *Imagined Communities: Reflections on the Origin and Spread of Nationalism*. London: Verso.

Appadurai, A. 2004. "The Capacity to Aspire: Culture and the Terms of Recognition." In *Culture and Public Action*, edited by Y. Rao and M. Walton, 59–84. Stanford, CA: Stanford University Press.

Assadourian, E., L. Starke, and L. Mastny. 2010. *State of the World, 2010: Transforming Cultures: From Consumerism to Sustainability. A Worldwatch Institute Report on Progress Toward a Sustainable Society*. New York: W. W. Norton.

Baltà Portolés, J. 2013. *Culture and Development: Review of MDG-F Joint Programmes Key Findings and Achievements*. New York: UNDP.

Bankes, N., and T. Koivurova, eds. 2013. *The Proposed Nordic Saami Convention: National and International Dimensions of Indigenous Property Rights*. Oxford: Hart Publishing.

Beland Lindahl, K., S. Bakere, L. Rist, and A. Zachrisson. 2015. "Theorizing Pathways to Sustainability." *International Journal of Sustainable Development and World Ecology* 23 (5): 1–13.

Belfiore, E. 2002. "Art as a Means of Alleviating Social Exclusion: Does it Really Work? A Critique of Instrumental Cultural Policies and Social Impact Studies in the UK." *International Journal of Cultural Policy* 8 (1): 91–106.

Belfiore, E., and O. Bennett. 2008. *The Social Impact of the Arts: An Intellectual History*. London: Palgrave MacMillan.

Bennett, O. 1996. *Cultural Policy and the Crisis of Legitimacy: Entrepreneurial Answers in the United Kingdom*. Working paper no. 2. Coventry: Centre for the Study of Cultural Policy, University of Warwick.

Blanc, N., and B. Benish. 2016. *Form, Art and the Environment: Engaging in Sustainability*. London: Routledge. Routledge Studies in Culture and Sustainable Development series.

Boström, M. 2012. "A Missing Pillar? Challenges in Theorizing and Practicing Social Sustainability: Introduction to the Special Issue." *Sustainability: Science, Practice, & Policy* 8 (1), 3–14.

Bourdieu, P. 1984. *Distinction: A Social Critique of the Judgement of Taste*. Cambridge, MA: Harvard University Press.

Boyer, R. H. W., N. D. Peterson, P. Arora, and K. Caldwell. 2016. Five Approaches to Social Sustainability and an Integrated Way Forward. *Sustainability* 8 (878), 1–18. doi:10.3390/su8090878

Caradonna, J. L. 2014. *Sustainability: A history*. New York: Oxford University Press.

Connelly, S. 2007. "Mapping Sustainable Development as a Contested Concept." *Local Environment* 12 (3): 259–278.

Council of Europe. 1978. *Socio-cultural Animation*. Strasbourg: Council for Cultural Co-operation, Education and Culture, Council of Europe.

Coutinho de Arruda, M. C., and M. Lino de Almeida Lavorato. 2016. "Sustaining the Sustainable: Creating the Culture of Sustainability." In *Understanding Ethics and Responsibilities in a Globalizing World*, edited by M. C. Coutinho de Arruda and B. Rok, 135–145. Springer.

De Beukelaer, C. 2015. *Developing Cultural Industries: Learning from the Palimpsest of Practice*. Amsterdam: European Cultural Foundation.

De Beukelaer, C., and R. Freitas. 2015. "Culture and Sustainable Development: Beyond the Diversity of Cultural Expressions." In *Globalization, Culture and Development: The UNESCO Convention on Cultural Diversity*, edited by C. De Beukelaer, M. Pyykkönen and J. P. Singh, 203–221. Basingstoke: Palgrave Macmillan.

De Beukelaer, C., and J. O'Connor. 2016. "Art, Culture and Development: 'Fast' Creative Economy Policy Slowing Down?" In *Art and International Development*, edited by P. Stupples and K. Teaiwa, 27–47. Abingdon: Routledge.

Dessein, J., K. Soini, G. Fairclough, and L. G. Horlings, eds. 2015. *Culture in, for and as Sustainable Development: Conclusions from the COST Action IS1007 Investigating Cultural Sustainability*. Jyväskylä: University of Jyväskylä. http://www.culturalsustainability.eu/conclusions.pdf

Dubois, V. 2015. "Cultural Policy Regimes in Western Europe." In *International encyclopedia of the behavioral and social sciences*. 2nd ed, edited by J. D. Wright, 460–465. London: Elsevier.

Duxbury, N., ed. 2002. "Special Issue: Making Connections: Culture and Social Cohesion in the New Millennium." *Canadian Journal of Communication* 27 (2–3): 117–399.

Elliott, J. A. 2006. *An Introduction to Sustainable Development*. 3rd ed. London: Routledge.

Evrard, Y. 1997. "Democratizing Culture or Cultural Democracy?" *The Journal of Arts Management, Law, and Society* 27 (3): 167–175.

Flew, T. 2012. *The Creative Industries: Culture and Policy*. London: Sage.

Gibson, R. B. 2006. "Beyond the Pillars: Sustainability Assessment as a Framework for Effective Integration of Social, Economic and Ecological Considerations in Significant Decision-Making." *Journal of Environmental Assessment Policy and Management* 08 (03): 259–280.

Gollmitzer, M., and C. Murray. 2009. *Work Flows and Flexicurity: Canadian Cultural Labour in the Era of the Creative Economy*. Vancouver: Center for Expertise on Culture and Communities.

Government of Australia. 1994. *Creative nation*. Canberra: Office for the Arts.

Gray, C. 2007. "Commodification and Instrumentality in Cultural Policy." *International Journal of Cultural Policy* 13 (2): 203–215.

Griggs, D., M. Stafford-Smith, O. Gaffney, J. Rockström, M. C. Öhman, P. Shyamsundar, W. Steffen, G. Glaser, N. Kanie, and I. Noble. 2013. "Policy: Sustainable Development Goals for People and Planet." *Nature* 495: 305–307.

Hasna, A. M. 2012. "Dimensions of Sustainability." *Journal of Engineering for Sustainable Community Development* 1 (2): 47–57.

Hosagrahar, J., 2012. *Culture: A Driver and an Enabler of Sustainable Development*. Thematic Think Piece for UNESCO. Developed for the UN System Task Team on the Post-2015 UN Development Agenda. https://en.unesco.org/post2015/sites/post2015/files/Think%20Piece%20Culture.pdf.

Hristova, S., M. Dragićević Šešić, and N. Duxbury, eds. 2015. *Culture and Sustainability in European Cities: Imagining Europolis*. London: Routledge. Routledge Studies in Culture and Sustainable Development series.

IFACCA (International Federation of Arts Councils and Cultural Agencies), United Cites and Local Governments – Committee on Culture, International Federation of Coalitions for Cultural Diversity, and Cultural Action Europe, 2013. *Culture as a Goal in the Post-2015 Development Agenda*. http://media.ifacca.org/files/cultureasgoalweb.pdf.

International Labour Organization, 1989. *Convention Concerning Indigenous and Tribal Peoples in Independent Countries* (C169). http://www.ilo.org/dyn/normlex/en/f?p=NORMLEXPUB:12100:0::NO::P12100_ILO_CODE:C169.

International Union for the Conservation of Nature and Natural Resources. 1980. *World Conservation Strategy: Living Resource Conservation for Sustainable Development*. Gland: IUCNNR.

Jeannotte, S. 2000. "Tango Romantica or Liaisons Dangereuses? Cultural Policies and Social Cohesion: Perspectives from Canadian Research." *International Journal of Cultural Policy* 7 (1): 97–113.

Johansson, P. 2016. "Indigenous Self-determination in the Nordic Countries: The Sami, and The Inuit of Greenland." In *Handbook of Indigenous Peoples' Rights*, edited by C. Lennox and D. Short, 424–442. Oxon and New York: Routledge.

Kangas, A. 2003. "Culture as a Local Tool and Public Service." *Kunnallistieteellinen aikakauskirja* 31 (4): 332–340.

Kangas, A., 2004. New Clothes for Cultural Policy. In *Construction of Cultural Policy*, edited by P. Ahponen and A. Kangas, 21–41. Jyväskylä: Minerva.

Landry, C. 2000. *The Creative City: A Toolkit for Urban Innovators*. London: Earthscan.

Langford, M. 2016. "Lost in Transformation? The Politics of the Sustainable Development Goals." *Ethics and International Affairs* 30 (02): 167–176.

Martínez i Illa, S., and Rius i Ulldemolins, J. 2011. "Cultural Planning and Community Sustainability: The Case of the Cultural Facilities Plan of Catalonia (PECCAT 2010-20)." *Culture and Local Governance* 3 (1): 71–82.

McGuigan, J. 2004. *Rethinking Cultural Policy*. Maidenhead: Open University Press.

MDG Achievement Fund, 2013. *Culture and Development: Thematic Window Development Results Report*. October. http://mdgfund.org/sites/default/files/Culture%20and%20Development%20-%20Development%20Results%20Report.pdf.

Meadowcroft, J. 2013. "Reaching the Limits? Developed Country Engagement with Sustainable Development in a Challenging Conjuncture." *Environment and Planning C: Government and Policy* 31: 988–1002.

Meadows, D. H., D. L. Meadows, J. Randers, and W. W. Behrens III. 1972. *Limits to Growth* Report to the Club of Rome. New York: New American Library.

Mennell, S. 1979. "Social Research and the Study of Cultural 'Needs'." In *Social Research and Cultural Policy*, edited by J. Zuzanek, 15–36. Waterloo: Otium.

Miller, T., and G. Yúdice. 2002. *Cultural Policy*. London: Sage.

Milz, S. 2007. "Canadian Cultural Policy-making at a Time of Neoliberal Globalization." *ESC* 3 (1–2): 85–107.

Moore, S., and A. Tickell. 2014. *The Arts and Environmental Sustainability: An International Overview*. D'Art Topics in Arts Policy, No. 34b. Sydney: Julie's Bicycle and the International Federation of Arts Councils and Culture Agencies. http://www.ifacca.org/topic/ecological-sustainability/

NESF (National Economic and Social Forum). 2007. *The Arts, Cultural Inclusion and Social Cohesion*. NESF Report no. 35. http://files.nesc.ie/nesf_archive/nesf_reports/NESF_35_full.pdf.

Nussbaum, M. C. 1995. "Human capabilities, female human beings." In *Women, Culture, and Development*, edited by M. Nussbaum and J. Glover, 61–104. Oxford: Clarendon Press.

Nussbaum, M. C. 2006. *Frontiers of Justice: Disability, Nationality, Species Membership*. Cambridge, MA: Belknap Press of Harvard University Press.

O'Brien, D. 2014. *Cultural Policy: Management, Value and Modernity in the Creative Industries*. London: Routledge.

Peck, J. 2005. "Struggling with the Creative Class." *International Journal of Urban and Regional Research* 29 (4): 740–770.

Peterson, N. 2016. "Introduction to the Special Issue on Social Sustainability: Integration, Context, and Governance." *Sustainability: Science, Practice, & Policy* 12(1): 3–7. Published online May 31.

Pilgrim, S., and J. Pretty. 2013. *Nature and Culture: Rebuilding Lost Connections*. Oxon: Routledge.

Plaza, B., and S. N. Haarich. 2009. "Museums for Urban Regeneration? Exploring Conditions for their Effectiveness." *Journal of Urban Regeneration and Renewal* 2 (3): 259–271.

Pronk, J. 2015. "From Post 1945 to Post 2015." *Journal of Global Ethics* 11 (3): 366–380.

Quental, N., J. M. Lourenço, and F. Nunes da Silva. 2011. "Sustainable Development Policy: Goals, Targets and Political Cycles." *Sustainable Development* 19: 15–29.

Rabinovich, V. 2007. "Four "Constants" in Canadian Cultural Policy." *Canadian Themes / Thèmes canadiens* (Winter) 4: 6–9.

Randle, K. 2015. "Class and Exclusion at Work: The Case of UK Film and Television." In *The Routledge companion to the cultural industries*, edited by K. Oakley and J. O'Connor, 330–343. London: Routledge.

Rao, V., and M. Walton. 2004. *Culture and Public Action*. Stanford: CA Stanford University Press.

Robertson, M. 2014. *Sustainability: Principles and Practice*. New York: Routledge.

Ross, A. 2010. *Nice Work if You Can Get it: Life and Labor in Precarious Times*. New York: NYU Press.

Roy Trudel, E., L. Heinämäki, and P. Kastner. 2016. Despite Gains, Europe's Indigenous People Still Struggle for Recognition. *The Conversation*. May 17. https://theconversation.com/despite-gains-europes-indigenous-people-still-struggle-for-recognition-54330.

Scott, A. J. 2000. *The Cultural Economy of Cities: Essays on the Geography of Image-Producing Industries*. London: Sage.

Seghezzo, L. 2009. "The Five Dimensions of Sustainability." *Environmental Politics* 18 (4): 539–556.

Sen, A. K. 1987. *On Ethics and Economics*. Oxford: Blackwell.

Sen, A. 1999. *Development as Freedom*. Oxford: Oxford University Press.

Sen, A. 2010. *The Idea of Justice*. London: Penguin Books.

Soini, K., and I. Birkeland. 2014. "Exploring the Scientific Discourse on Cultural Sustainability." *Geoforum* 51: 213–223.

Soini, K., and J. Dessein. 2016. "Culture-sustainability Relation: Towards a Conceptual Framework." *Sustainability* 8 (2): 167–179.

Sokka, S., and A. Kangas. 2007. "At the Roots of Finnish Cultural Policy: Intellectuals, Nationalism, and the Arts." *International Journal of Cultural Policy* 13 (2): 185–202.

Stevenson, N. 2003. *Cultural Citizenship: Cosmopolitan Questions*. Berkshire: Open University Press.

Støvring, K. 2012. "The Cultural Prerequisites of Social Cohesion: With Special Attention to the Nation of Denmark." *International Journal of Sociology and Social Policy* 32 (3/4): 134–152.

Throsby, D. 1997. "Sustainability and Culture Some Theoretical Issues." *International Journal of Cultural Policy* 4 (1): 7–19.

Throsby, D. 1999. "Cultural Capital." *Journal of Cultural Economics* 23 (1/2): 3–12.

Throsby, D., 2015. "Culture in Sustainable Development." In *Re|Shaping Cultural Policies: A Decade Promoting the Diversity of Cultural Expressions for Development [2005 Convention Global Report]*, edited by UNESCO, 151–170. Paris: UNESCO.

Throsby, D., and E. Petetskaya. 2016. "Sustainability Concepts in Indigenous and Non-indigenous Cultures." *International Journal of Cultural Property* 23 (02): 119–140.

Torggler, B., R. Murphy, C. France, and J. Baltà Portolés, 2015. *UNESCO's Work on Culture and Sustainable Development: Evaluation of a Policy Theme*. IOS/EVS/PI/145 REV.2. Paris: UNESCO Internal Oversight Service Evaluation Section.

UN (United Nations). 2015. *Transforming Our World: The 2030 Agenda for Sustainable Development*. https://sustainabledevelopment.un.org/post2015/transformingourworld.

UNCTAD. 2008. *Creative Economy Report 2008*. New York: United Nations.

UNCTAD. 2010. *Creative Economy Report 2010*. New York: United Nations.

UNCTAD. forthcoming. *Creative Economy Report 2016*. New York: United Nations.

UNCTAD, and UNESCO. 2013. *Creative Economy Report 2013 Special Edition: Widening Local Development Pathways*. New York: UNCTAD and UNESCO.

UNDP (United Nations Development Programme). 1990. *Human Development Report 1990*. New York: Oxford University Press.

UNESCO. 1969. *Cultural policy – a preliminary study*. Paris: UNESCO.

UNESCO. 1981. *The Training of Cultural Animators and Administrators*. Cultural Co-operation: Studies and Experiences, Joint Study no. 10. Paris: UNESCO.

UNESCO. 1982. *World Conference on Cultural Policies: Final Report. Mexico City, 26 July – 6 August 1982*. Paris: UNESCO.

UNESCO. 1998. *Action Plan on Cultural Policies for Development*. Stockholm: UNESCO.

UNESCO. 2001. *Universal Declaration on Cultural Diversity*. Paris: UNESCO.

UNESCO. 2003. *Convention for the Safeguarding of Intangible Cultural Heritage*. Paris: UNESCO.

UNESCO. 2005. *Convention on the Protection and Promotion of the Diversity of Cultural Expressions*. Paris: UNESCO.

UNESCO. 2015. *Re|Shaping Cultural Policies: A Decade Promoting the Diversity of Cultural Expressions for Development [2005 Convention Global Report]*. Paris: UNESCO.

Vancouver Board of Parks and Recreation. 2014. *Rewilding Vancouver: From Sustaining to Flourishing. An Environmental Education and Stewardship Action Plan for the Vancouver Park Board*. Vancouver: City of Vancouver.

Vestheim, G. 1994. "Instrumental Cultural Policy in Scandinavian Countries: A Critical Historical Perspective." *The European Journal of Cultural Policy* 1 (1): 57–71.

Vicario, L., and P. M. Martínez Monje. 2003. "Another 'Guggenheim Effect': The Generation of a Potentially Gentrifiable Neighbourhood in Bilbao." *Urban Studies* 40 (12): 2383–2400.

Vlassis, A. 2015. "Culture in the Post-2015 Development Agenda: the Anatomy of an International Mobilisation." *Third World Quarterly* 36 (9): 1649–1662.

Volkerling, M. 1996. "Deconstructing the Difference-engine: A Theory of Cultural Policy." *International Journal of Cultural Policy* 2 (2): 189–212.

Watene, K., and M. Yap. 2015. "Culture and Sustainable Development: Indigenous Contributions." *Journal of Global Ethics* 11 (1): 51–55.

WCCD (World Commission on Culture and Development). 1996. *Our Creative Diversity*. Paris: UNESCO Publishing.

WCED (World Commission for the Environment and Development). 1987. *Our Common Future*. New York: United Nations.

Wilks-Heeg, S., and P. North. 2004. "Cultural Policy and Urban Regeneration [special issue]." *Local Economy* 19 (4): 305–311.

Williams, R. 1958. *Culture and Society*. Harmondsworth: Penguin.

Index

Notes: Page numbers in *italics* refer to figures
Page numbers in **bold** refer to tables
Page numbers with "n" refer to endnotes

For Product Safety Concerns and Information please contact our EU
representative GPSR@taylorandfrancis.com
Taylor & Francis Verlag GmbH, Kaufingerstraße 24, 80331 München, Germany

www.ingramcontent.com/pod-product-compliance
Ingram Content Group UK Ltd.
Pitfield, Milton Keynes, MK11 3LW, UK
UKHW051830180425
457613UK00022B/1180